Through the Protestant principle we may achieve a new understanding of the human condition and of the forces that make the fate of modern man. Church and society will have to welcome natural criticism; even ostensibly antireligious movements, such as Marxism and secularism, must be valued and criticized as covert religious forces. To this end, states Tillich, religious socialism is offered as a challenge—not a program—to the churches and the democratic secular movements. Together they must find the elements, neglected or perverted by both capitalism and socialism, which will point the way beyond the present era.

The Protestant principle thus demands the shaping of a new philosophy of history and culture which can cope with the existential situation. Protestantism must undergo a transformation as disruptive and as boldly productive as the changes worked at the beginning of the Protestant era. This reformation may bring the end of the Protestant era as we have known it. But it will also demonstrate the enduring significance of the Protestant principle.

### About the Author . . .

Before coming to this country, PAUL TILLICH served as professor of philosophy and theology at Berlin, Marburg, Dresden, and Frankfurt. After the first World War, he became a leader in the religious-socialist movement in Germany. Since coming to the United States as an exile from Nazi Germany, he has been a visiting professor at many American universities and is now a University Professor at Harvard.

THE PROTESTANT ERA

# THE
# PROTESTANT ERA

*By*

PAUL TILLICH

*Translated and with a Concluding Essay by*

JAMES LUTHER ADAMS

THE UNIVERSITY OF CHICAGO PRESS
CHICAGO · ILLINOIS

THE UNIVERSITY OF CHICAGO PRESS, CHICAGO 37
James Nisbet & Co., Limited, London W. 1, England

*Copyright 1948 by The University of Chicago. All rights reserved*
*Published 1948. Fourth Impression 1957. Composed and printed*
*by* THE UNIVERSITY OF CHICAGO PRESS, *Chicago, Illinois,*
*U.S.A.*

*To*

WILHELM PAUCK

*friend and helper*

# TRANSLATOR'S NOTE

GRATEFUL acknowledgment is here expressed to Dr. Ernst Fraenkel for his invaluable assistance in the preparation of the translations included in this volume.

Acknowledgments are due also to the publishers who have graciously given permission for the inclusion here of essays that have previously appeared elsewhere either in German or in English. It should be noted, however, that the author has altered several of these essays for the present volume.

CHAPTER I, *Kant-Studien,* Vol. XXXIV (1929), Heft 3/4.
CHAPTER II is published here for the first time.
CHAPTER III, *Die Tat,* Vol. XIV (1922), Heft 5.
CHAPTER IV, *Journal of Religion,* Vol. XXVI (1946), No. 2.
CHAPTERS V, VII, VIII, XIII, and XIV, from the volume of Tillich's collected writings, *Religiöse Verwirklichung* (Berlin: Furche-Verlag, 1929).
CHAPTER VI, *Religion in Life,* Vol. X (1941), No. 1.
CHAPTER IX, *Crozer Quarterly,* Vol. XXII (1945), No. 4.
CHAPTER X, from *Religion and the Modern World* (Philadelphia: University of Pennsylvania Press, 1941).
CHAPTER XI, a translation of the brochure, *Protestantisches Prinzip und proletarische Situation* (Bonn: Friedrich Cohen, 1931).
CHAPTER XII, *The Protestant,* Vol. IV (1942), No. 5.
CHAPTER XV, originally published under the title "Protestantism in the Present World-Situation," *American Journal of Sociology,* Vol. XLIII (1937), No. 2.
CHAPTER XVI, *Anglican Theological Review,* Vol. XXV (1943), No. 1.
CHAPTER XVII, *Christianity and Society,* Vol. VII (1941), No. 2.
CHAPTER XVIII, *Christianity and Crisis,* Vol. II (1942), No. 14.

In an expository essay at the end of the volume the translator has attempted to relate Professor Tillich's concept of "The Protestant Era" to his general outlook and background, taking into account some of his many writings which are not available in English.

J. L. A.

THE MEADVILLE THEOLOGICAL SCHOOL
FEDERATED THEOLOGICAL FACULTY
UNIVERSITY OF CHICAGO

# AUTHOR'S INTRODUCTION

## I

THIS book would not have been published without the initiative and the work of James Luther Adams in Chicago. He has translated the German articles which are presented here for the first time to American readers. He has suggested the organization of the book and the selection of its parts. He has encouraged me again and again to go ahead with the publication. Before anything else I want to express my profound gratitude to him; and I want to include in my thanks some mutual friends who advised us. The hardest task was the translation of some extremely difficult German texts. In many cases the impossibility of an adequate translation made it imperative for me to reproduce whole passages and even articles without keeping to the original text. In all these cases I have used the paraphrasing translations of Dr. Adams, and in no case have I changed the train of thought of the original writing. This Introduction is intended to justify the selection and organization of the material by a retrospective and somewhat personal record of the development which is reflected in the different articles and which has led to the point of view from which the book is conceived.

This point of view, of course, is suggested in the title of the book, *The Protestant Era*. But, since this title itself needs interpretation and since the relation of several of the published articles to the title is not immediately evident, it seems advisable that the collection have an explanatory introduction. There is another, even more important, reason for such an introduction.

The collection includes material taken from about twenty years of theological and philosophical work. During these two decades some of the most monumental historical events have taken place—the victory of national socialism in Germany and the second World War. An immediate effect of the first event on my life was my emigration from Germany and my settlement in New York City. The change of country and continent, the catastrophe of a world in which I had worked and thought for forty-seven years, the loss of the fairly mastered tool of my

own language, the new experiences in a civilization previously unknown to me, resulted in changes, first, of the expression and then, to a
certain degree, of the content of my thinking. These changes were supported by the dramatic events in Germany under the rule of naziism,
especially the German church struggle, further by two extended trips
through the countries of western Europe and my active participation in
the Oxford conference of the world churches, and, finally, by the political and spiritual events preceding and accompanying the second World
War. The imminence and the outbreak of this war and the tremendous
problems of postwar reconstruction have forced upon me a larger participation in practical politics than I ever had intended to give. And,
since the key to the interpretation of history is historical activity, my
understanding of the world-historical situation has become broader and,
I hope, more realistic. Besides these dramatic events, American theology
and philosophy have influenced my thinking in several respects. The
spirit of the English language has demanded the clarification of many
ambiguities of my thought which were covered by the mystical vague-
ness of the classic philosophical German; the interdependence of
theory and practice in Anglo-Saxon culture, religious as well as secular,
has freed me from the fascination of that kind of abstract idealism
which enjoys the system for the system's sake; the co-operation with
colleagues and students of Union Theological Seminary, Columbia
University, and other universities and colleges has provided the experience of a type of Protestant religion and culture very different from
that of Continental Europe; the world perspective, almost unavoidable
on a bridge between the continents like New York and at a center of
world Protestantism like Union Theological Seminary, has had strong
effects on my thinking about the situation of the church universal in
our time.

All these influences—and, besides them, the natural growth of a
man's experience and thought in two decades—are mirrored in the
different articles of this book. They betray changes of style, of temper,
of emphasis, of methods, of formulations, which cannot escape any
reader.

But more obvious than the changes from the earlier to the more
recent articles in this collection is the continuity of the main line of
thought and the permanence of the basic principles. It sometimes
strikes me (and this is probably a very common experience), when I

read some of my earliest writings, how much of what I believed to be
a recent achievement is already explicitly or at least implicitly contained
in them. This is, first of all, true of the problem that controls the selection of the articles—the problem of Protestantism, its meaning and its
historical existence. Since my first years as a student of Protestant
theology, I have tried to look at Protestantism from the outside as well
as from the inside. "From the outside" meant in those earlier years:
from the point of view of a passionately loved and studied philosophy;
it meant in later years from the point of view of the powerfully developing comparative history of religion; and it meant, finally, from
the point of view of the experienced and interpreted general history of
our period. This outside view of Protestantism has deeply influenced
my inside view of it. If you look at Protestantism merely as a special
denominational form of Christianity to which you are bound by tradition and faith, you receive a picture different from the one you perceive
when looking at it as a factor within the world-historical process, influenced by and influencing all other factors. But the converse is also
true. The inside view of Protestantism, based on an existential experience of its meaning and power, strongly modifies the outside view.
None of the articles contained in this volume considers the situation of
Protestantism in a merely factual, "statistical" way, but each of them
betrays the author's concern and active involvement. This is not said
in order to depreciate detachment and scientific objectivity in the matters dealt with. There is a place for such an attitude even toward religion.
But it touches only the surface. There are objects for which the so-called
"objective" approach is the least objective of all, because it is based on a
misunderstanding of the nature of its object. This is especially true of
religion. Unconcerned detachment in matters of religion (if it is more
than a methodological self-restriction) implies an a priori rejection of
the religious demand to be ultimately concerned. It denies the object
which it is supposed to approach "objectively."

The inside and the outside views of Protestantism in their mutual
dependence have created an interpretation of its meaning which is set
forth, directly or indirectly, in all sections of this book. Protestantism
is understood as a special historical embodiment of a universally significant principle. This principle, in which one side of the divine-human
relationship is expressed, is effective in all periods of history; it is indicated in the great religions of mankind; it has been powerfully pro-

nounced by the Jewish prophets; it is manifest in the picture of Jesus as the Christ; it has been rediscovered time and again in the life of the church and was established as the sole foundation of the churches of the Reformation; and it will challenge these churches whenever they leave their foundation.

There is no question here as to whether we are now approaching the end of the Protestant principle. This principle is not a special religious or cultural idea; it is not subject to the changes of history; it is not dependent on the increase or decrease of religious experience or spiritual power. It is the ultimate criterion of all religious and all spiritual experiences; it lies at their base, whether they are aware of it or not. The way in which this principle is realized and expressed and applied and connected with other sides of the divine-human relationship is different in different times and places, groups, and individuals. Protestantism as a principle is eternal and a permanent criterion of everything temporal. Protestantism as the characteristic of a historical period is temporal and subjected to the eternal Protestant principle. It is judged by its own principle, and this judgment might be a negative one. The Protestant era might come to an end. But *if* it came to an end, the Protestant principle would not be refuted. On the contrary, the end of the Protestant era would be another manifestation of the truth and power of the Protestant principle. Will the Protestant era come to an end? Is *that* the judgment of the Protestant principle, as it was the judgment of the prophets that the nation of the prophets would be destroyed? This is a question which, of course, is not to be answered by historical predictions but by an interpretation of Protestantism, its dangers and its promises, its failures and its creative possibilities.

All articles of this collection are meant to contribute to the answer. Only a few of them deal directly with Protestantism, but all deal with the Protestant problem; for it is a presupposition of this book that no realm of life can be understood and formed without a relation to the Protestant principle, as it is a presupposition also that Protestantism cannot be understood and formed except in relation to all realms of life. This correlation, which is more fully developed in several places in the book, was decisive for the selection and organization of the articles, as it was decisive for the considerable number of different questions with which I have dealt in my thinking and writing and which appear in this collection as parts of the general problem of the Protestant era.

This Introduction does not intend to sum up the contents of the articles that follow. Its purpose is to show how the questions they ask and try to answer have arisen in connection with the rise of the Protestant problem in my thought. This cannot be done, however, without some autobiographical references, for the line of thought running through this book is based on a unity of experience and interpretation.

## II

The power of the Protestant principle first became apparent to me in the classes of my theological teacher, Martin Kaehler, a man who in his personality and theology combined traditions of Renaissance humanism and German classicism with a profound understanding of the Reformation and with strong elements of the religious awakening of the middle of the nineteenth century. The historians of theology count him among the "theologians of mediation"—often in a depreciating sense. But *the task of theology is mediation,* mediation between the eternal criterion of truth as it is manifest in the picture of Jesus as the Christ and the changing experiences of individuals and groups, their varying questions and their categories of perceiving reality. If the mediating task of theology is rejected, theology itself is rejected; for the term "theo-logy" implies, as such, a mediation, namely, between the mystery, which is *theos,* and the understanding, which is *logos.* If some biblicists, pietists, evangelicals, and lay Christians are opposed to the mediating function of theology, they deceive themselves, since, in reality, they live by the crumbs falling from the table of the theological tradition which has been created by great mediators. One of the methods of mediation in theology is called "dialectical." Dialectics is the way of seeking for truth by talking with others from different points of view, through "Yes" and "No," until a "Yes" has been reached which is hardened in the fire of many "No's" and which unites the elements of truth promoted in the discussion. It is most unfortunate that in recent years the name "dialectical theology" has been applied to a theology that is strongly opposed to any kind of dialectics and mediation and that constantly repeats the "Yes" to its own and the "No" to any other position. This has made it difficult to use the term "dialectical" to denote theological movements of a really dialectical, that is a mediating, character; and it has resulted in the cheap and clumsy way of dividing all theologians into naturalists and supernaturalists, or into liberals and orthodox. As a theologian who sometimes has been dealt with in this easy way of shelving somebody (for instance, by being called a "neo-supernaturalist") I want to state unambiguously my conviction that these divisions are completely obsolete in the actual work which is done today by every theologian who takes the mediating or dialectical task of theology seriously. Therefore, I would not be ashamed to be called a "theologian of mediation," which, for me, would simply mean: a "theo-logian." There is, of course, danger in all mediation performed by the church, not only in its theological function but also in all its practical functions. The church is often unaware of this danger and falls into a self-surrendering adaptation to its environment. In such situations a prophetic challenge like that given by the "neo-Reformation" theology (as it should be called instead of "dialectical theology") is urgently needed. But, in spite of such a danger, the church as a living reality must permanently mediate its eternal foundation with the demands of the historical situation. The church is by its very nature dialectical and must venture again and again a "theo-logy" of mediation.

The example of Martin Kaehler, in reference to whom this excursus on the mediating character of my theology has been made, shows clearly that mediation need not mean surrender. Kaehler's central idea was "justification through faith," the idea that separated Protestantism from Catholicism and that became the so-called "material" principle of the Protestant churches (the biblical norm being the "formal" principle). He was able not only to unite this idea with his own classical education but also to interpret it with great religious power for generations of humanistically educated students. Under his influence a group of advanced students and younger professors developed the new understanding of the Protestant principle in different ways. The step I myself made in these years was the insight that the principle of justification through faith refers not only to the religious-ethical but also to the religious-intellectual life. Not only he who is in sin but also he who is in doubt is justified through faith. The situation of doubt, even of doubt about God, need not separate us from God. There is faith in every serious doubt, namely, the faith in the truth as such, even if the only truth we can express is our lack of truth. But if this is experienced in its depth and as an ultimate concern, the divine is present; and he who doubts in such an attitude is "justified" in his thinking. So the paradox got hold of me that he who seriously denies God, affirms him. Without it I could not have remained a theologian. There is, I soon realized, no place *beside* the divine, there is no possible atheism, there is no wall between the religious and the nonreligious. The holy embraces both itself and the secular. Being religious is being unconditionally concerned, whether this concern expresses itself in secular or (in the narrower sense) religious forms. The personal and theological consequences of these ideas for me were immense. Personally, they gave me at the time of their discovery, and always since then, a strong feeling of relief. You cannot reach God by the work of right thinking or by a sacrifice of the intellect or by a submission to strange authorities, such as the doctrines of the church and the Bible. You cannot, and you are not even asked to try it. Neither works of piety nor works of morality nor works of the intellect establish unity with God. They follow from this unity, but they do not make it. They even prevent it if you try to reach it through them. But just as you are justified as a *sinner* (though unjust, you are just), so in the status of *doubt* you are in the status of truth. And if all this comes together and you are desperate about the meaning of life, the seriousness of your despair is the expression of the meaning in which you still are living. This unconditional seriousness is the expression of the presence of the divine in the experience of utter separation from it. It is this radical and universal interpretation of the doctrine of justification through faith which has made me a conscious Protestant. Strictly theological arguments for this idea are given in an early German article which I mention mainly because of its title: "Rechtfertigung und Zweifel" ("Justification and Doubt"). In that article (which does not appear in the present volume) the conquest of the experience of meaninglessness by the awareness of the paradoxical presence of "meaning in meaninglessness" is described. References to this idea are given wherever the Protestant principle is mentioned, especially in the chapters on "Realism and Faith," "The Protestant Message and the Man of Today," and "The Transmoral Conscience."

The radical and universal interpretation of the idea of justification through faith had important theological consequences beyond the personal. If it is valid, no realm of life can exist without relation to something unconditional, to an ultimate concern. Religion, like God, is omnipresent; its presence, like that of God, can be forgotten, neglected, denied. But it is always effective, giving inexhaustible depth to life and inexhaustible meaning to every cultural creation. A first, somewhat enthusiastic, expression of this idea was given in a lecture printed in the *Kant-Studien* under the title, "Über die Idee einer Theologie der Kultur" ("On the Idea of a Theology of Culture"). A short time later, in a more systematic fashion, the same idea was explained in a paper that appeared in the same magazine under the paradoxical title, "Die Überwindung des Religionsbegriffs in der Religionsphilosophie" ("Overcoming the Notion of Religion within the Philosophy of Religion"). Both articles (not reprinted here) try to introduce the larger concept of religion, challenging the undialectical use of the narrower definition.

It was natural that on the basis of these presuppositions the history of religion and of Christianity required a new interpretation. The early and high Middle Ages received a valuation that they never had received in classical Protestantism. I called them "theonomous" periods, in contrast to the heteronomy of the later Middle Ages and the self-complacent autonomy of modern humanism. "Theonomy" has been defined as a culture in which the ultimate meaning of existence shines through all finite forms of thought and action; the culture is transparent, and its creations are vessels of a spiritual content. "Heteronomy" (with which theonomy is often confused) is, in contrast to it, the attempt of a religion to dominate autonomous cultural creativity from the outside, while self-complacent autonomy cuts the ties of a civilization with its ultimate ground and aim, whereby, in the measure in which it succeeds, a civilization becomes exhausted and spiritually empty. The Protestant principle as derived from the doctrine of justification through faith rejects heteronomy (represented by the doctrine of papal infallibility) as well as a self-complacent autonomy (represented by secular humanism). It demands a self-transcending autonomy, or theonomy. These ideas have been developed in my "Religionsphilosophie" ("Philosophy of Religion") which appeared as a section of the *Lehrbuch der Philosophie* ("Textbook of Philosophy," edited by Max Dessoir). Expressions of the same point of view are given in the essays "Philosophy and Fate," "Philosophy and Theology," and "Kairos," in the present volume.

## III

Most important for my thought and life was the application of these ideas to the interpretation of history. History became the central problem of my theology and philosophy because of the historical reality as I found it when I returned from the first World War: a chaotic Germany and Europe; the end of the period of the victorious *bourgeoisie* and of the nineteenth-century way of life; the split between the Lutheran churches and the proletariat; the gap between the transcendent message of traditional Christianity and the immanent hopes of the revolutionary movements. The situation demanded interpretation as well as action. Both were attempted by the German religious-socialist movement, which was founded immediately after the war by a group of people, including myself. The first task we faced was an analysis of the world situation on the basis of contemporary events, viewed in the light of the great criticism of bourgeois culture during the nineteenth and early twentieth centuries, and with the help of the categories derived from the Protestant principle in its application to religion and culture. In this analysis the central proposition of my philosophy of religion proved its significance: Religion is the substance of culture, culture is the expression of religion. A large section of my published writings and unpublished lectures has been dedicated to such a "theonomous" interpretation of culture. The small, widely received book *Die Religiöse Lage der Gegenwart* (translated in 1932 under the title, *The Religious Situation*) tried to give an all-embracing analysis of the recent decades of our period. A similar, though shorter, analysis has recently appeared as the first section of a symposium, *The Christian Answer.* Among the articles collected in the present volume, practically all those brought together in the fifth part, "The Present Crisis," as well as "The Protestant Principle and the Proletarian Situation" and "The Idea and the Ideal of Personality," contribute to a theonomous interpretation of our period. An analysis of our situation could not have been attempted by me without my participation in the religious-socialist movement. In speaking about it, I first want to remove some misunderstandings concerning its nature and purpose. This is especially necessary in a country like the United States, where everything critical of nineteenth-century capitalism is denounced as "red" and, consciously or through ignorance, confused with communism of the Soviet type. The most unfortunate consequence of this attitude is the barrier that it erects against any real understanding of what is going on in our world, especially in Europe and Asia, and of the transformations that are taking place in all realms of life, in religion as well as in economy, in science as well as in the arts, in ethics as well as in education, in the whole of human existence. Religious socialism was always interested in human life as a whole and never in its economic basis exclusively. In this it was sharply distinguished from economic materialism, as well as from all forms of "economism." It did not consider the economic factor as an independent one on which all social reality is dependent. It recognized the dependence of economy itself on all other social, intellectual, and spiritual factors, and it created a picture of the total, interdependent structure of our present existence. We understood socialism as a problem not of wages but of a new theonomy in which the question of wages, of social security, is treated in unity with the question of truth, of spiritual security. On the other hand, we realized more than most Christian theologians ever did that there are social structures that unavoidably frustrate any spiritual appeal to the people subjected to them. My entrance into the religious-socialist movement meant for me the definitive break with philosophical idealism and theological transcendentalism. It opened my eyes to the religious significance of political Calvinism and social sectarianism, over against the predominantly sacramental character of my own Lutheran tradition. Religious socialism is not a political party but a spiritual power trying to be effective in as many parties as possible. It had and has sympathizers and foes on the Left as well as on the Right. Yet it stands unambiguously against every form of reaction, whether it be a semifeudal reaction as in Germany; a bourgeois status quo policy as in this country; or the clerical reaction that threatens to develop in large sections of postwar Europe. Religious socialism is not "Marxism," neither political Marxism in the sense of communism nor "scientific" Marxism in the sense of economic doctrines. We have, however, learned more from Marx's dialectical analysis of bourgeois society than from any other analysis of our period. We have found in it an understanding of human nature and history which is much nearer to the classical Christian doctrine of man with its empirical pessimism and its eschatological hope than is the picture of man in idealistic theology.

The most important theoretical work done by religious socialism was the creation of a religious interpretation of history, the first one, so far as I can see, of an especially Protestant character. There were Christian interpretations of history in the early and medieval church, an ecclesiastical or conservative type represented by Augustine and a sectarian or revolutionary type represented by Joachim of Floris. There were and are secular interpretations of history, conservative-pessimistic ones or evolutionary-optimistic ones or revolutionary-utopian ones (see the chapter on "Historical and Nonhistorical Interpretations of History"). Lutheranism had some affinity to the first type, Calvinism to the second, and sectarianism to the third. But a genuine Protestant interpretation of history was missing. It was the historical situation itself, the gap between conservative Lutheranism and socialist utopianism in Germany, which forced upon us the question of a Protestant interpretation of history. The answer given so far centers around three main concepts: "theonomy," "kairos," and the "demonic." The first of these concepts and its relation to the Protestant principle has already been explained. For the concept of "kairos" I can refer to the chapter "Kairos" in this book. The concept of the demonic is fully explained in my book, *The Interpretation of History*. In this introduction there remains the task of showing the relation of the concepts of "kairos" and of the "demonic" to the Protestant principle.

"Kairos," the "fulness of time," according to the New Testament use of the word, describes the moment in which the eternal breaks into the temporal, and the temporal is prepared to receive it. What happened in the one unique kairos, the appearance of Jesus as the Christ, i.e., as the center of history, may happen in a derived form again and again in the process of time, creating centers of lesser importance on which the periodization of history is dependent. The presence of such a dependent kairos was felt by many people after the first World War. It gave us the impulse to start the religious-socialist movement, the impetus of which was strong enough to survive its destruction in Germany and to spread through many countries, as the work and the decisions of the Oxford conference surprisingly proved. It is the basic trend of the European masses today, as all keen observers agree. "Kairos" is a biblical concept which could not be used by Catholicism because of the latter's conservative hierarchical interpretation of history; and it has not been used by the sects because of their striving toward the final end. The Protestant principle demands a method of interpreting history in which the critical transcendence of the divine over against conservatism and utopianism is strongly expressed and in which, at the same time, the creative omnipresence of the divine in the course of history is concretely indicated. In both respects the concept of "kairos" is most adequate. It continues the Protestant criticism of Catholic historical absolutism; it prevents the acceptance of any kind of utopian belief, progressivistic or revolutionary, in a perfect future; it overcomes Lutheran individualistic transcendentalism; it gives a dynamic historical consciousness in the line of early Christianity and the early Reformation; it provides a theonomous foundation for the creation of the new in history. The idea of "the kairos" unites criticism and creation. And just this is the problem of Protestantism (see the chapter entitled "The Formative Power of Protestantism").

The third concept decisive for my interpretation of history is that of "the demonic." It is one of the forgotten concepts of the New Testament, which, in spite of its tremendous importance for Jesus and the apostles, has become obsolete in modern theology. The thing responsible for this neglect was the reaction of the philosophers of the Enlightenment against the superstitious, abominable use of the idea of the demonic in the Middle Ages and in orthodox Protestantism. But abuse should not forbid right use. The idea of the demonic is the mythical expression of a reality that was in the center of Luther's experience as it was in Paul's, namely, the structural, and therefore inescapable, power of evil. The Enlightenment, foreshadowed by Erasmus' fight with Luther and by theological humanism, saw only the individual acts of evil, dependent on the free decisions of the conscious personality. It believed in the possibility of inducing the great majority of individuals to follow the demands of an integrated personal and social life by education, persuasion, and adequate institutions. But this belief was broken down not only by the "Storms of Our Times" (see the chapter of this title) but also by the new recognition of the destructive mechanisms determining the unconscious trends of individuals and groups. Theologians could reinterpret the badly named but profoundly true doctrine of "original sin" in the light of recent scientific discoveries. The powerful symbol of the demonic was everywhere accepted in the sense in which we had used it, namely, as a "structure of evil" beyond the moral power of good will, producing social and individual tragedy precisely through the inseparable mixture of good and evil in every human act. None of the concepts used by our interpretation of history has found as much response in religious and secular literature as has the concept of the demonic. This response may be interpreted as a symptom of the general feeling for the structural character of evil in our period. If evil has demonic or structural character limiting individual freedom, its conquest can come only by the opposite, the divine structure, that is, by what we have called a structure or "Gestalt" of grace. Luther's fight with Erasmus is typical for the Protestant interpretation of grace. We are justified by grace *alone,* because in our relation to God we are dependent on God, on God alone, and in no way on ourselves; we are grasped by grace, and this is only another way of saying that we have faith. Grace creates the faith through which it is received. Man does not create faith by will or intellect or emotional self-surrender. Grace comes to him; it is "objective," and he may be enabled to receive it, or he may not. The interest of early Protestantism was, however, so much centered around individual justification that the idea of a "Gestalt of grace" in our historical existence could not develop. This development was also prevented by the fact that the Catholic church considered itself as the body of objective grace, thus discrediting the idea of a "Gestalt of grace" for Protestant consciousness. It is obvious that the Protestant principle cannot admit any identification of grace with a visible reality, not even with the church on its visible side. But the negation of a visible "Gestalt of grace" does not imply the negation of the concept as such. The church in its spiritual quality, as an object of faith, is a "Gestalt of grace" (see the chapter on "The Formative Power of Protestantism"). And the church as "Gestalt of grace" is older and larger than the Christian churches. Without preparation in all history, without what I later have called the "church in its latency" (abbreviated to the "latent church"), the "manifest" church never could have appeared at a special time. Therefore, grace is in all history, and a continuous fight is going on between divine and demonic structures. The feeling of living in the center of such a fight was the basic impulse of religious socialism, expressing itself in a religious and, I think, essentially Protestant interpretation of history.

## IV

In all these ideas—theonomy, the kairos, the demonic, the Gestalt of grace, and the latent church—the Protestant principle appears in its revealing and critical power. But the Protestant principle is not the Protestant reality; and the question had to be asked as to how they are related to one another, how the life of the Protestant churches is possible under the criterion of the Protestant principle, and how a culture can be influenced and transformed by Protestantism. These questions are asked, in one way or another, in every article of the present book. And, in every answer suggested, the need for a profound transformation of religious and cultural Protestantism is indicated. It is not impossible that at some future time people will call the sum total of these transformations the end of the Protestant era. But the end of the Protestant era is, according to the basic distinction between the Protestant principle and Protestant reality, not the end of Protestantism. On the contrary, it may be the way in which the Protestant principle must affirm itself in the present situation. The end of the Protestant era is not the return to the Catholic era and not even, although much more so, the return to early Christianity; nor is it the step to a new form of secularism. It is something beyond all these forms, a new form of Christianity, to be expected and prepared for, but not yet to be named. Elements of it can be described but not the new structure that must and will grow; for Christianity is final only in so far as it has the power of criticizing and transforming each of its historical manifestations; and just this power is the Protestant principle. If the problem is raised of Protestantism as protest and as creation, a large group of questions immediately appear, all of them insufficiently answered in historical Protestantism and all of them driving toward radical transformations. Many of them are discussed in this book, several of them in other places by myself, some of them hardly at all. A short account of these problems may show their character and their importance. The sharp distinction between the principle and the actuality of Protestantism leads to the following question: By the power of what reality does the Protestant principle exercise its criticism? There must be such a reality, since the Protestant principle is not mere negation. But if such a reality does exist, how can it escape the Protestant protest? In other words: How can a spiritual Gestalt live if its principle is the protest against itself? How can critical and formative power be united in the reality of Protestantism? The answer is: In the power of the New Being that is manifest in Jesus as the Christ. Here the Protestant protest comes to an end. Here is the bedrock on which it stands and which is not subjected to its criticism. Here is the sacramental foundation of Protestantism, of the Protestant principle, and of the Protestant reality.

It is not by chance that a chapter on sacramental thinking appears in this book. The decrease in sacramental thinking and feeling in the churches of the Reformation and in the American denominations is appalling. Nature has lost its religious meaning and is excluded from participation in the power of salvation; the sacraments have lost their spiritual power and are vanishing in the consciousness of most Protestants; the Christ is interpreted as a religious personality and not as the basic sacramental reality, the "New Being." The Protestant protest has rightly destroyed the magical elements in Catholic sacramentalism but has wrongly brought to the verge of disappearance the sacramental foundation of Christianity and with it the religious foundation of the protest itself. It should be a permanent task of Christian theology, of preaching, and of church leadership to draw the line between the spiritual and the magical use of the sacramental element, for this element is the one essential element of every religion, namely, the presence of the divine before our acting and striving, in a "structure of grace" and in the symbols expressing it. C. G. Jung has called the history of Protestantism a history of continuous "iconoclasm" ("the destruction of pictures," that is, of religious symbols) and, consequently, the separation of our consciousness from the universally human "archetypes" that are present in the subconscious of everybody. He is right. Protestants often confuse essential symbols with accidental signs. They often are unaware of the numinous power inherent in genuine symbols, words, acts, persons, things. They have replaced the great wealth of symbols appearing in the Christian tradition by rational concepts, moral laws, and subjective emotions. This also was a consequence of the Protestant protest against the superstitious use of the traditional symbols in Roman Catholicism and in all paganism. But here also the protest has endangered its own basis.

One of the earliest experiences I had with Protestant preaching was its moralistic character or, more exactly, its tendency to overburden the personal center and to make the relation to God dependent on continuous, conscious decisions and experiences. The rediscovery of the unconscious in medical psychology and the insight into the unconscious drives of the mass psyche gave me the key to this basic problem of the Protestant cultus. The loss of sacraments and symbols corresponds to the exclusive emphasis on the center of personality in Protestantism; and both these facts correspond to the rise of the bourgeois ideal of personality, for which the Reformation and the Renaissance are equally responsible. At the same time, personal experience, the intimate observation of many individuals, the knowledge provided by psychotherapy, the trend of the younger generation in Europe toward the vital and pre-rational side of the individual and social life, the urgent desire for more community and authority and for powerful and dominating symbols—all these seemed to prove that the Protestant-humanist ideal of personality has been undermined and that the Protestant cultus and its personal and social ethics have to undergo a far-reaching transformation. This impression was and is supported by the general development of Western civilization toward more collectivistic forms of political and economic life. The demand for a basic security in social, as well as in spiritual, respects has superseded (though not removed) the liberal demand for liberty. And this demand can no longer be suppressed, for it is rooted in the deepest levels of the men of today, of personalities and groups. Reactionary measures may delay the development, but they cannot stop it. Organization of security (against the devastation coming from the atomic bomb or from permanent unemployment) is impossible without collectivistic measures. The question of whether Protestantism as a determining historical factor will survive is, above all, the question of whether it will be able to adapt itself to the new situation; it is the question of whether Protestantism, in the power of its principle, will be able to dissolve its amalgamation with bourgeois ideology and reality and create a synthesis, in criticism and acceptance, with the new forces that have arisen in the present stage of a revolutionary transformation of man and his world.

This is a challenge for both the individual and the social ethics of Protestantism. In the section on "Religion and Ethics" the attempt has been made to meet this challenge, most comprehensively in the chapter on "The Idea and the Ideal of Personality." Here the relation of the personal center, first, to nature, second, to community, and, third, to its own unconscious basis is discussed, and ideas for the transformation of these relations in the coming period of history are suggested. A special point is elaborated in the chapter on "The Transmoral Conscience," which tries to connect Luther's experience of the "justified conscience" with the psychotherapeutic principle of "accepting one's self" and with the emphasis on the creative venture of thinking and acting in the different forms of "the philosophy of life" and pragmatism. With respect to social ethics the chapter on "The Protestant Principle and the Proletarian Situation" is the most representative, though all chapters of the last section, "The Present Crisis," bear on the subject. Protestantism has not developed a social ethics of its own as Roman Catholicism has done (and codified) in terms of Thomism. The Protestant principle cannot admit an absolute form of social ethics. But, on the other hand, it need not surrender its development to the state, as it did on Lutheran soil, or to society, as it did on Calvinistic soil. Protestantism can and must have social ethics determined by the experience of the kairos in the light of the Protestant principle. The chapter on "Ethics in a Changing World" deals with this problem. The main answer given there is: Ethics out of the kairos is ethics of love, for love unites the ultimate criterion with the adaptation to the concrete situation.

It is a shortcoming of Protestantism that it never has sufficiently described the place of love in the whole of Christianity. This is due to the genesis and history of Protestantism. The Reformation had to fight against the partly magical, partly moralistic, partly relativistic distortion of the idea of love in later Catholicism. But this fight was only a consequence of Luther's fight against the Catholic doctrine of faith. And so faith and not love occupied the center of Protestant thought. While Zwingli and Calvin, by their humanistic-biblicistic stress on the function of the law, were prevented from developing a doctrine of love, Luther's doctrine of love and wrath (of God and the government) prevented him from connecting love with law and justice. The result was puritanism without love in the Calvinistic countries and romanticism without justice in the Lutheran countries. A fresh interpretation of love is needed in all sections of Protestantism, an interpretation that shows that love is basically not an emotional but an ontological power, that it is the essence of life itself, namely, the dynamic reunion of that which is separated. If love is understood in this way, it is the principle on which all Protestant social ethics is based, uniting an eternal and a dynamic element, uniting power with justice and creativity with form. In the chapter on "Ethics in a Changing World" the attempt is made to lay the foundation of a Protestant doctrine of love.

The formative power of Protestantism in theology and philosophy is indicated in several articles but is not applied constructively. It is my hope that parts of the theological system, on which I have been work-ing for many years, will appear in a not distant future. In the present volume only some results are anticipated, especially in the chapter on "Philosophy and Theology." I have traveled a long way to my present theological position, a way that started in my first larger book, *Das System der Wissenschaften nach Gegenständen und Methoden* ("The System of Knowledge: Its Contents and Its Methods"). In many respects the ideas developed in this book have determined my thinking up to the present moment, especially those on biology, technical sciences, history, and metaphysics. Theology is defined as "theonomous metaphysics," a definition that was a first and rather insufficient step toward what I now call the "method of correlation." This method tries to overcome the con-flict between the naturalistic and supernaturalistic methods which im-perils not only any real progress in the work of systematic theology but also any possible effect of theology on the secular world. The method of correlation shows, at every point of Christian thought, the interdepend-ence between the ultimate questions to which philosophy (as well as pre-philosophical thinking) is driven and the answers given in the Christian message. Philosophy cannot answer ultimate or existential questions *qua* philosophy. If the philosopher tries to answer them (and all creative philosophers have tried to do so), he becomes a theologian. And, conversely, theology cannot answer those questions without ac-cepting their presuppositions and implications. Question and answer determine each other; if they are separated, the traditional answers be-come unintelligible, and the actual questions remain unanswered. The method of correlation aims to overcome this situation. In the chapter on "Philosophy and Theology" (as well as in all my work in systematic theology) the method is explained and applied. Such a method is truly dialectical and therefore opposed to the supernaturalism of later Bar-thianism as well as to any other type of orthodoxy and fundamentalism. Philosophy and theology are not separated, and they are not identical, but they are correlated, and their correlation is the methodological prob-lem of a Protestant theology.

In this connection I want to say a few words about my relationship to the two main trends in present-day theology, the one called "dialectical" in Europe, "neo-orthodox" in America, the other called "liberal" in Europe (and America) and sometimes "humanist" in America. My theology can be understood as an attempt to overcome the conflict between these two types of theology. It intends to show that the alternative expressed in those names is not valid; that most of the contrasting statements are expressions of an obsolete stage of theological thought; and that, besides many other developments in life and the interpretation of life, the Protestant principle itself prohibits old and new orthodoxy, old and new liberalism. Since the latter point is especially important in the context of this book I want to enlarge on it in a few propositions which, at the same time, show the main lines of my own theological position.

It was the Protestant principle that gave liberal theology the right and the good conscience to approach the Holy Scripture with the critical methods of historical research and with a complete scientific honesty in showing the mythical and legendary elements in both Testaments. This event, which has no parallel in other religions, is an impressive and glorious vindication of the truth of the Protestant principle. In this respect Protestant theology must always be liberal theology.

It was the Protestant principle that enabled liberal theology to realize that Christianity cannot be considered in isolation from the general religious and cultural, psychological and sociological, development of humanity; that Christianity, as well as every Christian, is involved in the universal structures and changes of human life; and that, on the other hand, there are anticipations of Christianity in all history. This insight, which is deadly for ecclesiastical and theological arrogance, is strengthening for Christianity in the light of the Protestant principle. In this respect also Protestant theology must be liberal theology.

It was the Protestant principle that destroyed the supra-naturalism of the Roman Catholic system, the dualism between nature and grace, which is ultimately rooted in a metaphysical devaluation of the natural as such. And it was the Protestant principle that showed liberal theology a way of uniting the antidualistic emphasis of the Reformation with the ontological universalism and humanism of the Renaissance, thus destroying holy superstitions, sacramental magic, and sacred heteronomy. In this respect above all, Protestant theology must be liberal theology and must remain so even if challenged and suppressed by a period which will prefer security to truth.

But it is also the Protestant principle that has induced orthodox theologians (both old and new) to look at Scripture as Holy Scripture, namely, as the original document of the event which is called "Jesus the

Christ" and which is the criterion of all Scripture and the manifestation of the Protestant principle. In this respect Protestant theology must be "ortho-dox" and must always maintain the ground in which the critical power of the Protestant principle is rooted.

It was the Protestant principle that showed orthodox theologians (both old and new) that the history of religion and culture is a history of permanent demonic distortions of revelation and idolatrous confusions of God and man. Therefore, they emphasized and re-emphasized the First Commandment, the infinite distance between God and man, and the judgment of the Cross over and against all human possibilities. In this respect also, Protestant theology must be always orthodox, fighting against conscious and unconscious idolatries and ideologies.

Again, it was the Protestant principle that forced the orthodox theologians (both old and new) to acknowledge that man in his very existence is estranged from God, that a distorted humanity is our heritage, and that no human endeavor and no law of progress can conquer this situation but only the paradoxical and reconciling act of the divine self-giving. In this respect above all, Protestant theology must be orthodox at all times.

Is the acceptance of these propositions liberal, is it orthodox theology? I think it is neither the one nor the other. I think it is Protestant and Christian, and, if a technical term is wanted, it is "neo-dialectical."

This Introduction is written in the confusing period after the end of the second World War. What are the chances of historical Protestantism in this period? What are its possible contributions to this period? Will the new era be in any imaginable sense a Protestant era, as the era between the Reformation and the first World War certainly was? Only a few indications for the immediate future and its spiritual needs are given in the last chapter. Much more could be derived from the whole of this book. A few things are obvious. The wars and the revolutions that mark the first half of the twentieth century are symptoms of the disintegration of life and thought of the liberal *bourgeoisie* and of a radical transformation of Western civilization. In so far as Protestantism is an element in the changing structure of the Western world—and nothing beyond it—it takes part in the processes of disintegration and transformation. It is not untouched by the trend toward a more collectivistic order of life, socially as well as spiritually. It is threatened by the dangers of this trend, and it may share in its promises. We are not yet able to have a picture of this coming era and of the situation of Christianity and Protestantism within it. We see elements of the picture which certainly will appear in it, but we do not see the whole. We do not know the destiny and character of Protestantism in this period. We do not know whether it will even desire or deserve the name "Protestantism." All this is unknown. But we know three things: We know the Protestant principle, its eternal significance, and its lasting power in all periods of history. We know, though only fragmentarily, the next steps that Protestantism must take in the light of its principle and in view of the present situation of itself and of the world. And we know that it will take these steps unwillingly, with many discords, relapses, and frustrations, but forced by a power that is not its own.

May I conclude with a personal remark? It was the "ecstatic" experience of the belief in a kairos which, after the first World War, created, or at least initiated, most of the ideas presented in this book. There is no such ecstatic experience after the second World War, but a general feeling that more darkness than light is lying ahead of us. An element of cynical realism is prevailing today, as an element of utopian hope was prevailing at that earlier time. The Protestant principle judges both of them. It justifies the hope, though destroying its utopian form; it justifies the realism, though destroying its cynical form. In the spirit of such a realism of hope, Protestantism must enter the new era, whether this era will be described by later historians as a post-Protestant or as a Protestant era; for, not the Protestant era, but the Protestant principle is everlasting.

# TABLE OF CONTENTS

## I. RELIGION AND HISTORY

## II. RELIGION AND CULTURE

## III. RELIGION AND ETHICS

## IV. PROTESTANTISM

## V. THE PRESENT CRISIS

## TILLICH'S CONCEPT OF THE PROTESTANT ERA

## INDEX

# I. RELIGION AND HISTORY

# Chapter I

## PHILOSOPHY AND FATE[1]

TO HAVE a philosophical understanding of one's fate, to defy fate with philosophy, appears to be the usual and obvious answer to the question as to the relation between fate and philosophy. This answer has a strong justification. Since the days of the Greeks it has been considered the task of philosophy to give its followers the power to resist fate; to be a philosopher means to adopt an attitude that is superior to fate. Philosophical knowledge is a knowledge that is not subject to fate, it is fateless; for it is knowledge of the eternal structure of reality which, as the condition of all historical change, is changeless itself.

Can we maintain the idea that knowledge is fateless because its object is beyond fate? Can we even maintain the idea that being, the object of philosophy, is fateless? Is truth fateless? Can we say that both thought and being are fateless, or is truth subject to fate? And if it is subject to fate, what does this imply? What does truth look like if it is dominated by fate, and what sort of thing is a knowledge that is bound by fate? And what powerful changes must philosophy have experienced, what trying course of fate must it have traveled in passing from the idea that truth is fateless to the idea that it is fate-bound? These are questions that confront us.

### I. THE CONCEPT OF FATE

Our theme "Philosophy and Fate" might have permitted a different sort of treatment. We might have directed our attention to the philosophical concept of fate. This question, however, is not the one with which we are concerned. Yet it cannot be entirely ignored.

Fate is the transcendent necessity in which freedom is entangled. This involves three things: first, fate is related to freedom. Where there

1. [Inaugural address, given in June, 1929, on assuming the chair of Professor of Philosophy at the University of Frankfort on the Main. The word *Schicksal*, here rendered as "fate," combines the meaning of "fate" and "destiny."—TRANSLATOR.]

3

is no freedom, there is no fate; there is simply necessity. A merely physical object that is conditioned in all respects is entirely without fate because it is wholly bound to necessity. The more freedom there is, that is, the more the self-determination (or the greater the autonomous power), the more the susceptibility to fate. Just because philosophy is free, because it is determined by itself, it is susceptible to fate. *Not only the philosopher as a man but also the philosopher as philosopher has a fate, and this means that philosophy itself has a fate.* If freedom is taken from philosophy, if philosophy is made a necessary function of something else—of material, psychological, sociological laws—it has lost a fate or destiny of its own.

Second, fate signifies that freedom is subjected to necessity. It puts freedom into an embracing frame of reference. It negates the freedom of the philosopher as a philosopher; it negates the freedom of philosophy. Only one whose freedom was absolute would have no fate. Only a being with unconditioned power over itself, only a being with unconditional freedom, would be above fate. Philosophy has often tried to put itself into such a position; it has yielded to the temptation of *eritis sicut Deus* and has believed it would be able to become fateless. It has supposed that its processes of thinking are identical with the divine self-consciousness. But here, too, pride goes before a fall, as may be seen most strikingly in the collapse of Hegel's absolute system.

Third, fate signifies that freedom and necessity are not separated but that, in every fateful event, freedom and necessity interpenetrate each other. Man feels that that side of his being upon which he has put his own stamp, his "character," is largely responsible for what happens to him, even external and accidental things. And he feels, at the same time, that his character is conditioned by events that in their origin go far back to past generations, back to much earlier manifestations of the continuing and living fabric of humanity. He feels that the necessity implied in the concept of fate is a universal necessity, a necessity that transcends every special chain of events. If philosophy has a fate, it is subjected to such a universal necessity. At the same time, it is true that nothing can condition philosophy which is not also conditioned by the freedom of philosophy. Even the most accidental thing that arises within the life of philosophy is conditioned by the character of philosophy itself, by the stamp that comes from its own nature.

We have analyzed the concept of fate as we wish to consider it here, and we have also indicated the sense in which one can speak of the "fate" of philosophy: the freedom of philosophy is bound up with an embracing universal necessity, so that freedom and necessity are conditioned by each other and are inextricably interwoven.

We now turn to a discussion of the relation between philosophy and fate as it is found in history. We must see how the question of the relation between philosophy and fate arose. First, we must ask what kind of fate has impelled philosophy to conceive of itself as conditioned by fate. Second, we must raise the question as to how philosophy can give a conceptual formulation to its own relationship to fate and whether philosophy, in the fulfilment of its own function, can make use of the fact that it is subject to fate.

## II. PHILOSOPHY AND FATE IN GREEK THOUGHT

Greek philosophy, like Greek tragedy, religion, and mystery cult, is a struggle against fate, an attempt to rise above fate. The origin of the mysteries cannot be understood if they are viewed merely as cultus, nor can the origin of tragedy be understood merely from the point of view of aesthetics, or the origin of philosophy merely from a scientific point of view. To be sure, all these concerns became the basis of various cultic, aesthetic, and scientific developments, but they did not originate in the separation. They grew out of a common, deeper level of existence, out of the life-and-death struggle, out of a wrestling with fate. To the Greek the struggle against fate was unavoidable, for fate had for him demonic qualities. It was a holy and destructive power. It entangled man in an objective guilt that was working out its baleful consequences without regard for the individual subject, avenging his guilt by dire punishment even though the guilt was not a matter of his freedom. The mystery cult offers purification at the hands of a god who, although himself subject to fate, overcomes fate. Tragedy presents the hero who in freedom endures and overcomes his fate. Philosophy gives knowledge, a knowledge by means of which man is united with the eternal One, beyond fate. This attitude of Greek philosophy, whereby it deprived all things and all forms of life of their ultimate power and concentrated the power of being in one substance, in the result of the highest abstraction, in "Pure Being," is not intelligible except as the consequence of a dire need. It is the need to overcome the bondage to fate and tragedy. This connection is clearly expressed in the words of

Anaximander, the very first words of Greek philosophy. He speaks of "things perishing into that from which they have their birth, for they pay to one another the penalty of their injustice according to the order of time." This world of objective guilt and tragic punishment beclouded the Greek mentality. Echoes of a deep pessimism vibrate from the lyrics and from many of the aphorisms of pre-philosophical wisdom. But the Greek's passionate will to live, aided by the unique clarity of the Greek mind, broke through the spell which threatened to fetter it. Not in vain had the Greeks lived through the days when the sun of Homer's Olympus had shone over a world that was almost free from demonic fear. It is true that this golden sun was almost eclipsed when, in the period of religious revolutions, the Greeks touched the deeper levels of religious experience. But the Homeric sun had not shone in vain. The Greek spirit overcame the demonic again, but no longer with the help of the Olympic gods. In philosophy it was done in terms of pure being, as substance or as number, as idea, as logos, as pure form, as element and atom, as the ultimate One. Bold and courageous thinking here struggles with the melancholy subjection to tragedy and fate. Every step forward in knowledge has an exorcising effect. Knowledge restricts the power of fate, it deprives things of their frightful mystery, it makes them into mere things and subjects them to the control of the mind. In a titanic assault, carried through with great courage and brilliant clarity, Greek philosophy assails the mystery of fate and reveals it step by step with admirable power. In such a struggle a number of different attitudes were held by the philosophers. Some attempted the critical dissolution of the old powers of fate, as with the Sophists and the Cynics; some attempted to transform them into measured things, as with the Pythagoreans, into quantity and law, as with Democritus; some attempted it by resistance to the powers of fate, as with the Stoics, or by inner freedom from them, as with Socrates; others attempted it by the skilful exploitation or utilization of these powers, as with the Epicureans, or by the attempt to subject them to form, as in Plato's *Republic;* others attempted it by a paradoxical affirmation of them, as with Heraclitus, or by a flight from them, as with the Skeptics; and still others attempted it by rising above existence as such, as with Parmenides, Plato, Aristotle, and Plotinus. In all this diversity of attitude, however, one thing remains the same: the struggle of the philosopher against a fate-entangled, demonically controlled existence. For this reason the highest ideal for human life is found in the realm of thought, in the rising above existence, not in the realm of action, not in transforming existence. Never before or afterward has the struggle of philosophy against the fear of fate achieved so rapid and decisive a victory, and never again has victorious philosophy, in turn, been defeated so severely by fate.

Just as the gods of the Homeric world banished the demonic powers of the past but did not eliminate them, so Greek philosophy suppressed the power of fate without being able to eliminate it. Just as the gods of Homer banished the demons into the underworld, the philosophers relegated the intractable and resisting element of existence into the realm of nonbeing, into the *mē on,* into that which is without any power of being. But this *mē on* retained in its very impotence the power to resist form and knowledge, just as the underworld was the impotent, and yet always threatening, opponent of the world of Olympus; and in due time the opponent reappeared in power. Fate became powerful again. *Tyche* and *heimarmene* ("chance" and "necessity") darkened the heavens of late antiquity. The astrological preoccupation with fate subjected man to fate. The fear of demons hovered like a cloud over his spirit. The Epicureans exalted their master to a savior, because through his materialism he had freed them from fear. But it was not a lasting salvation. By establishing the element of absolute chance, Epicurus himself reserved a place for fear in his system. The Neo-Platonists were not able to come to terms with the demonic powers except by taking them up into their system.

In this situation, philosophy became aware of its own fate. It surveyed its own history and saw that its struggle to achieve a certainty by which it might form human life was futile. The battle of the schools had driven even the Platonic Academy into skepticism, and the attempt to create new forms of life was out of the question in a time when Rome, like a superhuman power of fate, was bringing one nation after the other under its heel. From the depths of this skepticism men cried out for revelation. The old schools invested their leaders with a religious aura. But oriental revelations gave deeper certainty than the old philosophers. Threatened by a demonic fate, men were reaching out for a saving fate—for "grace."

### III. PHILOSOPHY AND FATE IN OCCIDENTAL THOUGHT

The victory of Christianity is the victory of the idea that the world is a divine creation over the belief in the resisting power of an eternal matter. It is the victory of the belief in the perfection of created being in all its levels over the tragic fear of resistant matter, hostile to the divine. It is the radical denial of the demonic character of existence as such. It places an essentially positive valuation on existence. And this implies that it places a positive valuation on the whole temporal order of events, that the "order of time" harbors within itself not only, as with Anaximander, a becoming and a passing-away but also the possibility of real novelty, a creative and formative power, a purpose and end that give it meaning. In Christianity, time triumphs over space. The irreversible, unrepeatable character of time, its meaningful directedness, replaces the cyclic, ever recurrent becoming and passing-away. A "gracious" destiny that brings salvation in time and history subdues a demonic fate which denies the new in history. Thus the Greek view of life and the world is overcome, and with it the presupposition of Greek philosophy as well as of Greek tragedy. Never again can philosophy be what it was originally. The philosophy that wished to overcome fate is itself seized by fate and becomes something different. Whoever does not see this, whoever imagines that philosophy has taken a unilinear course through history, misses the essential and the most profound thing in the history of ideas in the Occident, he misses the destiny of the Western mind.

Philosophy in its despair had called out for revelation. Now revelation laid hold of philosophy and adapted it to its own purposes. It purged away what was demonic in it, and at the same time it took over its logical forms and its empirical contents. But the metaphysical elements in it, the element that gives philosophy its real significance, was suppressed. Philosophy became formalistic; and by that very fact it became fitted to serve the sacred. If it had itself claimed to be sacred, the "sacred" that had now become triumphantly victorious would have repulsed it and annihilated it. It was its destiny to become merely a bond-slave. And this fate was imposed upon it not only from the outside. Philosophy was not merely the innocent victim of abuse at the hands of religion. The fate that befell philosophy arose out of the inner logic of its own historical development. That philosophy should become the handmaid of theology was in a genuine sense its proper fate.

The memory of what had befallen it in its skeptical period made serf-dom easy for it. The memory of the catastrophe of Greek culture which took place in late antiquity echoes through the thought of the Middle Ages as a constantly recurring overtone. It was the negative presupposi-tion of ecclesiastical authority in the Middle Ages. But, finally, this overtone faded away, the catastrophe that once had decided the fate of philosophy was forgotten, and the brilliance of its first great triumphant march to victory fascinated the mind and spirit of the West. *Everything Greek came back again; yet nothing was in reality Greek, for the reli-gious foundation was no longer the same.* Not the idea of becoming and passing away but rather that of the divine creation of the world and the belief in a divine providence, in a divine purpose, working to-ward salvation in time and through history, had become fundamental for the character of the occidental mentality. What was created was not Hellenism, but *Christian humanism.* This concept, whose command-ing importance for the proper understanding of the whole modern era has not yet been adequately recognized, sheds light on the problem that we are dealing with here. Christian humanism, even in its most anti-religious and anti-Christian forms, is still Christian in substance. In Christian humanism the fate of Christianity and the fate of philosophy are bound together.

Greek philosophy had developed categories and methods of universal significance. But the religious character of Greek culture prevented them from being used for world transformation. They were used either for aesthetic intuition of the world, for ethical resignation from it, or for mystical elevation above it. In contrast to these uses, Christian humanism employed Greek concepts for the technical control and the revolutionary transformation of reality. Especially useful for this pur-pose was the mathematical-quantitative interpretation of nature as pro-moted by the Pythagoreans and Plato. It was not an accident, but deep-ly rooted in Greek spirituality, that this view was suppressed by the biological-qualitative point of view as represented by Aristotle. Modern philosophy goes the opposite way. It overcomes the existential skepti-cism of the last period of Greek philosophy by a methodological skep-ticism as the basis of mathematical science and its technical application. And there is no better and more continuous test for the truth of this type of scientific approach to nature than the fact that the technical creations which are based on it *do* work and work more effectively every day. Ethical theories for the individual and legal theories for the state, fitting the world-transforming activism of modern culture, are added to the dominant philosophy of science. Disturbing interferences from the transcendent are eliminated. To this end an empiricist or rationalistic metaphysics pushes the divine out to the fringe of the world —or subordinates it to technical and moral purposes. Philosophy, in this period of its development, believed not only that it had ceased to be the "handmaid" of theology but also that it had become completely autonomous, determined only by the laws of reason and free from any religious element. But this was an illusion. During the whole course of modern culture, which is the expression of the fighting and victorious *bourgeoisie,* philosophy maintained the belief in providence. It did not call it "providence," it called it "pre-established harmony" or the "law of progress and perfectibility." It did not make the development dependent on divine actions but on the political and educational activities of man. Like philosophy itself, these activities follow the demands of reason. And reason, according to rationalistic belief, has no fate. Its principles are unchangeable. It can be realized more or less perfectly. Its understanding can and must grow. In periods like the Middle Ages reason had bad luck, in modern times, good luck. But it never had and never can have a fate, a unity of freedom and necessity. Truth and fate are separated.

But the claim of modern philosophy to be beyond fate and tragedy was refuted by its own history. The self-assured rationalism of the eighteenth century was shattered by the blows of Hume, Kant, Comte, and others. Even in its great days of revolution and victory, rationalism had not been able to remove the religious and classical traditions. Now it was weakened in itself, and some of these traditions became powerful again. Romanticism was longing for the Middle Ages. Aesthetic classicism reappeared; orthodox Protestantism and pietistic mysticism experienced a resurrection. But more decisive for the future was another trend, a trend that had lurked under the surface of rationalism in the days of its weakness, a trend toward irrationalism, in some cases even toward antirationalism. An old, almost forgotten, tradition, which runs from Duns Scotus and the nature philosophy of the Renaissance down through Luther and Jacob Boehme to Oetinger and Schelling, came suddenly to the fore. Under the influence of this tradition new motifs began to attract attention: the ambiguous character of existence, the irrational will that destroys any static conception of the world of ideas, the conflict of the unconscious and the conscious will, the demonic depth in the divine nature itself. A vigorous protest was raised against Cartesian rationalism.

A discovery, decisive for the question of philosophy and fate, had been made. The place, so to speak, was found at which fate could again determine philosophy—at the nonrational level of existence and thought. In the Middle Ages the nonrational level of existence was spoken of as "the deeps of the soul." Here divine grace and demonic possession were effective. This level of existence now reappeared in various forms, as a dark urge, as "Life," as vitality, as the unconscious, as the will to power, as the infinite desire, as the collective unconscious, as the class struggle. The mind became aware of the relationship between itself and the prerational levels of the psyche, those levels through which fate determines thought. The way in which this happens has been described in different ways since the breakdown of Hegel's renewal of an all-embracing system of reason, and mostly in opposition to him. It appeared as Feuerbach's materialistic analysis of religion, as Marx's theory of the economic determinism of political thought, as the pragmatist theory of knowledge in Nietzsche and William James, as the depth psychology of Freud, Jung, and their schools, supported by the great French and Russian novelists and poets. Each of these tendencies forced upon philosophy the question of its historical existence, of its dependence on fate. Only academic philosophy was deaf to the question. It expounded an epistemology and an ethical theory that gave it a sense of being secure against the bludgeonings of fate. Today we are inescapably confronted with this question. We cannot evade it any longer. There is no place of shelter from it, not even in the field of formal logic, as there is no longer any refuge to which bourgeois society can withdraw in order to escape the question of its own fate. The question may be stated thus: What is truth if it is determined by historical destiny?

IV. TRUTH AND FATE

Hegel gives the first significant answer to the question concerning the way in which truth is involved in fate. He gives this answer in his philosophy of history: History is the place where the eternal ideas, the divine reason, appear in dialectical succession within time and finitude.

And history is the place where nations with their will to power fight each other. History is not alone the place of ideas and the logical necessity of their succession. Nor is it determined alone by the irrational will to live. Both are united in history; nations are the bearers of the ideas. This occurs through what Hegel calls the "cunning" of the idea. The idea uses the vital forces of individuals and nations in order to realize itself. The theory of the cunning of the idea is no myth; rather is it a paradoxical expression for faith in providence, but in its idealistic metamorphosis. The believer in the traditional idea of providence also knew that the ways of providence are dark, contradictory, and obscure; nevertheless, he believed in it and was certain that it would arrive at its goal. Hegel goes one step further. He knows of the ways in which the idea develops; he is aware of its cunning and of the true meaning of the devious and roundabout course which history follows. He stands at the end and can look back upon the whole development. Thus it is in his, the final philosopher's, thought that philosophy finds its full realization and achieves its freedom from fate. Every external necessity disappears in the "absolute" system. Participation in the unconditioned freedom of the unconditioned is now possible, the threat of fate is annulled, history is taken up into the system, freedom triumphs over necessity.

But this solution had to break down; it was in itself contradictory, for, once granting the existence of fate, why should it come to a halt before the thought of Hegel? Actually, it did not come to a halt, it pushed on through to its own opposite. One needed only to reverse the symbol of the cunning of the idea. One could ask whether the really "cunning" thing is not perhaps the will of the national group, the will to power of the classes, or the instinctive urges of the individual soul? Is not the idea merely an illusion that the vital powers use in order to achieve their purposes? This could be said in psychological, as well as in sociological, terms. Where it is said, truth itself—every nonfactual truth—is sacrificed: ideas are ideologies, illusionary expressions of will to power or libido. Philosophy is subjected to a completely external necessity. It has no freedom to follow its own structures and demands, no genuine fate; for fate, as was said before, presupposes the unity of necessity and freedom. It is, of course, impossible to maintain this general doctrine of ideology. If it is a true theory (and it claims to be that), it presupposes truth, at least at *one* point, and ceases to be general. In *this* point necessity is united with freedom. It is no longer external necessity. The philosopher who undermines philosophy must also show why he does not undermine his own undermining. He must show the place on which he stands. And all the irrationalists in philosophy have always tried to do just this. As Hegel called the place at the end of philosophy the "place of truth," so Marx thought that the proletariat occupies this favored position, and the psychoanalyst attributes it to the completely analyzed personality, and the philosopher of vitalism to the strongest life, to the process of growth, to an élite or a race. There are, according to these ideas, favored moments and positions in history when truth appears and reason is united with the irrational. There are moments, as I myself have emphasized on different occasions, in which "kairos," the right time, is united with "logos," the "eternal truth," and in which the fate of philosophy is decided for a special period.

Max Scheler, a representative of vitalism, a man of great intuitive power, tried to give a solution in a different way. He thought the dominant forces, the economic forces, the vital instincts, and the like, decide *what* can be thought in each period but do not decide about the meaning and the validity of thought itself. These irrational forces determine which ideas can have reality, but they do not determine their truth. So far as the world of reality is concerned, development is strictly determined. No idea has the power to resist it. Scheler argues for the "impotence of the idea" and the exclusive power of the vital forces in determining history. There is, so to speak, an unlimited reservoir of ideas that are possible of conception. Out of this reservoir the historical process draws whatever fits the special situation. In this view, obviously, idea and existence are divorced; philosophy and fate are only externally related to each other. But there is a double, untenable presupposition in this solution: the realm of historical processes is entirely determined by a necessity that in itself has no relation to meaning. But, if this were the case, how could there be an affinity of special situation to special ideas? The historical process must be intrinsically related to ideas in order to be able to receive them. And, on the other hand, ideas are not static possibilities but dynamic forces whose eternity does not prevent them from becoming temporal, whose essence drives them to appear in existence. In this, Aristotle and Hegel are right, against Plato and Descartes. Fate is not strange to truth, it does not concern only the outer court of philosophy, leaving untouched the sacred precincts themselves.

Fate obtrudes even into the sacred inclosure of philosophy, into the truth itself, and it stops only before the holy of holies. It stops only before the certainty that fate is divine and not demonic, that it is meaning-fulfilling and not meaning-destroying. Without this certainty, which is the inmost kernel of Christianity, we should be thrown back to the Greek situation and should have to begin to traverse the whole fateful path of philosophy over again. But this eternal truth, this logos above fate, is not at man's disposal; it cannot be subjected, as Hegel thought it could, to the processes of human thinking; it cannot be described or presented as the meaningful world process. To be sure, this eternal logos does pulsate through all our thinking; there can be no act of thought without the secret presupposition of its unconditional truth.

But this unconditional truth is not in our possession. It is the hidden criterion of every truth that we believe we possess. There is an element of venture and of risk in every statement of truth. Yet we can take this risk in the certainty that this is the only way in which truth can reveal itself to finite and historical beings.

But truth is not itself an idea with whose help a philosophy free from fate can be created. It stands critically over against every realization, as is clearly understood by genuine Protestantism. It is the "justification" of thought, it is that through which thought meets its finite limit and also receives its infinite right.

If philosophy maintains its relation to the eternal logos, if philosophy is not afraid of the demonic threat of fate, then it can quite readily accept the place of fate within thinking. It can acknowledge that it has from the beginning been subject to fate, that it has always wished to escape it, though it has never succeeded in doing so. The union of kairos and logos is the philosophical task set for us in philosophy and in all fields that are accessible to the philosophical attitude. The logos is to be taken up into the kairos, universal values into the fulness of time, truth into the fate of existence. The separation of idea and existence has to be brought to an end. It is the very nature of essence to come into existence, to enter into time and fate. This happens to essence not because of something extraneous to it; it is rather the expression of its own intrinsic character, of its freedom. And it is essential to philosophy to stand in existence, to create out of time and fate. It would be wrong if one were to characterize this as a knowledge bound to necessity. Since existence itself stands in fate, it is proper that philosophy should also stand in fate. Existence and knowledge both are subject to fate.

The immutable and eternal heaven of truth of which Plato speaks is accessible only to a knowledge that is free from fate—to divine knowledge. The truth that stands in fate is accessible to him who stands within fate, who is himself an element of fate, for thought is a part of existence. And not only is existence fate to thought, but so also is thought fate to existence, just as everything is fate to everything else. Thought is one of the powers of being, it is a power within existence. And it proves its power by being able to spring out of any given existential situation and create something new! It can leap over existence just as existence can leap over it. Because of this characteristic of thought, the view perhaps quite naturally arose that thought may be detached from existence and may therefore liberate man from his hateful bondage to it. But the history of philosophy itself has shown that this opinion is a mistaken one. The leap of thought does not involve a breaking of the ties with existence; even in the act of its greatest freedom, thought remains bound to fate. Thus the history of philosophy shows that all existence stands in fate. Every finite thing possesses a certain power of being of its own and thus possesses a capacity for fate. The greater a finite thing's autonomous power of being is, the higher is its capacity for fate and the more deeply is the knowledge of it involved in fate. From physics on up to the normative cultural sciences there is a gradation, the logos standing at the one end and the kairos at the other. But there is no point at which either logos or kairos alone is to be found. Hence even our knowledge of the fateful character of philosophy must at the same time stand in logos and in kairos. If it stood only in the kairos, it would be without validity and the assertion would be valid only for the one making it; if it stood only in the logos, it would be without fate and would therefore have no part in existence, for existence is involved in fate.

And this holds for all knowledge, for every task in which we are engaged in this university. As the Greeks devoted themselves to philosophy, obedient to the logos within the limits of the kairos; as the Middle Ages subordinated the logos to the great kairos upon which their culture was built; as modern philosophy through *its* kairos adapted itself to the logos of a world-dominating science and technique, so *our* task is to serve the logos out of the depths of our new kairos, a kairos that is now emerging in the crises and catastrophes of our day. Hence, the more deeply we understand fate—our own personal fate and that of our society—the more our intellectual work will have power and truth.

# Chapter II

## HISTORICAL AND NONHISTORICAL
## INTERPRETATIONS OF HISTORY
## A COMPARISON[1]

IF I correctly understand the title of my address, it demands a comparative analysis of Christian and non-Christian interpretations of history, including those which are not directly Christian but which prepare the way for the Christian interpretation or are influenced by it. This means that a large field must be covered and consequently that I can give only a short and rather schematic description of the main types of interpreting history. It means also that this paper cannot attempt any constructive interpretation of history. It is, of course, unavoidable that the arrangement and description of the different types is influenced by my own theological understanding. A merely objective typology is impossible in the realm of the spiritual life. Understanding spiritual things means participating in them, deciding about them, and transforming them.

The many forms of the interpretation of history can be reduced to two main types: the first type in which *history is interpreted through nature* and the second in which *history is interpreted through itself.*

The first type gives an interpretation of history which I like to call "the nonhistorical interpretation of history" because it is set forth in natural terms and denies an original and independent character to history. "Natural" in this context comprises nature as well as supra-nature in the sense of a higher transcendent nature.

The second type acknowledges history as an original reality which cannot be derived either from nature or from supernature, which, on the contrary, tries to draw nature as well as supernature into its own development. These two types exhibit entirely different structures. In the first type space is predominant; in the second, time is predominant. This does not overlook the fact that no pure types appear in history, that always elements of the one type can be found in the other type,

1. Address delivered at the annual meeting of the American Theological Society, Eastern Branch, April 14, 1939.

since there is no time without space and no space without time in human existence. Nevertheless, the difference in fundamental structure is very evident. Religion as well as philosophy must choose between these two possibilities which ultimately are exclusive. And this choice is the decision against or for Christianity.

No reference is made in this paper to the difference between religious and philosophical interpretations of history. In every religious interpretation of history, philosophical elements are implied—first of all, a philosophy of time; and in every philosophical interpretation of history religious elements are implied—first of all, an interpretation of the meaning (or meaninglessness) of existence. Wherever *existence* itself is to be interpreted, the difference between philosophy and theology decreases, and both meet in the realm of myth and symbol.

### I. THE NONHISTORICAL TYPE OF INTERPRETING HISTORY

The nonhistorical type of interpreting history is represented in four doctrines of world-historical significance: in the Chinese Tao doctrine, in the Indian Brahma doctrine, in the Greek nature doctrine, in the late-European life-doctrine.

### A

The Tao is the eternal law of the world which is both the norm and the power of human life. The emperor as the Son of Heaven is supposed to mediate between the cosmic Tao and the human historical life, which are united in his empire. The Tao is eternal, the law of all motions, itself beyond motion and therefore beyond history. As far as history is dealt with, the past is glorified. The ancient emperors and the classical writers are the patterns for all the future in politics and culture. The ancestors determine life more than those who are living. The past is predominant over the future. The present is a consequence of the past, but not at all an anticipation of the future. In Chinese literature there are fine records of the past but no expectations of the future.

### B

In India the Brahman experience and speculation deprive all things in time and space, gods as well as men and animals, of their ultimate reality and meaning. They have reality—but from the point of view of Maya; they are not simply the products of imagination, but they become transparent for the ascetics who have discovered the principle of

Brahma-Atman in themselves and in their world. Consequently, no event in time can have ultimate significance. Even the incarnations of the gods, the appearance of Bodhisattvas, are repeated again and again and will be repeated in the future. We have very few historical records in Indian literature. If there is historical expectation, as, for example, in Vishnuism, it expresses itself in the doctrine of world cycles: the breath of Brahma alternately produces and swallows the world. Between these cosmic tides the world develops in four ages, or Yugas, from the best to the worst in continuous deterioration. We are living in the beginning of the fourth period, the Kali Yuga, which leads inescapably either to a miraculous return of the first age (where the whole process starts again) or immediately to the burning of the world and after it to the repetition of the same process. Time (Kala, often identified with the evil principle, "Kali") is a power of deterioration, not of improvement and salvation. Salvation means being saved from time and history, from the wheel of repetition; but it is not salvation *through* time and history. India is the least history-conscious of all the great cultures.

C

In Greek philosophy, "nature" is a rational category, designating everything as far as it exists by growth ($\phi\acute{v}\sigma\epsilon\iota$) or by essential necessity, not artificially ($\theta\acute{\epsilon}\sigma\epsilon\iota$) or by arbitrary thinking and acting. Nature is the structural necessity in which empirical reality participates. But empirical reality participates within the limitations of its material nature; by the latter it is prevented from realizing fully its essential nature. The mark of perfection in nature is the circular motion of a thing, in which it returns to itself. "Being" as such has the form of a sphere, equally perfect in all parts, not needing higher perfection, immovable and eternal, without genesis and decay. Temporal things, conversely, show contradictory, irregular motions without a circular connection of end and beginning and therefore with genesis and decay, self-destruction and death. History cannot claim any point of perfection because it is not a circular motion. The great Greek historiography shows the genesis, acme, and decay of cities and nations. It is, of course, more interested in the present than are the Chinese analysts. It wants to shape the present according to the experiences of the past, as, for instance, Aristotle's *Politics* shows. But there is no expectation of a more perfect future.

Aristotle describes Greece as the country of the "center" between north and south, east and west. He knows a center of space, but he does not know a center of time. "Time is nearer to decay than to genesis," he says, quoting a Pythagorean. Time for him is endless, repeating itself infinitely, while space is limited, full of plastic power, formed, defying infinity. In Stoicism the doctrines of the four world ages, the burning and the rebirth of the world, reappear. The present age is the worst, as it is assumed to be in India. But, instead of quietly surrendering to the inescapable fate of self-destruction, Stoicism (especially Roman Stoicism) tries to transform individuals and society by moral and political activities. In the Rome of Augustus, even prophetic hopes for the return of the golden age through the emperor became effective. A trend toward a historical interpretation of history spread over the ancient world—for a short time only. The political disappointment and the lack of any transcendent hope re-established the tragic and nonhistorical feeling. This becomes obvious in the last creation of original Greek thought, Neo-Platonism, in which the horizontal line is entirely negated by the vertical one, and society is entirely devaluated for the sake of the individual soul. The emanation of the different degrees of reality from the ultimate One to mere matter and the return of the soul through the different spheres from matter to the ultimate One stabilize a vertical direction of thinking and acting which has nothing to do with the horizontal line and the directed time of history. Mystical supra-naturalism at the end of Greek philosophy is no less unhistorical than classical naturalism at the beginning of Greek philosophy.

D

Modern European naturalism since the Renaissance is different from Greek naturalism in so far as it has overcome, under Christian influence, that dualistic and tragic element in Greek thinking which drives the human soul beyond the world and history to seek for salvation from the tragic circle, in the immovable "One." Modern naturalism is monistic and describes the world as a unity and totality, either in mathematical terms, as Spinoza and Leibniz do, or in organic terms, as Bruno and Shaftesbury do, or in dynamic terms, as Nietzsche and Bergson do, or in sociological terms, as Spengler does. For all these people the future signifies the evolution of all possibilities as implied in the present stage of the world. There may be infinite varieties, there may be self-destruction or circular motion or infinite repetition; but in no case is the directed line of history decisive. Billions of years of physical time frustrate any possible meaning for the utterly small sum of historical years. In the mathematical type, time has been made a dimension of space. He who knows the mathematical world formula in principle knows all the future. In the organic and dynamic types of modern naturalism, time is considered a deteriorizing force. In the organic and historical process, life becomes more complex, more self-conscious, more intellectualized. It loses its vital power and is driven toward self-destruction. In Spengler's prophecy of the decline of the West the great cultures are posited like trees beside each other. They arise, grow, decay, and die like trees, each for itself. There is no universal history, crossing the life-and-death curve of each culture, overcoming the spatial "Beside" by a temporal "Toward." On this basis even the tragic outlook of Greece tries to return. In nationalism the gods of space revolt against the Lord of time. Nation, soil, blood, and race defy the idea of a world-historical development and a world-historical aim. This recent development shows that a nonhistorical interpretation of history, even if arising in Christian countries, must return to paganism in the long run, for Christianity is essentially historical, while paganism is essentially nonhistorical.

## E

The main characteristics of the nonhistorical type of interpreting history, in all forms we have dealt with, are as follows:

1. Nature (or supernature) is the highest category of interpreting reality.

2. Space is predominant against time; time is considered to be circular or repeating itself infinitely.

3. The temporal world has a lesser reality and no ultimate value.

4. The true being and the ultimate good are eternal, immovable, above becoming, genesis, and decay.

5. Salvation is the salvation of individuals from time and history, not the salvation of a community through time and history.

6. History is interpreted as a process of deterioration, leading to the inescapable self-destruction of a world era.

7. The religious correlate to the nonhistorical interpretation of history is either polytheism (the deification of special spaces) or pantheism (the deification of a transcendent "One," negating space as well as time).

## II. THE HISTORICAL TYPE OF INTERPRETING HISTORY

The historical type of interpreting history appears first in the religion of Zoroaster, although still mixed with nonhistorical elements. In the religion of the Jewish prophets history gains its full meaning and power, although in a continuous struggle against religious nationalism, which belongs to the opposite type. In original Christianity the historical interpretation of history gets its final foundation and its universal significance. In church history nonhistorical elements have penetrated and have created the conservative ecclesiastical form of interpreting history. The conservative type has been challenged through all church history by the revolutionary sectarian type of interpreting history. This fight has continued in secular forms as the fight between political conservatism, on the one hand, and political radicalism, revolutionary or progressive, on the other hand. We shall now examine those different forms of a historical interpretation of history, to find out the characteristics that are constitutive for all of them and to compare them with the characteristics we have found essential in the nonhistorical group of interpretations of history.

### A

Although the contrast of divine and demonic powers can be found in many religions, only in Persia has a dualistic religion developed. This fact is amazing, not only because it has given rise to the first and only historical interpretation of history besides the Jewish-Christian line of thought but also because it shows the limitation under which the human mind is able to stand an ultimate dualism. With respect to the latter point, it is obvious that the final victory of the good presupposes its ontological superiority over the evil principle. A complete dualism would destroy the unity of the human mind, would be a metaphysical schizophrenia. The Persian interpretation of history shows a group of ideas which, since the time of Zoroaster, have returned in all historical interpretations of history: a struggle between two dynamic principles, God and Satan; the idea of the deterioration of the world, going on in different periods of some thousand years, up to the turning-point before the last period, the last period being brought about by the appearance of a prophetic messenger; the expectation of a divine savior who will bring the ultimate decision in the world-historical struggle; the victory of the good, the end of history, resurrection, individual judgment, and the burning of the evil. But there is one idea in the Iranian religion which limits its historical character—the doctrine of a dual creation, a good one and an evil one. This means that there is some evil in the world which cannot be overcome by the historical process but only by the material extinction of whole sections of beings, of special animals, plants, and material things, which are evil in themselves. The good God is not the sovereign Lord of history, because he is not the creator of nature as a whole. This limitation of the divine power makes grace impossible. Only the unconditioned God can forgive sins. A conditioned god must defend himself. He is bound to the law of his special nature.

B

This question is treated differently in Jewish prophetism, which therefore must be considered as the real birthplace of a universal historical consciousness in world history. An exclusive monotheism, rooted in the idea of justice as the characteristic of the true, universal God; the faith in the unrestricted sovereignty of this God to rule over history according to his purpose; the idea of *one* creation which is essentially good and *one* mankind which, although fallen from its original innocence and unity, shall be blessed through the history of the elected nation—all these give a framework for an entirely historical interpretation of history, as developed in the Old Testament: the call of Abraham, implying the demand to separate himself from the spatial gods of his father's house and to follow the God of time and the future who is the God of all nations; the exodus from Egypt as the fundamental event, the center of history, for Israel; the covenant between God and his nation; the prophetic threat that God might punish and destroy even his elected nation; the promise that the exiled remnants will become the bearers of the world-historical aims of God, that a messianic king out of David's seed will arise, that in the last day, in the day of Yahweh, all his enemies will be overcome and Jerusalem will become the center of true adoration, justice, and peace, peace even in nature. This is the Old Testament interpretation of history. Here it is obvious that God reveals himself not only *in* history but also *through* history as a whole. The gods of space are overcome; history has a beginning, a center, and an end. Although the elected nation is the main bearer of history, its history has meaning for all nations.

## C

The prophetic interpretation of history expresses itself in terms which remain within the limits of this world, of time and space—although some miraculous elements belong to the prophetic world view: for instance, the coming peace of nature, the future participation of everybody in the gift of the Holy Spirit, the final victory of one of the smallest nations over the great empires. Later apocalypticism emphasizes those miraculous elements, thus breaking through all limitations of time and space. This takes place to a great extent under the direct influence of the Persian interpretation of history. The historical conflicts, as envisaged in the prophetic description of the future, are replaced by the struggles of transcendent powers—God, Satan, good and evil angels. The Messiah, more and more, becomes a divine being, ceasing to be a historical king; the end of the world process becomes more important than the end of history, which is only a consequence of the former. In the Revelation of John the prophetic and the apocalyptic interpretations of history are combined. History as such comes to its goal and fulfilment in the thousand-year reign of Christ and his saints when Satan is bound but not finally overcome. The final victory occurs in a world catastrophe in which the heavenly powers conquer the satanic powers, and the Kingdom of God, uniting the elect out of all nations, including a new nature, is established forever.

## D

The tension between these two forms of historical interpretation of history—the prophetic and the apocalyptic—has become tremendously important for church history. The conservative, ecclesiastical form, represented by Augustine, has removed the dangerous consequences of the idea of the thousand-year reign of Christ by assuming that it is fulfilled in the Christian church—first of all, in the church hierarchy. From this point of view history has already reached its last period. Nothing really new can be expected before the end of history and nature. Therefore, no radical criticism of the church is possible. There is no historical goal before us from which the critique could be launched. The expectation of one's individual death has replaced the expectation of the end of history. A nonhistorical element has penetrated into the Christian interpretation of history through the elimination of chiliasm. This element was strong enough to devaluate historical activity and the struggle for social justice and to separate the individual destiny from that of the whole.

## E

In opposition to the ecclesiastical interpretation of history the sectarian interpretation re-establishes the doctrine of the thousand years by stressing the famous idea of a "third stage," in which history will be fulfilled on earth. The prophecy of Joachim of Floris gave the first impulse which was received and intensified by the radical Franciscans and taken over in the pre-Reformation and Reformation period by Taborites, Anabaptists, and revolutionary peasants; it was used during the English revolution and finally secularized and transformed into bourgeois and proletarian utopianism. In all these movements the future is the decisive mode of time. Something entirely new is expected, for which past and present are preparations. The turning-point of history is at hand; the last stage will start very soon; justice will be victorious either through divine power alone or through human revolutionary actions under the guidance of God. Universal peace will become actual, the Holy Spirit will be given to everybody and will bring to an end all earthly authorities. No mediators, priests, or teachers are necessary because everybody will have a true knowledge of God.

## F

It is easy to draw the line from these two attitudes within the church to the corresponding attitudes outside the church. Ecclesiastical conservatism has become the foundation of political conservatism in almost all Christian countries. It is typical for this conservatism that some event of the past (which originally had a revolutionary character) is considered to be *the* final event in which the meaning of history is fully expressed. Therefore, the situation brought about by this event must be preserved and defended against revolution and radical progress. This is true not only of old Prussian feudalism—an outstanding example of political conservatism on a Lutheran basis—but it is also true of those Sons or Daughters of the American Revolution who, in the name of a revolution in the past, try to prevent forever any kind of revolution in the future—an outstanding example of political conservatism on a Calvinistic-sectarian background. In both cases and in the many varieties of outlook between them, everything essential in history is supposed to be achieved. The future is a relatively unimportant actualization of what potentially is always given (according to the pattern of natural events). It is obvious that this attitude can easily fall back into some form of nonhistorical naturalism—as happened in nineteenth-century Europe.

## G

The line from the revolutionary sectarian interpretation of history to political radicalism is even more obvious. The idea of the "third stage" played a tremendous role, first, in the struggling *bourgeoisie* and then in the struggling proletariat. In the period of the Enlightenment and the bourgeois revolution the "third stage" was identified with the control of reason over nature and society. Autonomous thinking is potentially the gift of everybody, and it will become actualized by social changes and education. On this basis, democracy is possible, authority is replaced by persuasion, and hierarchy by leadership. The inner light of the spiritual sectarian is transformed into the autonomous reason of the enlightened bourgeois. Freedom and equality, universal peace and social justice, are necessary consequences of the leap from the prerational to the rational stage of mankind. After the *bourgeoisie* had become victorious, conservative elements penetrated and transformed the revolutionary impulse into a progressivistic attitude (it ceased to be "sect" and became "church"). The progressive interpretation of history is moderate utopianism, following the radical utopianism of the period of struggle. It is utopianism in so far as it believes in continuous progress as the general law of history. It is moderate in so far as it believes that the decisive step has already been taken, the step from the prerational to the rational (bourgeois) stage of mankind.

Against this moderate element, socialism and communism have re-established the radical, revolutionary interpretation of history. The "classless" society is the analogy to the "third stage." It is supposed to be the fulfilment of the original purpose of the bourgeois revolution, which has been betrayed by the bourgeois class interest. It will be the realization of justice, peace, freedom, and humanity not only for a few but for everybody. Marx calls this stage the beginning of real history, while the second stage—namely, all earlier history—is only prehistory, the self-estrangement of man from himself in continuous class struggles. Sometimes the first stage is described as original communism, a stage of innocence expressed in sociological terms. The turning-point in history is the appearance of the proletariat, which has messianic qualities, not because of its moral qualities but because of its historical function, namely, to pursue the interest of the whole by pursuing its special interest. The determining forces in history are interest and passion—as Hegel had already emphasized. But, like him, Marx discovers a meaningful—so to speak, providential—trend in history, which directs all the struggling interests toward a final harmony. Revolutionary catastrophes will bring about the classless society, the aim and end of history, through a co-operation of free human activities and dialectical (nonmechanical) necessity. In this interpretation of history most of the elements of the directly religious interpretations of history are implied, but with two differences: the transcendence of the struggling powers is transformed into the immanence of contrasting principles and the transcendent fulfilment beyond history is replaced by the immanent fulfilment within history. These differences make it possible for the Marxist interpretation of history to be put into a naturalistic, nonhistorical framework, as can happen to the progressivistic world view also. Both of them are in danger of falling back to a nonhistorical naturalism. Without a transcendent element the ultimate meaning of history cannot be maintained.

## H

Religious socialism has tried to apply the religious principles of the prophetic interpretations of history to the concrete understanding of the present situation in socialist terms, keeping itself, however, within the framework of biblical thought. So it has united the main forms of a historical interpretation of history and has reintroduced the problem of history into theological thought. A description of the system of religious socialism is beyond the scope of this paper. Some of its aspects will be dealt with in the concluding section. But, before considering these aspects, we have to find out the main points which characterize the historical interpretation of history in contrast to the main points we have discovered in the nonhistorical attitude.

## I

1. History is an independent and, finally, the outstanding category of interpreting reality.

2. Time is predominant against space. The movement of time is directed, has a definitive beginning and end, and is moving toward an ultimate fulfilment.

3. The temporal world is a battlefield between good and evil powers (expressed in mythological or in rational terms). Ontologically, or as creation, the world is good.

4. The true being, or the ultimate good, is in a dynamic process of self-realization within and above temporal existence.

5. Salvation is the salvation of a community from the evil powers *in* history *through* history. History is essentially "history of salvation."

6. History has a turning-point or a center in which the meaning of history appears, overcoming the self-destructive trend of the historical process and creating something *new* which cannot be frustrated by the circular motion of nature.

7. The religious correlate to the historical interpretation of history is exclusive monotheism: God as the Lord of time controlling the universal history of mankind, acting in history and through history.

APPENDIX

SOME NEW TESTAMENT CATEGORIES OF INTERPRETING HISTORY
THEIR GREEK AND THEIR CHRISTIAN MEANING

The New Testament is a document of that event in which the historical interpretation of history has received its final and perfect foundation: Christ as the center of history. This document is written in the same language in which the nonhistorical interpretation of history has found its most consistent and most rational expression—in Greek. It is, therefore, tremendously interesting to compare the meaning of the main terms in which the New Testament expresses its understanding of history with the meaning of the same or similar terms in classical Greek. Such a comparison is the best way of making visible the peculiar attitude of the New Testament to history and its difference from all types of nonhistorical interpretation of history.

A. *kairos*, "RIGHT TIME"

Aristotle in the *Nicomachean Ethics* defines *kairos* as "the good in the category of time." If a special moment of time is good for the fulfilment of something, this moment is its kairos. Everything and every action can have its good moment, which is not given before or after but only *en kairo,* in the right moment. But time as such has no kairos for Aristotle, because the world process as a whole has no good and no perfection. The ultimate good is *above* it, not *in* it, and does not appear in any special moment. In Paul, kairos designates the fulfilment of time as a whole. The good in the category of time appears fully in one moment of time, dividing history into a period of preparation and of reception, creating a center of history, cutting off the two infinities of physical time, the infinity of the past and the infinity of the future, thus establishing a "definitive" time. This use of the word "kairos" makes it a main category of the New Testament interpretation of history. Time has a direction, periodization, qualitative differences, by the very fact of having a kairos.

B. *telos*, "END, FULFILMENT"; *teleios*, "FINISHED, PERFECT"

Aristotle defines *to teleion* as something of which no part can be found outside of it. In connection with his metaphysics, this means that all potentialities of a thing are actualized. As, for example, the fixed stars show by their circular motion that they are not lacking something beyond them, although their motion indicates that there is still a difference in them between their potentiality and their actuality. Absolutely perfect *teleios* is only the pure actuality; in it there is no potentiality at all, and it is therefore immovable. *Telos* is the immanent aim of the life-process, the form in which it is fulfilled and which is its essential good. The word *telos* has been used at the same time for the highest offices in the state, for the initiations into the Eleusinian mysteries, and for the ethical ideal of every individual. In all these cases it points to the perfect realization of an essential possibility. Its direction is vertical; the horizontal meaning of "ending," "finishing," is secondary. In the New Testament the emphasis is shifted to the horizontal meaning. Paul speaks of the end of the ages in our days (I Cor. 10:11). In I Cor. 15:24 the *telos* is the moment in which God receives the Kingdom from Christ. Similar is its meaning in Matt. 24:14. The *telos* lies in the horizontal line, as something new coming from above; it has eschatological, not ontological, character. Therefore *teleios* in Eph. 4:14 is measured not by human potentialities but by the fulness of Christ who is in history. *Telos* in Greece negates history; in the New Testament it is the fulfilment of history.

C. *parousia*, "PRESENCE, APPEARANCE"

In his *Gorgias*, Plato speaks of the *parousia tou agathou*, the presence of the good which appears in things, although it is at the same time beyond all things. Things have being by the presence of the good in them; the true being of things is their good, appearing in them but at the same time concealed by them. The pure good itself is beyond all things and cannot be seen directly; it can be seen only in so far as it appears in things. The same word *parousia* is used in the New Testament for the appearance of Christ in his glory, not hidden by the humility of his flesh. In Plato the emphasis is laid on the presence of the good in all things in so far as they exist. It designates the eternal relation between idea and reality. In the New Testament the word points to the eschatological event in which the meaning of the one historical event, namely, the coming of Christ in the flesh, is presupposed. The Greek use of the word is nonhistorical. The New Testament use of the word is based on an interpretation of history in terms of its center and its end.

### D. *ktizein,* "FOUNDING, CREATING"; *demiourgein,* "SHAPING"

The word *ktizein* in classical Greek means "founding a city." Something new is made, but it is made at a given place, with a given material. Similar is the meaning of *demiourgein,* "making a public work," "giving a public service by shaping," "forming," "fashioning." The latter word and not the former is used by Plato when he speaks of the shaping of the world by the *demiourgos.* The *demiourgos* has shaped the world by forming and ordering the matter according to the picture of the idea of the good. In doing so, he elevates the matter which is controlled by necessity to the greatest possible similarity with the idea. But he can succeed only in a limited way. He cannot overcome the evils which are rooted in the resistance of matter. The Septuagint and the New Testament use the word *ktizein* for the creative activity of God, emphasizing the idea of a new foundation and dropping entirely the connotation of something "given" by the idea of a creation out of nothing. The world is *ktisis,* it is created, not shaped; therefore it is good in itself; the evil has no ontological, but only moral, foundation, and thus a history of salvation is possible.

### E. *logos,* "WORD, REASON"

*Logos* in Greek philosophy designates the reasonable word which grasps being itself, its true, essential nature, its form and structure. The word, in order to do so, must carry the truth of things in itself; being and the speaking of being or being and the thought in which being is grasped are the same. Reason in things and reason in mind are identical. This universal reason, which is objective in things and subjective in the human mind, is called *logos*. In Heraclitus and the Stoics it is the law of nature as well as the law for human thinking and acting. It is in all things, everything participates in it. It becomes self-conscious and distorted in man. It is the active, divine power which forms and shapes the passive matter. It is always present, although in different degrees. By its very being, everything participates in it. The use of the same word in the Fourth Gospel for the character of Christ shows better than anything else the turn from the nonhistorical to the historical interpretation of reality. The logos becomes history, a visible and touchable individuality, in a unique moment of time. The logical relation between universal and individual is completely transformed. The individual is not only an exemplar of the universal, unable to express its fulness, but the individual adds something entirely new to the universal. History is possible because the individual man or the individual event is more than an exemplar of the genus "man" or the genus "event." When the word becomes flesh, the contrast between universal and individual disappears. History is not less than the universal logos but united with it. History and true being are not in contrast to each other. True being, or logos, appears in its fulness in history.

### f. *aletheia,* "TRUTH"

The transformation of the meaning of *logos* is accompanied by a transformation of the idea of truth. *Alethes,* in Greek, means "not hidden." Knowing the truth means penetrating to that level of reality which is hidden to the natural world view and can be discovered only by methodological knowledge. This level of reality is behind the surface of things; but it is always and everywhere present and approachable in the depths of things. The historical situation does not mean anything for this approach. The same word is used in the New Testament. But its meaning cannot be derived from its Greek origin. It must be understood by referring to the Hebrew word of which it is the translation: *emunah,* which has the same root as "Amen" and designates the trustworthy, unshakable character, especially of a person and a promise given by him. It points to the practical certainty which follows from absolute confidence in somebody. Therefore, the Fourth Gospel can speak of the "becoming of the truth," namely, as a divine act in history; while for Greek thinking, *aletheia* is just the opposite of becoming, namely, "eternal being." The Bible can speak further of "doing the truth," and Jesus can say "I am the truth." Truth is not universal but identical with the historical fact Jesus Christ. It cannot be discovered by a methodological approach but only by faith and obedience. And it cannot be discovered always and everywhere but only in the unique historical community, the church.

### G. *ecclesia,* "ASSEMBLY (CHURCH)"

This leads to the last and decisive concept in which the change from nonhistorical to historical thinking becomes visible: *ecclesia,* "assembly." In the Greek city-state it designates the assembly of the free citizens who are called out of their houses in order to make political decisions and to carry on the life of the city. Only those who are free belong to it. And one is free by birth because one has received by inheritance a virtue which the slave and the barbarian lack. For Aristotle the free Greek citizen, who belongs to the city assembly, represents the genus of the élite. Later on, in Stoicism, everybody is considered to be free by having reason. Human beings as such belong to the élite genus because they participate in the universal reason. But, despite the difference between these two meanings of freedom as well as of election, both of them have a nonhistorical character. In both cases, nature makes the election—in Aristotle in a more vitalistic and aristocratic interpretation, in Stoicism in a more rationalistic and democratic interpretation. In the New Testament, *ecclesia* is often used with the addition *"ecclesia* of God or of Christ." As such it is the continuation of the assembly of God in the Old Testament, namely, the elected nation or the elected remnants of that nation. In the New Testament the "assembly of God" is called the "true people of God," consisting of the elect from all nations. This election is not a matter of race or of reason. It is a matter of historical destiny. The free members of this assembly of God are free by salvation. Their virtue is the grace they receive in the church. The church is *one* historical reality starting with the promise of God to Abraham, centered in the appearance of Christ, and moving toward the final fulfilment. The spatial *ecclesia* of Greece has been replaced by the historical *ecclesia* of Christianity, the bearer of historical consciousness in all periods and nations.

# Chapter III

## KAIROS

THE ideas here set forth present a summons to a thinking that is conscious of history, to a consciousness of history whose roots reach down into the depth of the unconditional,[1] whose conceptions are created from the primordial concerns of the human spirit, and whose ethos is an inescapable responsibility for the present moment in history. The form of this summons will not be that of a sermon; it will not be propaganda or romanticism or poetry but serious intellectual work, striving for a philosophy of history that is more than a logic of the cultural sciences and yet does not lag behind it in sharpness and objectivity. It would be a meaningless beginning to wish to undertake such a task in the brief limits of an essay if more were intended than to bring *one* concrete conception into a sharp light, a conception that, if it alone has been made to stand out clearly, can be illuminating for many others —the conception of "kairos." A summons to a consciousness of history in the sense of the kairos, a striving for an interpretation of the meaning of history on the basis of the conception of kairos, a demand for a consciousness of the present and for action in the present in the spirit of kairos—that is what is intended here.

1. The term "unconditional" which is often used in this book points to that element in every religious experience which makes it religious. In every symbol of the divine an unconditional claim is expressed, most powerfully in the command: "Thou shalt love the Lord thy God with *all* thy heart and with all thy soul, and with all thy mind." No partial, restricted, conditioned love of God is admitted. The term "unconditioned" or the adjective made into the substantive, "the unconditional," is an abstraction from such sayings which abound in the Bible and in great religious literature. The unconditional is a quality, not a being. It characterizes that which is our ultimate and, consequently, unconditional concern, whether we call it "God" or "Being as such" or the "Good as such" or the "True as such," or whether we give it any other name. It would be a complete mistake to understand the unconditional as a being the existence of which can be discussed. He who speaks of the "existence of the unconditional" has thoroughly misunderstood the meaning of the term. Unconditional is a quality which we experience in encountering reality, for instance, in the unconditional character of the voice of the conscience, the logical as well as the moral. In this sense, as a quality and not as a being, the term is used in all the following articles.

# I

It was a fine feeling that made the spirit of the Greek language signify *chronos,* "formal time," with a different word from *kairos,* "the right time," the moment rich in content and significance. And it is no accident that this word found its most pregnant and most frequent usage when the Greek language became the vessel for the dynamic spirit of Judaism and primitive Christianity—in the New Testament. His "kairos" had not yet come, is said of Jesus; and then it had once at some time or other come, *en kairo,* in the moment of the fulness of time. Time is an empty form only for abstract, objective reflection, a form that can receive any kind of content; but to him who is conscious of an ongoing creative life it is laden with tensions, with possibilities and impossibilities, it is qualitative and full of significance. Not everything is possible at every time, not everything is true at every time, nor is everything demanded at every moment. Various "rulers," that is different cosmic powers, rule at different times, and the "ruler," conquering all the other angels and powers, reigns in the time that is full of destiny and tension between the Resurrection and the Second Coming, in the "present time," which in its essence is different from every other time of the past. In this tremendous, most profoundly stirred consciousness of history is rooted the idea of the kairos; and from this beginning it will be molded into a conception purposely adapted to a philosophy of history.

It is no superfluous undertaking if a summons to a consciousness of history is made, for it is by no means obvious to the human mind and spirit that they are historical; rather, a spiritual outlook that is unaware of history is far more frequent, not only because of dulness and lack of spirit—these we have always had and always will have—but also because of deep instincts of a psychic and metaphysical kind. This outlook that is unconscious of history has two main roots. It may be rooted in the awareness of what is beyond time, the eternal. This type of mentality knows no change and no history. Or it may be rooted in the bondage of all time to this world, to nature and to her eternally recurrent course and change, to the ever continuing return of times and things. There is a mystical unawareness of history which views everything temporal as a transparent cover, as a deceptive veil and image of the eternal, and which wants to rise above such distractions to a timeless contemplation of the timeless; and then there is what we may call a naturalistic unawareness of history, which persists in a bondage to the course of nature and lets it be consecrated in the name of the eternal by priest and cult. For wide areas of Asiatic culture mystical unawareness of history is the basic spiritual attitude. In contrast to this, consciousness of history is relatively rare. In principle, it is a characteristic element in the development of the Semitic-Persian and Christian-occidental outlook. But even there it appears only at those times when a new vitality has emerged, in the supreme moments of the creative apprehension of the world. All the more important is it for the whole development of mankind at large that this consciousness should in the Occident again and again emerge in full vigor and depth. For one thing is certain: Once it has definitely emerged, it will by degrees bring all nations under its spell; for an action conscious of history can be countered only by an action conscious of history; and if Asia in proud self-consciousness because of an age-old possession defends itself against the Occident, then, to the extent in which this opposition takes place consciously, it is already transported to the soil of historical thinking, and therefore it is by virtue of the very struggle itself brought into the domain of historical consciousness.

But in the Occident itself an opponent has risen against historical thinking, an opponent issuing from the mystical view of the world, nourished by the naturalistic attitude, and shaped by the rational, mathematical method of thinking—the technical-mathematical explanation of the world by means of natural science, the rational conception of reality as a machine with eternally constant laws of movement manifest in an infinitely recurring and predictable natural process. The mentality that has produced this conceptual framework as its creation has, in turn, come so much under its spell that it has made itself into a part of this machine, into a piece of this eternally identical process. It has so surrendered itself to its own creation that it has considered itself as a mechanism and has forgotten that this machine was created by it. This is a great threat to occidental culture. It means the loss of a precious possession, a greater catastrophe than that of never having had it. These words are directed to the materialistically minded among the socialists, and they are needed in order to reveal the contradiction in which the socialists stand if, as heirs of a powerful philosophy of history and as bearers of the present consciousness of history, they turn to worship a philosophy that excludes meaningful history and accepts a meaningless natural process. A "materialistic interpretation of history" would be a contradiction in itself, if it were meant to be anything other than an "economic" interpretation of history or if it were meant to have anything to do with metaphysical materialism. Unfortunately, the word has here often become a deception, hiding the actual situation. No system has a better right to raise a protest against the late bourgeois materialism that has no consciousness of history than does socialism, a movement that is unprecedently aware of history. The stronger it raises this protest and the more it gives evidence of the kairos, the further it gets away from all metaphysical materialism, and the more clearly it reveals its belief in the creative power of life.

## II

The first great philosophy of history was born out of a keen sense of duality and conflict. The struggle between light and darkness, between good and evil, is its essence. World history is the effect of this conflict; in history the entirely new occurs, the unique, the absolutely decisive; defeats may be suffered on the way, but in the end comes the victory of the light. Thus did Zarathustra, the Persian prophet, interpret history. Jewish prophecy brought into this picture the ethical drive of its God of justice. The epochs of the struggle are the epochs of history. History is determined by supra-historical events. The most important period is the final one, that of the struggle for the ultimate decision, an epoch beyond which no new epoch can be imagined. This type of historical consciousness thinks in conceptions of an absolute character: the absolute opposition between light and darkness, between good and evil; the final decision; the unconditional "No" and the unconditional "Yes" which are struggling with each other. It is an attitude toward history which is moved by a tremendous spiritual tension and by an ultimate responsibility on the part of the individual. This is the great, early expression of man's historical consciousness: the philosophy of history expressed in absolute terms.

It can take on two basic forms. The first form of the absolute philosophy of history is defined by a tense feeling that the end of time is near: the Kingdom of God is at hand, the time of decision is imminent, the great, the real kairos is appearing which will transform everything. This is the revolutionary-absolute type. It sees the goal of history in the "kingdom from above" or in the victory of reason within this world. In both cases an absolute "No" is pronounced upon all the past, and an absolute "Yes" is pronounced upon the future. This interpretation of history is fundamental for all strong historical consciousness, as is the interpretation in which the conception of the kairos was first grasped.

The second form of the absolute philosophy of history can be called a conservative transformation of the revolutionary form as it was achieved by Augustine in his struggle against the chiliastic revivals of the early Christian belief in the imminent coming of the Kingdom of God in history. The background of this type is the same as that of the revolutionary type: the vision of a struggle between two forces in all epochs of history. But, according to the conservative type, the decisive event has already happened. The new is victoriously established in history, although it is still attacked by the forces of darkness. The church in its hierarchical structure represents this new reality. There are still improvements, partial defeats, and partial victories to be expected and, of course, the final catastrophe, in which the evil is destroyed and history will come to an end. But nothing really new can be expected within history. A conservative attitude toward the given is demanded.

The dangerous element in both forms of the absolute philosophy of history, in the conservative as well as in the revolutionary form, is the fact that a special historical reality is set up as absolute, whether it be an existing church or the expected rational society. This, of course, brings a continuous tension into the historical consciousness; but, at the same time, it depreciates all other historical realities. In the Augustinian interpretation, which in principle corresponds with the inner feeling and self-consciousness of all predominantly sacramental churches, only the history of a special church is, in the strict sense, significant for the philosophy of history. Her inner conflicts and their resolution, her fights against external enemies—these are the viewpoints under which all other events are envisaged and estimated. The fight for God and against the world, which is the present historical task, means, in practice, a fight for the church, for a pure doctrine, for a hierarchy. Against this ecclesiastical interpretation of history we must conceive of the kairos in universal terms, and we must not limit it to the past but raise it to a general principle of history, to a principle that is also relevant to the present.

Again and again sectarian revolutionary impulses have opposed the ecclesiastical-conservative mentality, in religious or in secular terms. Whether the great revolution is thought of as from beyond and is expected through the action of God exclusively, or as prepared for by human action, or as being a creation of the human spirit and an act of political revolution; whether the utopias are based on ideas of natural law, such as democracy, socialism, and anarchism (heirs of the religious utopias) or on a transcendent myth, the consciousness of the kairos is equally strong and equally unconditional in all of them. But, in contrast to the conservative interpretation, the kairos in this view lies in the present: "The kingdom is at hand." This excitement, however, about the present and the exclusive orientation toward the future in the revolutionary movements blinds them with respect to the past. The sects are opposed to the ecclesiastical traditions, the *bourgeoisie* destroys the aristocratic forms of life, socialism fights against the bourgeois heritage. The history of the past disappears in the dynamic thrust toward the future. This is the reason why a strong historical consciousness has often accompanied ignorance about past history—for instance, in the proletarian masses—and this is the reason why, on the other hand, a tremendous amount of historical knowledge has not overcome an attitude of detachment and misapprehension with respect to the present moment of history, for instance, in the bourgeois historians of the last decades (in contrast to the great bourgeois historians of the eighteenth century, with their revolutionary visions). For these scholars history was an object of causal explanation or of exact descriptions, but it did not concern them existentially. It was not a place of actual decisions (in spite of their great achievements in historical research). But oppressed and ignorant people, and those few from the educated classes who identified themselves with the people, created the revolutionary-absolute interpretation of history. So it was in early Christianity, in most of the medieval sects, and in our own period. But the lack of a sense of tradition was also the reason for the strong elements of utopianism in all these movements. Their ignorance of the past betrayed them into the feeling that the period of perfection had already started, that the absolute transformation was only a matter of days or of a few years, and that they were its representatives and bearers.

Both forms of an absolute philosophy of history are judged by the absolute itself. The unconditional cannot be identified with any given reality, whether past or future; there is no absolute church, there is no absolute kingdom of reason and justice in history. A conditional reality set up as something unconditional, a finite reality to which divine predicates are attributed, is antidivine; it is an "idol." This prophetic criticism, launched in the name of the unconditional, breaks the absolute church and the absolute society; conservative ecclesiasticism and revolutionary utopianism are alike idolatry.

This is the message of the so-called "theology of crisis," represented by Karl Barth in his powerful commentary on Paul's Epistle to the Romans. No finite reality can claim an absolute status. Everything conditioned is judged by the unconditional in terms of "Yes" and "No." There is a permanent crisis going on in history, a crisis in the double sense of the Greek word: judgment and separation. No moment of history is without this tension, the tension between the unconditional and the conditional. The crisis is permanent. The kairos is always given. But there are no outstanding moments in history with respect to the manifestation of the unconditional (except the *one* moment which is called "Jesus Christ" and which has a supra-historical character). History as such loses its absolute significance; hence it loses the tremendous weight it has in the revolutionary interpretations of history. From the absolute point of view, history becomes indifferent. A third type of absolute philosophy of history appears in this doctrine of "crisis," the "indifference" type. It is indifferent to the special heights and depths of the historical process. A kind of "divine humor" toward history is praised, reminding one of romantic irony or of Luther's understanding of history as the realm of God's strange acting. In this attitude the concept of crisis has no actuality; it remains abstract, beyond every special criticism and judgment. But this is not the way in which the crisis can be effective and the negative can be overcome. The latter is possible only by a new creation. Not negation but affirmation conquers the negative. The appearance of the new is the concrete crisis of the old, the historical judgment against it. The new creation may be worse than the old one which is brought into crisis by it; and, whether better or worse, it is subjected to judgment itself. But in the special historical moment it is *en kairo* ("at the right time") while the old creation is not. In this way history receives the weight and seriousness which belong to it. The absolute—to vary a famous saying of Hegel—is not so impotent as to remain in separation from the relative. It appears in the relative as judgment and creation. This leads to the description of relative interpretations of history.

## III

We may distinguish three types in the relative form of philosophy of history: the classical, the progressive, and the dialectical type. The common characteristic of relative interpretations of history is their relativizing attitude toward historical events and, accordingly, the loss of absolute tensions. Instead of absolute judgments, there appears a uniform and universal evaluation of all phenomena on the basis of a historical understanding which is able to have an intuitive feeling for the meaning of every single phenomenon. Thus the relative interpretations comprehend the richness and abundance of historical reality, and they offer the possibility of integrating it into a universal philosophy of history.

The classical philosophy of history can be subsumed under the motto that "every epoch is immediately under God." In every epoch human nature develops the fulness of its possibilities; in every epoch, in every nation, an eternal idea of God is realized. History is the great process of growth of the tree of mankind. This is the vision of people like Leibniz, Goethe, and Ranke. But epochs and nations are not revelations of human nature in the same way in all times. There are differences between blossom and decay, between creative and sterile periods; the vitality of the creative process is the criterion according to which the various periods are judged. This links the classical interpretation of history to the nonhistorical naturalism of the Greeks, as is especially obvious in Spengler's physiognomy of the cultural cycles. Here every culture is a tree by itself with a thousand-year span of life and a final disappearance. History is torn into separate processes originating in different geographical areas and having nothing to do with one another. Crisis is in a rather negative sense the transition from the creative to the technical period of development, which leads to inescapable self-destruction. In spite of this relationship between the classical and the naturalistic interpretation of history, they are different in their basic attitude. The modern form of the classical philosophy of history belongs to Christian humanism and betrays its Christian background in spite of its longing for the Greek way of life. In contrast to the tragic pessimism of the ancient world, it maintains the independent meaning of history.

This is the point of contact which it has with the progressive-relative philosophy of history. Just as the religious enthusiasm of early Christian (and many sectarian) expectations of the end became weakened after the continuous delay of the end and the establishment of the church in the world (or of the sect as a large denomination), so also the secular revolutionary movements become relativistic after their political victory and after the necessary disappointment about the gap between expectation and reality. At this moment "crisis" becomes restricted criticism, radical change becomes slow transformation, the ideal is projected into a remote future, the enthusiasm is replaced by the clever calculation of possibilities, the belief that the turning-point has arrived is exchanged for the certainty of a continuous progress. The religious idea of a history of revelation in several stages is secularized into the idea of a progressive education of the human race (Lessing).

The progressive-relative attitude can emphasize the restricting elements of the idea of progress. Then it tends to become more and more conservative, defending the status quo, clinging to the given, praising the positive against the negative and critical, developing a positivistic behavior and philosophy. If, on the contrary, progressivism emphasizes the negative-critical element of the idea of progress, two ways are open to it. Either it becomes an attitude of, so to speak, professional criticism which is unable to accept anything positive and to express any affirmation—an empty, often cynical, often oversophisticated, often desperate criticism. Or it becomes an attitude of an intensive will to create something new, not to accept the "positively given." In this case it easily loses its relative character and becomes absolute and revolutionary. The consciousness of a kairos becomes possible. Thus the ambiguity of the progressive interpretation of history is its danger and its power.

A connecting of the classical with the progressive interpretation of history results in the dialectical interpretation: this is the highest type of the relative interpretations. It operates in three forms, the theological, the logical, and the sociological, each depending in many respects upon the others.

The theological form is anticipated in the proclamation of the three eras of the Father, the Son, and the Spirit by the Abbé Joachim of Floris in the twelfth century; it is taken up in the idea of the three ages expounded by the leaders of the Enlightenment and of German idealism; and it appears again in the three stages (the theological, the metaphysical, and the positivistic stages) of Comte's philosophy of history. The logical form of the dialectical philosophy of history is so typically and impressively represented by Hegel that it is sufficient merely to mention him, while the sociological form is represented in the French socialistic romanticism with its distinction between the critical and the organic periods and, above all, in the economic interpretation of history by Karl Marx.

A common element in these three forms of the dialectical interpretation of history is their positive valuation of all periods. Every period is more than a transitory moment in the historical process. It has a meaning of its own, an eternal significance. But, besides its relation to the absolute, it is related to the other periods. It is more or less perfect in relation to them. There is "immediacy" with respect to the unconditional, and, at the same time, there is progress with respect to other periods in every period of history. The classical and the progressive philosophy of history are united in the dialectical method.

The dialectical interpretations of history (theological, logical, and sociological) betray an ambiguity similar to that of the progressive interpretation. They can be understood in absolute and in relative terms. According to Joachim, Hegel, Marx, and Comte, the last period of history is "at hand." It can already be recognized in the womb of the present period. (For Hegel his own philosophy is the moment of its birth.) The epoch of the Holy Spirit, the stage of perfect self-consciousness, the classless society, the foundation of the religion of positive science, are final stages; they are *kairoi* in the absolute sense. A revolutionary impulse is visible in all these dialecticians of history, even in Hegel, in his principle of negation. From this side of their thinking they belong to the revolutionary-absolute interpreters of history. Joachim and Marx were so esteemed by their revolutionary followers. But there is another side to the picture. Dialectical thinking subjects every moment of time to its "Yes and No." It does not negate the past unconditionally, and it does not affirm the future unconditionally. The period of the Spirit, in Joachim's vision, is prepared for by the periods of the Father and the Son. But what prevents the history of salvation from preparing something new in the womb of the period of the Spirit? The Germanic nations, according to Hegel, are the last bearers of the process in which the absolute idea actualizes itself. But why should the principle of negation be impotent in face of the Germanic peoples alone? The alternation of organic and critical periods in French socialism gives a high valuation to the Middle Ages. But why should the next organic period, socialism, be protected against a new "critical" period? And why should the period of positive sciences, which is an offspring of religion and metaphysics, not produce another higher period?—a question directed to Comte. And why, finally, should the classless society, which Marx expects, be the end of historical dialectics? Why should the proletariat, after its victory, not succumb to cleavages similar to those experienced by the victorious *bourgeoisie?* An absolute stage as the end of the dialectical process is a contradiction of the dialectical principle. It is an idea taken from the revolutionary-absolute interpretations of history. In this ambiguity the limits of the dialectical interpretation of history become manifest: either it must stop the dialectical process arbitrarily, or it must fall back to a doctrine of infinite repetition.

### IV

The last considerations have shown us the struggle for an interpretation of history which is in accord with the meaning of the kairos. We have described and schematized the different interpretations in order to draw from them the demands that the idea of kairos poses for any interpretation of history. There are, first of all, two demands that can be derived from the two main groups of interpretations of history. From the absolute types we derive the demand for an absolute tension in the historical consciousness; from the relative types we derive the demand for a universal historical consciousness; from the relative types we derive the demand for a universal historical thinking. We reject any attempt to absolutize *one* historical phenomenon over against all the others, challenging, at the same time, the leveling of all epochs into a process of endless repetition of relativities. A twofold demand may therefore be made upon a philosophy of history that is aware of the kairos. The tension characteristic of the absolute interpretation of history must be united with the universalism of the relative interpretations. But this demand contains a paradox. What happens in the kairos should be absolute, and yet not absolute, but under judgment of the absolute.

This demand is fulfilled when the conditioned surrenders itself to become a vehicle for the unconditional.

The relation of the conditioned to the unconditional, in individual as well as in social life, is either an openness of the conditioned to the dynamic presence of the unconditional or a seclusion of the conditioned within itself. The finite life is either turned toward the infinite or turned away from it toward itself. Where there is an acceptance of the eternal manifesting itself in a special moment of history, in a kairos, there is openness to the unconditional. Such openness can be expressed in religious as well as in secular symbols as the expectation of the transcendent Kingdom of God, or the thousand years of the reign of Christ, or the third epoch of world history, or the final stage of justice and peace. However different the historical consciousness involved in the use of the one or the other of these symbols may be, the consciousness of the kairos, of the outstanding moment in history, can express itself in each of them.

Openness to the unconditional, turning toward it, receiving and bearing it, are metaphors that all express the same reality. But they express it only in a highly abstract way and require a much more concrete interpretation of their meaning. An age that is open to the unconditional and is able to accept a kairos is not necessarily an age in which a majority of people are actively religious. The number of actively religious people can be greater in a so-called "irreligious" than in a religious period. But an age that is turned toward, and open to, the unconditional is one in which the consciousness of the presence of the unconditional permeates and guides all cultural functions and forms. The divine, for such a state of mind, is not a problem but a presupposition. Its "givenness" is more certain than that of anything else. This situation finds expression, first of all, in the dominating power of the religious sphere, but not in such a way as to make religion a special form of life ruling over the other forms. Rather, religion is the life-blood, the inner power, the ultimate meaning of all life. The "sacred" or the "holy" inflames, imbues, inspires, all reality and all aspects of existence. There is no profane nature or history, no profane ego, and no profane world. All history is sacred history, everything that happens bears a mythical character; nature and history are not separated. Equally, the separation of subject and object is missing; things are considered more as powers than as things. Therefore, the relation of them is not that of technical manipulation but that of immediate spiritual communion and of "magical" (in the larger sense of the word) influence. And the knowledge of things has not the purpose of analyzing them in order to control them; it has the purpose of finding their inner meaning, their mystery, and their divine significance. Obviously, in such a situation, the arts play a much greater role than in a scientific or technical age. They reveal the meaning of the myth on the basis of which everybody lives. In the same way social and political acts cannot be imagined without the powers of the divine sphere. The individual is entirely surrounded and carried by this all-penetrating spiritual substance out of which blessedness (and also curse) comes to him. He cannot escape it. Only in extreme cases of vocation or revolt can the individual extricate himself from the whole to which he belongs. Merely individual religion, individual culture, individual emotional life, and individual economic interests are impossible in such a social and spiritual situation. We shall call such a situation "theonomous," not in the sense that in it God lays down the laws but in the sense that such an age, in all its forms, is open to and directed toward the divine. How could such a stage of history disappear? What has destroyed primitive theonomy? The answer is the always present, always driving, always restless principle of "autonomy." Just as theonomy does not mean a situation in which God gives laws, so autonomy does not mean lawlessness. It means the acceptance of the structures and laws of reality as they are present in human mind and in its structures and laws. Autonomy means obedience to reason, i.e., to the "logos" immanent in reality and mind. Autonomy operates in the theoretical, as well as in the practical, spheres of culture. It replaces mystical nature with rational nature; it puts in the place of mythical events historical happenings, and in the place of the magical sense of communion it sets up technical control. It constitutes communities on the basis of purpose, and morality on the basis of individual perfection. It analyzes everything in order to put it together rationally. It makes religion a matter of personal decision and makes the inner life of the individual dependent upon itself. It releases also the forces of an autonomous political and economic activity.

Autonomy is always present as a tendency; it acts under the surface of every theonomy. "The secret impressionist that lives in every true artist" (Hartlaub) is the model for the secret astronomer in every true astrologer, and the secret physician in every true medicine man. The power of scientific and technical needs, in war and in industry and agriculture; the rationalizing energy inherent in the centralization of religion and government; the individualizing power of all strong piety; the struggle of ethical as against ritualistic "holiness"—all these forces are at work every moment, and they try to break through the bonds of the theonomous situation. The outcome of this struggle varies greatly. The theonomous situation can be so strong that autonomy cannot even start, as in many primitive cultures. Or it can achieve a certain degree of rationalization, at which point it comes to a standstill, and the forms thus created receive a final sanction, as, for example, in China. Or the rationalization can pierce directly through the finite world and become an all-devouring principle, as in Indian mysticism. Or autonomy can remain in the religious realm, as in Protestantism. Or it can achieve a complete victory, as in ancient Greece and in the modern Enlightenment. Or it can, after a victorious period, be partly conquered again, as at the end of the ancient world and in the anti-autonomous attitudes of Protestant orthodoxy and of the Counter Reformation. Each of these events is a turning-point in history. It was felt so by the contemporaries, and it appears as such in the historical tradition. Each of them can be called a "kairos," an outstanding moment in the temporal process, a moment in which the eternal breaks into the temporal, shaking and transforming it and creating a crisis in the depth of human existence.

Autonomy is the dynamic principle of history. Theonomy, on the other hand, is the substance and meaning of history. How are they related to each other? First of all, it must be stated that autonomy is not necessarily a turning-away from the unconditional. It is, so to speak, the obedient acceptance of the unconditional character of the form, the logos, the universal reason in world and mind. It is the acceptance of the norms of truth and justice, of order and beauty, of personality and community. It is obedience to the principles that control the realms of individual and social culture. These principles have unconditional validity. Obedience to them is obedience to the logos-element in the unconditional. The difference, however, between autonomy and theonomy is that in an autonomous culture the cultural forms appear only in their finite relationship, while in a theonomous culture they appear in their relation to the unconditional. Autonomous science, for instance, deals with the logical forms and the factual material of things; theonomous science deals, beyond this, with their ultimate meaning and their existential significance. Autonomy is not "irreligious," although it is not a vehicle of religion. It is indirectly religious through the form; it is not directly religious. The humility of the scientific empiricist is religious, but it does not appear as such; it is not theonomous. The heroism of Stoic self-control is religious, but it is not theonomous. The mystery of Leonardo's "Mona Lisa" is religious, but it does not show that it is. If both theonomy and autonomy are related to the unconditional, can we choose between them according to our taste, our psychological inclination, or our sociological tradition? This question is itself its own answer. Where it can be raised, theonomy already has been lost. As long as theonomy is in power, no alternative is open. If its power is broken, it cannot be re-established as it was, the autonomous road must be traveled to its very end, namely, to the moment in which a new theonomy appears in a new kairos.

A new theonomy is not the negation of autonomy, nor is it the attempt to suppress it and its freedom of creativity. For such attempts, which often have been made, with or without success, we use the term "heteronomous." Heteronomy imposes an alien law, religious or secular, on man's mind. It disregards the logos structure of mind and world. It destroys the honesty of truth and the dignity of the moral personality. It undermines creative freedom and the humanity of man. Its symbol is the "terror" exercised by absolute churches or absolute states. Religion, if it acts heteronomously, has ceased to be the substance and life-blood of a culture and has itself become a section of it, which, forgetting its theonomous greatness, betrays a mixture of arrogance and defeatism.

Theonomy does not stand against autonomy as heteronomy does. Theonomy is the answer to the question implied in autonomy, the question concerning a religious substance and an ultimate meaning of life and culture. Autonomy is able to live as long as it can draw from the religious tradition of the past, from the remnants of a lost theonomy. But more and more it loses this spiritual foundation. It becomes emptier, more formalistic, or more factual and is driven toward skepticism and cynicism, toward the loss of meaning and purpose. The history of autonomous cultures is the history of a continuous waste of spiritual substance. At the end of this process autonomy turns back to the lost theonomy with impotent longing, or it looks forward to a new theonomy in the attitude of creative waiting until the kairos appears.

Kairos in its *unique* and universal sense is, for Christian faith, the appearing of Jesus as the Christ. Kairos in its *general* and special sense for the philosopher of history is every turning-point in history in which the eternal judges and transforms the temporal. Kairos in its *special* sense, as decisive for our present situation, is the coming of a new theonomy on the soil of a secularized and emptied autonomous culture.

In these concepts and their dialectical relations the answer is given to the basic question of the philosophy of history: How can the absolute categories which characterize a genuine kairos be united with the relativity of the universal process of history? The answer is: History comes from and moves toward periods of theonomy, i.e., periods in which the conditioned is open to the unconditional without claiming to be unconditioned itself. Theonomy unites the absolute and the relative element in the interpretation of history, the demand that everything relative become the vehicle of the absolute and the insight that nothing relative can ever become absolute itself.

This solution concedes a limited truth to the interpretations of history discussed before.

The conservative-absolute philosophy of history is right in tracing the fight for and against theonomy, the "struggle between belief and unbelief," as it has been called, through all history. But it is wrong in identifying theonomy with a historical church.

The revolutionary-absolute philosophy of history is right in emphasizing the absolute tension toward absolute fulfilment, experienced in every kairos. In each kairos the "Kingdom of God is at hand," for it is a world-historical, unrepeatable, unique decision for and against the unconditional. Every kairos is, therefore, implicitly the universal kairos and an actualization of the unique kairos, the appearance of the Christ. But no kairos brings the fulfilment in time.

The warning against the idolatrous elevation of *one* moment in history, given by the indifferent-absolute philosophy of history, has a decisive influence on the solution: Everything can be a vessel of the unconditional, but nothing can be unconditioned itself. This, however, does not produce indifference toward history; it creates an attitude that takes history absolutely seriously.

The classical-relative philosophy of history is right in its idea of humanity as a whole, in its emphasis on autonomy, and in its recognition of the national, regional, and traditional differentiations within mankind. It understands the universality and individuality of human history and the special conditions of each kairos; but it fails in not accepting the absolute categories and absolute decisions connected with the experience of the kairos.

In every transforming activity a belief in progress is implied. Progressivism is the philosophy of action. Acting out of the kairos means acting in the direction of theonomy. And there is progress from what is not yet or no longer true theonomy toward its realization. In this the progressive-relative philosophy of history is right. But it is wrong in making the law of acting a law of being, for there is no law of universal progress. The fight between theonomy and its foes always goes on and grows more refined and more disastrous, the more the technical progress changes the surface of the earth, binding together all nations for common creation and common destruction at the same time.

The philosophy of the kairos is closely related to the dialectical interpretations of history. Theonomy, autonomy, and heteronomy are dialectically related to one another, since each of these ideas drives beyond itself. But there are some important differences. There is, in the doctrine of the kairos, no final stage in which dialectics, against its nature, ceases to operate. There is, in the doctrine of the kairos, not only the horizontal dialectic of the historical process but also the vertical dialectic operating between the unconditional and the conditioned. And, finally, there is no logical, physical, or economic necessity in the historical process, according to the doctrine of the kairos. It moves through that unity of freedom and fate which distinguishes history from nature.

V

We are convinced that today a kairos, an epochal moment of history, is visible. This is not the place to give reasons for this conviction, although we should refer to the ever growing literature that is critical of our culture and to movements in which the consciousness of the crisis has taken a living form. These may not be proofs that are objectively convincing; proofs of that sort cannot exist. Indeed, the consciousness of the kairos is dependent on one's being inwardly grasped by the fate and destiny of the time. It can be found in the passionate longing of the masses; it can become clarified and take form in small circles of conscious intellectual and spiritual concern; it can gain power in the prophetic word; but it cannot be demonstrated and forced; it is deed and freedom, as it is also fate and grace.

The movement most strongly conscious of the kairos seems to us today to be socialism. "Religious socialism" is our attempt at interpreting and shaping socialism from the viewpoint of theonomy, from the vision of the kairos. It proceeds from the presupposition that in present-day socialism there are certain elements that are incompatible with the idea of the kairos, that are "untimely elements" in which originally creative ideas are perverted or corrupted. Religious socialism for that reason energetically carries on the cultural criticism characteristic of all socialism and seeks to lead the latter to its own real depth, while directing this criticism also against socialism itself.

In present-day socialism are brought together the revolutionary-absolute type in the this-worldly form and the dialectical-relative type in the form of an economic interpretation of history. But a balancing of the two has not been achieved. The unconditional is not grasped in its positive and negative power. It is not grasped in its positive significance as the principle of theonomy, judging and transforming *all* sides of our industrial civilization, including economics and politics. And the negative power of the unconditional is not appreciated, which brings the bearers of the crisis under judgment along with those who are criticized by them, and which judges also every future state of society. The reason for this twofold failure is that socialism, in spite of all its criticism of the bourgeois epoch, has been unable to keep itself free from its negative element, namely, its attempt to exclude the unconditional from the spheres of thought and action and, accordingly, to create the new epoch merely through technology and strategy. Socialism was not aware that precisely in this fashion it was prolonging the old epoch. Socialism saw the kairos, but it did not see its depth; it did not recognize the extent to which it stood itself under the crisis. When it fought against "bourgeois" science, it did not see how it itself shared the basic presupposition of this science, the purely objectifying relationship to the world, to spirit, and to history; and it did not see how, in spite of a different basic impulse, it was fettered within the bonds of that attitude. When it rejected the aesthetic aristocratic practice of art, it was not aware of the fact that, in its promotion of an art determined by its content and oriented to a particular type of ethics and politics, it stood simply at the other pole of the same axis. If in its theory of education it made its focal point the "enlightenment" and the technical discipline of intellect and will for the purpose of an economic and political acquisition of power, it did not realize that it was thereby adopting the basic attitude of its enemies or that it was trying to resist them by the very weapons with the help of which their enemies had deadened the souls of men and had made their bodies into mere cogs in a machine. If it made the highest possible increase of economic welfare into the all-determining and foremost aim, it did not see that it became thereby a mere competitor of capitalism, which believed that it could better accomplish the same thing through social welfare and technical progress. If socialism intended to deprive the spiritual and religious life of its intrinsic value, considering it as a mere ideology, it did not sense that it thereby strengthened the attitude toward economics and life in general that is characteristic of materialistic capitalism. When socialism viewed the atomistic individual as an ultimate reality and then tried to unite him with others through the solidarity of mere interests, it was not aware of its dependence upon the decomposition of "liberal" society and upon the false assumption that human groups may be ultimately motivated by the "struggle for existence." If socialism fought against religion in its ecclesiastical and dogmatic forms, and for that purpose took over all the means of combat and the slogans of the old liberal struggle against the churches, it did not see that it thereby came into the danger of cutting off the roots out of which alone enthusiasm, consecration, "holiness," and unconditional devotion can flow into it: the unconditional "Yes" to the unconditional, regardless of what its forms or symbols might be.

In all these things religious socialism is willing to push the criticism further, to carry it through deeper, to bring it to its ultimate and decisive point. It strives to be more radical, more revolutionary, than socialism, because it wishes to reveal the crisis from the viewpoint of the unconditional. It wishes to make socialism conscious of the present kairos.

With this aim, it follows that religious socialism is always ready to place itself under the criticism of the unconditional. By far the greatest danger for the religious-socialist movement seems to me to be where "religion" is used as a matter of strategy. Here the bourgeois element which socialism drags along with it is in a fateful way encouraged. A merging between the present-day socialism and the churches of our day impedes the coming of the kairos by mutually strengthening the very elements that must be eliminated. Religious socialism must not, for the present, become either a church-political movement or a state-political

party, since it loses thereby the unrestricted power to bring both the
churches and the parties under judgment.

Religious socialism should, in any case, avoid considering socialism
as a religious law, by appealing to the authority of Jesus or to the primitive Christian community. There exists no direct way from the unconditional to any concrete solution. The unconditional is never a law or a
promoter of a definite form of the spiritual or social life. The contents
of the historical life are tasks and ventures of the creative spirit. The
truth is a living truth, a creative truth, and not a law. What we are
confronted with is never and nowhere an abstract command; it is living
history, with its abundance of new problems whose solution occupies
and fulfils every epoch.

One question may still be raised, and we offer a brief answer to it:
"Is is possible that the message of the kairos is an error?"

The answer is not difficult to give. The message is always an error;
for it sees something immediately imminent which, considered in its
ideal aspect, will never become a reality and which, considered in its
real aspect, will be fulfilled only in long periods of time. And yet the
message of the kairos is never an error; for where the kairos is proclaimed as a prophetic message, it is already present; it is impossible for
it to be proclaimed in power without its having grasped those who proclaim it.

II. RELIGION AND CULTURE

# Chapter IV

## RELIGION AND SECULAR CULTURE[1]

THE technical problem of a lecture on religion and secular culture is the implicit demand to give in one paper the content of at least two volumes, namely, that of a philosophy of religion and that of a philosophy of culture. Since this cannot be done except in terms of an abstract and unconvincing summary, I intend to limit myself to one central concept, namely, that of a "theonomous" culture, and to develop this concept in a kind of autobiographical retrospect from the end of the first World War to the end of the second, adding some systematic analyses of the theonomous character of symbols.

### I

When we returned from the first World War, we found a deep gap between the cultural revolution and the religious tradition in central and eastern Europe. The Lutheran and the Roman and Greek Catholic churches rejected the cultural and—with some exceptions on the part of Roman Catholicism—the political revolutions. They rejected them as the rebellious expression of a secular autonomy. The revolutionary movements, on the other hand, repudiated the churches as the expression of a transcendent heteronomy. It was very obvious to those of us who had spiritual ties with both sides that this situation was intolerable and, in the long run, disastrous for religion as well as for culture. We believed that it was possible to close the gap, partly by creating movements such as religious socialism, partly by a fresh interpretation of the mutual immanence of religion and culture within each other. History, however, has shown that it was too late for such an attempt to be successful at that time. It proved impossible to break down the secular ideology and the mechanistic (non-Marxist) materialism of the labor parties. The Old Guard prevailed against us and against the youth of their own movement. In the religious realm not only the conservative representatives of "ruling-class Christianity" (the European counterpart to American "suburban Christianity")

1. [A lecture given in January, 1946, for the Hiram W. Thomas Foundation at the University of Chicago.—EDITOR.]

55

ostracized us; we were also attacked by that dynamic theology which in this country is called "neo-orthodoxy" and which united prophetic powers with a non-prophetic detachment from culture, thus confirming and deepening the gap. Our attempt was frustrated; but we did not and do not accept defeat in so far as the truth of our conception is concerned; for we do not accept the idea, which a consistent pragmatism can hardly avoid, that victory is a method of pragmatic verification.

The first of my attempts to analyze the mutual immanence of religion and culture was made in a lecture which I read in Berlin immediately after the end of the war, entitled "The Idea of a Theology of Culture." It was written with the enthusiasm of those years in which we believed that a new beginning, a period of radical transformation, a fulfilment of time, or, as we called it with a New Testament term, a *kairos* had come upon us, in spite of breakdown and misery. We did *not*, however, share the feeling of many American religious and secular humanists of the twenties; we did *not* believe that the Kingdom of God, consisting in peace, justice, and democracy, had been established. Very early we saw those demonic structures of reality which during the past months have been recognized by all thoughtful people in this country. But we also saw a new chance, a moment pregnant with creative possibilities. The breakdown of bourgeois civilization in central and eastern Europe could pave the way for a reunion of religion and secular culture. That was what we hoped for and what religious socialism fought for, and to it we tried to give a philosophical and theological basis. The idea of a "theonomous culture" seemed to be adequate for this aim; it became the principle of philosophies of religion and of culture which proposed to fill the gap from both sides.

The churches had rejected the secularized autonomy of modern culture; the revolutionary movements had rejected the transcendent heteronomy of the churches. Both had rejected something from which, in the last analysis, they themselves lived; and this something is theonomy. The words "autonomy," "heteronomy," and "theonomy" answer the question of the *nomos* or the law of life in three different ways: Autonomy asserts that man as the bearer of universal reason is the source and measure of culture and religion—that he is his own law. Heteronomy asserts that man, being unable to act according to universal reason, must be subjected to a law, strange and superior to him. Theonomy asserts that the superior law is, at the same time, the innermost law of man himself, rooted in the divine ground which is man's own ground: the law of life transcends man, although it is, at the same time, his own. Applying these concepts to the relation between religion and culture, we called an autonomous culture the attempt to create the forms of personal and social life without any reference to something ultimate and unconditional, following only the demands of theoretical and practical rationality. A heteronomous culture, on the other hand, subjects the forms and laws of thinking and acting to authoritative criteria of an ecclesiastical religion or a political quasi-religion, even at the price of destroying the structures of rationality. A theonomous culture expresses in its creations an ultimate concern and a transcending meaning not as something strange but as its own spiritual ground. "Religion is the substance of culture and culture the form of religion." This was the most precise statement of theonomy.

With these distinctions it was possible to create a theonomous analysis of culture, a "theology of culture," so to speak, which shows its theonomous ground not only where it is clearly indicated, as in the archaic periods of the great cultures and the early and high Middle Ages of our Western civilization, but also in those periods in which heteronomy was victorious, as in the later Middle Ages and in Arabic and Protestant orthodoxy, and even in autonomous or secular epochs, such as classical Greece, the Renaissance, the Enlightenment, and the nineteenth century. No cultural creation can hide its religious ground or its rational formation. Against ecclesiastical heteronomy it is always possible to show that all the rites, doctrines, institutions, and symbols of a religious system constitute a religious culture which is derived from the surrounding general culture—from its social and economic structure, its character traits, its opinions and philosophy, its linguistic and artistic expressions, its complexes, its traumas, and its longings. It is possible to show that, if such a special religious culture be imposed on dissenters or foreign cultures, it is not the ultimate, with its justified claim to grasp the hearts of men, but something provisional and conditioned which uses the religious ultimacy for *its* claims. The Thomistic philosophy, as well as the Protestant ideal of personality, is a transitory form of religious culture, but neither has any claim to ultimacy and finality; and the same holds true of the Greek concepts in the dogma of the church, of the feudal pattern of the Roman hierarchy, of the patriarchalistic ethics of Lutheranism, of the democratic ideals of sectarian

Protestantism, and even of the cultural traditions which, for instance, are embodied in the biblical language and world view. Theonomous thinking sides with autonomous criticism, if such forms of religious culture present themselves as absolutes.

But more important in our situation was and is the other task of a theonomous analysis of culture: to show that in the depth of every autonomous culture an ultimate concern, something unconditional and holy, is implied. It is the task of deciphering the style of an autonomous culture in all its characteristic expressions and of finding their hidden religious significance. This we did with all possible tools of historical research and comparative interpretation and empathic understanding and with a special effort in regard to such stages of civilization as were utterly secular, as, for instance, the later nineteenth century. Autonomous culture is secularized in the degree to which it has lost its ultimate reference, its center of meaning, its spiritual substance. The Renaissance was a step toward autonomy, but still in the spiritual power of an unwasted medieval heritage. The Enlightenment quickly lost its Protestant and sectarian substance and became in some—though not in many—of its expressions completely secular. The later nineteenth century, with its subjection to the technical pattern of thought and action, shows the character of an extremely emptied and secularized autonomy in an advanced stage of disintegration. But even here the religious substance, a remnant of something ultimate, was noticeable and made the transitory existence of such a culture possible. However, more than in the disintegrating bourgeois autonomy, the religious reference was effective in the movements which protested—often with a prophetic passion—against this situation. Theonomous analysis was able to decipher puzzling experiences, such as the visionary destruction of bourgeois idealism and naturalism in art and literature by expressionism and surrealism; it was able to show the religious background of the rebellion of the vital and unconscious side of man's personality against the moral and intellectual tyranny of consciousness; it was able to interpret the quasi-religious, fanatical, and absolutistic character of the reactions of the twentieth century as against the nineteenth. It was able to do all this without special reference to organized religion, the churches being only a part of the whole picture, but with a decisive reference to the religious element which was and is hidden in all these antireligious and anti-Christian movements. In all of them there is an ultimate, unconditional, and all-determining concern, something absolutely serious and therefore holy, even if expressed in secular terms.

So the gap between religion and culture is filled: religion is more than a system of special symbols, rites, and emotions, directed toward a highest being; religion is ultimate concern; it is the state of being grasped by something unconditional, holy, absolute. As such it gives meaning, seriousness, and depth to all culture and creates out of the cultural material a religious culture of its own. The contrast between religion and culture is reduced to the duality of religious and secular culture with innumerable transitions between them. The revolutionary movements, for instance, represent an ultimate concern, a religious principle, hidden but effective within them. The Lutheran churches, for example, represent a special cultural period in which an ultimate concern, a religious principle, has embodied itself manifestly and directly. Both are religious and both are cultural at the same time. Why, then, the difference? The answer can only be that the Kingdom of God has not yet come, that God is not yet all in all, whatever this "not yet" may mean. Asked what the proof is for the fall of the world, I like to answer: religion itself, namely, a religious culture beside a secular culture, a temple beside a town hall, a Lord's Supper beside a daily supper, prayer beside work, meditation beside research, *caritas* beside *eros*. But although this duality can never be overcome in time, space, and history, it makes a difference whether the duality is deepened into a bridgeless gap, as in periods in which autonomy and heteronomy fight with each other, or whether the duality is recognized as something which should not be and which is overcome fragmentarily by anticipation, so to speak, in a theonomous period. The kairos which we believed to be at hand was the coming of a new theonomous age, conquering the destructive gap between religion and secular culture.

But history took another path, and the question of religion and culture cannot be answered simply in those terms. A new element has come into the picture, the experience of the "end." Something of it appeared after the first World War; but we did not feel it in its horrible depth and its incredible thoroughness. We looked at the beginning of the new more than at the end of the old. We did not realize the price that mankind has to pay for the coming of a new theonomy; we still believed in transitions without catastrophes. We did not see the possibility of final catastrophes as the true prophets, the prophets of doom, announced them. Therefore, our theonomous interpretation of history had a slight tinge of romanticism, though it tried to avoid any kind of utopianism. This has come to an end because the end itself has appeared like a flash of lightning before our eyes; and not only among the ruins of central and eastern Europe but also within the abundance of this country has it been seen. While after the first World War the mood of a new beginning prevailed, after the second World War a mood of the end prevails. A present theology of culture is, above all, a theology of the end of culture, not in general terms but in a concrete analysis of the inner void of most of our cultural expressions. Little is left in our present civilization which does not indicate to a sensitive mind the presence of this vacuum, this lack of ultimacy and substantial power in language and education, in politics and philosophy, in the development of personalities, and in the life of communities. Who of us has never been shocked by this void when he has used traditional or untraditional secular or religious language to make himself understandable and has not succeeded and has then made a vow of silence to himself, only to break it a few hours later? This is symbolic of our whole civilization. Often one gets the impression that only those cultural creations have greatness in which the experience of the void is expressed; for it can be expressed powerfully only on the basis of a foundation which is deeper than culture, which is ultimate concern, even if it accepts the void, even in respect to religious culture. Where this happens, the vacuum of disintegration can become a vacuum out of which creation is possible, a "sacred void," so to speak, which brings a quality of waiting, of "not yet," of a being broken from above, into all our cultural creativity. It is not an empty criticism, however radical and justified such criticism may be. It is not an indulgence in paradoxes that prevents the coming-down to concreteness. It is not cynical detachment, with its ultimate spiritual dishonesty. It is simple cultural work out of, and qualified by, the experience of the sacred void. This is the way—perhaps the only way—in which our time can reach a theonomous union between religion and culture.

One thing is clear: the experience of the end by no means undermines the idea of theonomy. On the contrary, it is its strongest confirmation. Two events may illustrate this. The first is the turn of Karl Barth from a theology of radical detachment from culture, religious as well as secular, to an equally radical attachment to the fight against a demonically distorted cultural system. Barth suddenly realized that culture can never be indifferent toward the ultimate. If it ceases to be theonomous, it first becomes empty, and then it falls, at least for a time, under demonic control. The demand for a merely matter-of-fact culture is dishonesty or illusion, and a catastrophic illusion at that. This leads to the second event to which I want to refer: the change of attitude toward culture in this country. It was truly symbolic for the collapse of our secular autonomy when the atom scientists raised their voices and preached the end, not unconditionally but with conditions of salvation which present-day humanity is hardly willing to fulfil. It was and is a symptom of a changed mood when some of these men and others with them, statesmen, educators, psychologists, physicians, sociologists, not to speak of artists and poets, whose visions anticipated our cultural predicament long ago—when these people cry for religion as the saving power of our culture. They do it often in the ugly and false phraseology which demands the undergirding of culture by religion, as if religion were a tool for a higher purpose. But even in this inadequate form the ideal of a theonomous culture is transparent.

## II

After this historical and dialectical interpretation of the relation between religion and secular culture, I want to show the truth of the underlying assertion by analyzing some religious symbols and their significance for the cultural situation out of which they are taken. Religious symbols use a finite reality in order to express our relation to the infinite. But the finite reality they use is not an arbitrary means for an end, something strange to it; it participates in the power of the ultimate for which it stands. A religious symbol is double edged. It expresses not only what is symbolized but also that through which it is symbolized.

The terms for "salvation" in many languages are derived from roots like *salvus, saos,* whole, *heil,* which all designate health, the opposite of disintegration and disruption. Salvation is healing in the ultimate sense; it is final cosmic and individual healing. In such theonomous terminology the work of the physician stands symbolically for the ultimate restitution. But the decisive question is whether it stands so by chance or by inner necessity. If it is a symbol by chance, it can be replaced by any other symbol and is in reality not even a symbol but only a metaphor. This is the situation in a secularized culture, in which religious salvation and medical healing are separated. In a theonomous culture, healing is an expression of salvation and, consequently, can become a genuine symbol of the saving power of the ultimate. It is perhaps a symptom of the longing for a new theonomy that everywhere attempts at co-operation among ministers, physicians, and psychiatrists are being made.

Medieval historians know that the official welcome offered to princes, kings, and emperors by city authorities often was given in messianic terminology. Not this or that king was greeted but *the* king of peace, the messianic king. Now, it is obvious that the term "king," applied, for instance, to Yahweh or to his Messiah, is a symbol of something which infinitely transcends every human king. Nevertheless, the symbol is not arbitrary. The king is called by God. The grace that is upon him is divine grace. The symbol works in both directions. It gives the king—and that means the political realm—theonomous dignity; and it makes the kingship of God a genuine symbol. When the king became a functionary of an autonomous state, he became either a tyrant (and was removed) or a puppet without the power of religious symbolism. We use kingship still as a traditional, but no longer as a genuine, symbol.

The Christian church as the mystical body of Christ is a strictly theonomous symbol. It has meaning only so long as the organic unity, including a spiritual center, is seriously applied to human communities. In this case human relations have the character of a mutual edification on the basis of a common ultimate concern. "Body" is a genuine symbol and not an exchangeable metaphor. It lost its symbolic power when the church became a voluntary covenant of individuals and society became the realm of social contracts for preliminary purposes. The nineteenth-century philosophical and political organologists made a mistake when they tried to save the idea of the organic "body politic" without its theonomous foundation. And this is, generally speaking, the reason for the unavoidable frustration of all politics and ethics and philosophies of restoration. They try to re-establish theonomy on an autonomous foundation.

Personality is the most emphasized ideal of modern religious and secular humanism. Personality is considered as the most necessary symbol for God. God is even described as the person in whom all human perfections are perfectly embodied. In this case the disintegration of a symbol has occurred, and the result has been its large-scale removal. In classical theology, "person" was used only for the three principles in the divine life, not for God himself; and "personality" was not used at all in this connection. The idea of God in classical theology united personal with supra-personal traits. God was less and more than personal, as well as personal; he was the unity of all potentialities. In this sense personal symbolism could be applied to him on the basis of man's real existence, which unites prepersonal and postpersonal elements with personality. In the degree to which first Protestantism, then humanism, neglected the nonpersonal elements in man—his vital and mystical side—for the sake of consciousness, God became one person alongside others. He ceased to be the supporting and transcending center of every personal life. But as such he was superfluous, one more autonomous personality beside the others, although exceeding them in power and value. The persons were left alone, centered in themselves and very soon unable to stand this situation of monadic loneliness. The symbol and, along with it, the reality from which it was taken disintegrated in mutual interdependence. When God became *a* person, man's personality was driven into neurotic disintegration.

In classical theology God is, first of all, Being as such. *Deus est esse*. Being in this sense is not the most abstract category, as a mistaken nominalism asserts; it is the power of Being in everything that is, in everything that participates in Being. So long as this is the basic statement about God, we are in a theonomous situation because it implies that every finite reality is rooted in the creative ground, in Being itself. Therefore, it is possible to find the traces of the ultimate in everything, and the scientific approach to Being is an approach to that which concerns us unconditionally. When Being lost its symbolic power under the influence of nominalism and when, more definitely in the second half of the Renaissance, Being became the object for a subject, to be calculated and controlled, God ceased to be Being itself and Being ceased to be divine. If today you say that God is Being, it sounds almost blasphemous. The consequence of this whole development was that science observed the relation of all beings to one another and the calculable rules of their behavior, but that it lost Being itself, its unity, its power, its meaning. Science had destroyed the unity of reality *before* it learned to split up any given structure of reality. Science openly confesses that it no longer has anything to do with Being, but only with equations. When Being as a symbol was lost, Being itself was lost. If it is denied that *Deus est esse, Deus* as well as *esse* is given up.

If God is called *ipsum esse,* Being itself, he can also, and must, be called *ipsum verum,* the true itself. But if God is a being beside others which may or may not exist, or a person beside others whom we may or may not discover, a statement like *Deus est veritas,* "God is truth," has no meaning. There is perhaps no point in the history of human thought at which the transition from theonomy to a cleavage between autonomous culture and heteronomous religion is more obvious and more clearly discussed than in this question. In a recent paper about the two types of philosophy of religion, I have tried to show how the first slight break in theonomous thinking occurred when Thomas Aquinas interpreted the Augustinian-Franciscan principle that God is truth (and, therefore, immediately certain more than anything else, including myself) in Aristotelian terms and said that God is immediately certain for himself but not for us.[2] We need mediating discourse and ecclesiastical authority to reach him. This gap was deepened by Duns Scotus and made insuperable by the nominalists who in this, as in many other respects, opened the way toward a secular culture. If the statement that God is the true has itself lost its symbolic power, two consequences follow. The first one is that there is no truth about God in terms of the prius of all other truth, that the truth about God is secondary, and this necessarily leads to a secular world without God. The second consequence is that within this secular world the idea of truth is reduced to the realm of observable and, if possible, calculable relations, while the truth about existence itself and its meaning for us is left to emotions and opinions, a situation most useful for the rise and victory of uncontrolled authorities. Being and truth are lost if they cannot be applied to God any more, and God is lost if Being is mere objectivity and truth mere subjectivity. The two-edged character of any symbol used for God is manifest even in concepts like "being" and "truth" which, if applied to God, unite a symbolic and a nonsymbolic element.

I want to close with a few words concerning that realm of culture which is not an independent realm but is the way of communicating

2. ["The Two Types of Philosophy of Religion," *Union Seminary Quarterly Review,* I, No. 4 (May, 1946), 3–13.—EDITOR.]

all other realms to those who are to be shaped by them, namely, education. In doing so, I give, at the same time, homage to the genius of this place. The theonomous word for education is "initiation." While the word "education" points to the *terminus a quo,* the "where from," the word "initiation" points to the *terminus ad quem,* the "where to." Secular culture has lost an ultimate and commanding *terminus ad quem,* because it has lost an ultimate and unconditional concern. In the Diotima speech in Plato's *Symposium* we see, still retained, the steps of initiation into the ultimate wisdom. And in his myth of the cave in the *Republic* we learn that the way to wisdom implies a radical transformation, a liberation from bondage and darkness. Such ideas presuppose that there is a level in life, the most and ultimately the *only* important one, which cannot be approached directly. It is the level of gnosis or *sapientia* or "wisdom," in distinction from the level of *episteme* or *scientia* or "science." It is the level of Being and truth as such before they split into subject and object; and, therefore, it has the character of a mystery. Everything which is merely object can be approached directly with scientific reasoning and technical tools. That which precedes mere objectivity needs initiation. Innumerable rites of initiation in all nations up to Christian baptism and confirmation show that mankind was conscious of the sacred depth in things which cannot be approached in ordinary ways. When the element of initiation was lost, education lost the *terminus ad quem* and is now desperately looking for it. But no abundance of highest possibility shown to the coming generations can replace something ultimate that is necessary. Are we able to show it to them by initiation as well as by education? We *cannot* do it today in terms of special contents, whether they be religious or secular. But we *can* do it by accepting the void which is the destiny of our period, by accepting it as a "sacred void" which may qualify and transform thinking and acting. I have not tried to present a well-balanced synthesis between religion and secular culture. I have tried to show their *one* theonomous root and the void which necessarily has followed their separation, and perhaps something of the longing of our time for a new theonomy, for an ultimate concern in all our concerns.

# Chapter V

## REALISM AND FAITH

### I. THE IDEA OF A SELF-TRANSCENDING REALISM

FOR those who have followed with sympathy or enthusiasm the development of painting in the first three decades of the nineteenth century, two events will stand out in memory: first, the emergence and success of "expressionism," then the flagging of its energies and the rise of a style called *neue Sachlichkeit* ("the new objectivity"). When expressionism appeared, it was largely rejected as repulsive, dark, and ugly. But slowly it began to fascinate many people because of the riddle implied in it and the radicalism of its solutions. Finally, it won most enthusiastic adherence from groups who saw in it a new mysticism or the way to a new religious cultus. This is understandable. Expressionism was a revolution against the realism of the nineteenth century. It was a rebellion against the naturalistic-critical, as well as against the idealistic-conventional wing of realism, and it also trespassed the limits of the subjective-impressionistic realism from which it came. Things were interpreted by the expressionistic painters in their cosmic setting and their immeasurable depth. Their natural forms were broken so that their spiritual significance could become transparent. Colors, expressing divine and demonic ecstacies, broke through the gray of the daily life. It seemed as if the period of the myth had returned, and developments in other realms seemed to confirm the visions of the artists. But this feeling lasted no longer than to the middle of the third decade. At this time, works of art appeared which kept much closer to the natural forms of things than the expressionists did. They could, however, not be considered as a relapse to the nineteenth-century naturalism. They represented a post-expressionistic, not a pre-expressionistic style. They repudiated the elements of subjectivism and romanticism in the preceding period without giving up the depth and cosmic symbolism of their predecessors. Those who expected from this development a return to the idealizing naturalism of bourgeois liking were destined to disappointment, for the new realism was not interested in the natural forms of things for their own sake but for their power of expressing the profounder levels and the universal significance of things. Nineteenth-century realism had deprived reality of its symbolic power; expressionism had tried to re-establish this power by shattering the surface of reality. The new realism tries to point to the spiritual meaning of the real by using its given forms. In these movements art is driving toward a self-transcending realism. There is no guaranty that this goal will be reached; many tendencies in our period work against it, some of them honest, some of them merely ideological. But it is a tendency which should be understood and supported by Protestantism because it has a genuinely Protestant character.

Self-transcending realism is a universal attitude toward reality. It is neither a merely theoretical view of the world nor a practical discipline for life; it lies underneath the cleavage between theory and practice. Nor is it a special religion or a special philosophy. But it is a basic attitude in every realm of life, expressing itself in the shaping of every realm.

Self-transcending realism combines two elements, the emphasis on the real and the transcending power of faith. There seems to be no wider gap than that between a realistic and a belief-ful attitude. Faith transcends every conceivable reality; realism questions every transcending of the real, calling it utopian or romantic. Such a tension is hard to stand, and it is not surprising that the human mind always tries to evade it. Evasion is possible in two ways—in the way of a realism without self-transcendence or in the way of a self-transcendence which is not realistic. For the latter I want to use the word "idealism," for the former the word "self-limiting realism." Neither of these attitudes is necessarily irreligious. Positivism, pragmatism, empiricism—the different forms of realism which refuse self-transcendence—may accept religion as a realm beside the philosophical and scientific interpretation of reality, or they may connect the two realms in terms of a theology of immanent experience (the former more an English, the latter more an American, type). Idealism, on the other hand, in its different forms, such as metaphysical, epistemological, moral idealism (the first a classical German, the second a universal bourgeois, the third an Anglo-Saxon type) is essentially religious but in such a way that genuine religion must be critical of it. Faith is an ecstatic transcending of reality in the power of that which cannot be derived from the whole of reality and cannot be approached by ways which belong to the whole of reality. Idealism does not see the gap between the unconditional and the conditioned which no ontological or ethical self-elevation can bridge. Therefore it must be judged from a prophetic and Protestant point of view as religious arrogance and from the point of view of a self-limiting realism as metaphysical arrogance. In this double attack, from the side of faith and from the side of realism, idealism breaks down, historically and systematically, practically and theoretically. It is the glory of idealism that it tries to unite an autonomous interpretation of reality with a religious transcending of reality. Idealism is always on the way to "theonomy." Most of the theological, philosophical, and political critics of idealism have not even understood its problems. Their feeling of superiority over idealism is based on their ignorance about the depth of its questions and answers. The limitation and tragedy of idealism lie in the fact that it idealizes the real instead of transcending it in the power of the transcendent, i.e., in faith. Hence we are led to the result that faith and realism, just because of their radical tension, belong together. For faith implies an absolute tension and cannot be united with any attitude in which the tension is weakened. Idealism relativizes, self-limiting realism denies, but self-transcending realism accepts the tension.

## II. THREE TYPES OF REALISM

Knowing is a union between the knower and the known. The cognitive will is the will of a separated life to unite itself with other life. *Theoria* is not detached observation, although different degrees of separation and detachment are a necessary element in knowledge; but *theoria* is union with the really real, with that level of a thing in which the "power of being" (*ousia, "Seinsmächtigkeit"*) is situated. Every real has different levels with more or less power of being. This (Platonic) doctrine has been challenged by Neo-Kantianism because it seems to confuse being and value. But we confront here just the question whether values must not have an ontological foundation and whether the understanding of being as power is not the way to give such a foundation to values and, at the same time, to give back to *theoria* the "existential" significance which it formerly had. Of course, if being is defined as "object of thought" no matter what content it has, the idea of "degrees of being" is senseless. But if being is "power" the assertion

of such degrees is natural, and it is a vital necessity for the mind to penetrate into the strata in which the real power of a thing reveals itself.

It is characteristic of Greek thought that from the beginning it sought
the power of a thing, the "really real" of it, in that element which can
be grasped by the "logos," the word, the speech, the notion. The "rational" (that which is susceptible to the logos) is the really real. The
power of a thing is to be discovered in that which can be grasped by
word and concept. This view is unique in comparison with the attitude
of the largest part of mankind, for whom a magical, psychic, mystical
element, something like *mana,* is the inner power of things. For this
reason it is understandable, although not justified, that Greek philosophy could be interpreted as the way of depriving things of their power
and that the Platonic ontology could be conceived of as epistemological
logic (Natorp). But for the Greek philosophers from Parmenides to
Plotinus, the rationality and the inner power of things are identical,
which is clearly expressed in their belief that the highest goal of reason
is, at the same time, the highest goal of the movement of every life.
Only in the light of this identity of the will to knowledge and the will
to union is the role of Greek philosophy in the ancient world understandable. Only on the basis of this assumption is it possible to understand the transition of Greek classicism into the Neo-Platonic synthesis of the mystical and the rational. There is, however, one point in
Plotinus which shows that he represents the end of autonomous
Greek thought, namely, the fact that he finds the ultimate power of
being beyond the *nous* (the power of reason) in the abyss of the form-
less One. In this he is oriental and not Greek.

The unity of rationality and the power of being may be interpreted
in different ways. Since the power of being is discovered by thought,
the thinking subject may become, intentionally or unintentionally, the
bearer of all power. In this case the things are subjected to control and
use by the rational man. They become powerless means for him who
analyzes them or enjoys them or transforms them or rises above them or
retires from them. From the critical and ethical schools of Greek
philosophy this attitude is transmitted through late nominalism to
modern technical science and the technocratic world view. One concedes to things only so much power as they should have in order to be
useful. Reason becomes the means of controlling the world. The really
real (*ousia*) of things is their calculable element, that which is deter-

mined by natural laws. Anything beyond this level is without interest and not an object of knowledge. This relation to reality is called "realistic" today. Through technical science and its economic utilization this realism is so predominant in our social and intellectual situation that the fight against it seems romantic and almost hopeless. Later Neo-Kantianism and, more consistently, positivism are the philosophical expressions of this radical reduction of the power of things to their theoretical calculability and their practical utility. Even theology was largely drawn into the orbit of this "technological realism."

But reason as the way of grasping the power of things may be understood in a quite different way. The power of being within reality may be preserved also in a rationalized and spiritualized form. In this case the true being, discovered by the logos, becomes a matter of contemplation and union. There are degrees of the power of being (Plato, Aristotle, and Plotinus agree on this point), and on these degrees the human mind climbs theoretically and practically to the highest one, the supreme power of being. Mere vital existence, the control and transformation of reality, practice generally, and even physical and mathematical knowledge are transcended, and the eternal essences and their unity and ground are sought. Here "matter" exercises a permanently retarding and often preventive influence on the ascending mind. Matter, although without form or essential being, has a negative, half-demonic power which cannot be overcome in the material world. Therefore, the mind must transcend the visible cosmos as a whole, in order to find the ultimate power of being in that which is beyond being, the "good," the "pure actuality," "the One." Their longing for the true power of being drives the Greeks into a flight from the ambiguous half-demonic power of things. This is the conceptual foundation of Neo-Platonic asceticism and of that type of realism which we should call "mystical realism."

Mystical realism was dominant in the early and high Middle Ages before its nominalistic disintegration. It was not a radical, but a moderate, realism which the Middle Ages accepted. On the basis of biblical religion it was impossible to follow Greek mysticism in its ultimately negative attitude toward individuality and personality. But mystical realism was "realism" and not romanticism or idealism. Although our present terminology makes it difficult for us to use the word "realistic" for something that seems to be just the opposite of what the word generally means today, we must understand that medieval realism was as much right in using the word "real" for its attitude as modern realism is in using it for its attitude. In both cases realism gives an answer to the question of the really real or the essential power of things, but the place where this power is sought and found is different. We are prevented, however, from acknowledging this if we interpret the belief that the universals are the really real merely as a logical theory (which it also is) instead of understanding it primarily as the ontological expression of a social and spiritual situation.

The mystical realism of the Middle Ages is still alive in our time. The technological concept of reality is permanently challenged by the mystical concept, which reappears in many transformations. Theories of intuitive knowledge, classicist and romantic revivals of ancient or medieval forms of thought, phenomenology, the philosophy of life (aesthetic or vitalistic), the "theory of Gestalt," some types of the psychology of the "unconscious"—all these seek for the inner power of things beyond (or below) the level at which they are calculable and dominable. The fight between the two types of realism is continuously going on, with changing results. On the whole, however, technological realism is victorious because the real situation of the man of today, his personal and his social situation, and his relation to things are determined by its effects. But though not yet victorious, the struggles of the modern offsprings of mystical realism have not been in vain, as is noticeable in all fields of knowledge. The fate of our culture is, in the long run, bound up with this conflict and with our ability to go forward to a new kind of realism.

Both technological and mystical realism have, according to their Greek origin, one thing in common. They do not look at concrete existence, its "here and now," in order to discover the power of things. They abstract from it—technological realism for the sake of means and ends, mystical realism for the sake of essence and intuition. It is, of course, a necessary quality of all thinking to go beyond the given as given, but it is possible to seek for the power of reality within the concreteness of its existence. This is the nature of historical knowledge on which a third type of realism, namely, "historical realism," is based. Historical realism is a creation of the Occident, and especially of the Occident in so far as it stands under Protestant influence. The really real is asked for in time and space, in our historical existence, in that sphere from which all Greeks had taken flight. It was now no longer necessary to flee, since the world is divinely created and no demonic ambiguity can be found in the material world as such.

For historical realism the really real appears in the structures created by the historical process. Historical logic is still in a beginning stage, but this much is already clear: History cannot be understood in terms of technological realism. It cannot become an object of calculation and control like some levels of natural objects. History, on the other hand, cannot be grasped in a mystical contemplation of its essence. It is open to interpretation only through active participation. We can grasp the power of historical being only if we are grasped by it in our own historical existence. Detached observation of historical events and registration of assumed historical laws removes us from the possibility of approaching history.

Historical realism transcends technological, as well as mystical, realism. Its decisive characteristic is consciousness of the present situation, of the "here and now." It sees the power of being, in the depth of "our historical situation." It is contemporaneous, and in this it differs from the technological, as well as from the mystical, idea of reality.

Neither technological nor mystical realism knows the principle of contemporaneity. The technological does not, because it relates every moment in the historical process to a purpose the fulfilment of which lies in the future. There is no "present" in the vicious circle of means and ends, as the doctrine of infinite progress clearly indicates. Life, in so far as it occurs in the present, is concerned only with the surface, the accidental, with the experience of pleasure and pain, the mere impression. It is just the lack of contemporaneity that subjects us to the bondage of the passing moment. There is no contemporaneity in mystical realism either. It transcends the concrete historical existence and tries to create a union of the mind with the eternal essences in which individual things and events participate in a transitory way and for which they are only examples. The Christian, especially the Protestant, understanding of history as the history of salvation, has overcome this attitude of indifference toward our historical existence. The prophetic-Christian interpretation of history is the background of historical realism.

Contemporaneity is not bondage to the passing moment, it is not living in mere impressions. Not only historical realism but every intellectual penetration into things transcends the accidental, the mere flux of events. Such a transcending is presupposed in all our relations to reality, even before philosophy has created methods and discovered categories. Our very being as "minds" divides our world into essential and accidental elements, into that level which contains the power of being and that level which is without power. But what is the power of the here and now? It is its unique, unrepeatable, and fateful character. It is the merging of the still actual past and the already actual future in the present moment which creates the power of a historical situation. Even nature has one side which makes a historical interpretation of it possible. Although the particular event in nature is subject to the law of repetition, the natural process as a whole runs forward and is irreversible.

### III. HISTORICAL REALISM AND KNOWLEDGE

The principle of contemporaneity as emphasized by historical realism has important consequences for the relation of the cognitive sphere to the whole of human existence. Neither mystical nor technological realism demands the participation in all elements of life, the mystical because of its ascetic attitude toward the dynamics of life, the technological because of its domineering attitude toward reality. Only historical realism makes the participation in the whole of human existence a condition of true knowledge.

This applies to the personal, as well as to the social, reality of man in history. Nobody is able to penetrate into the deeper levels of a historical situation without penetrating into the deeper levels of his personality. Knowing the really real of our historical existence presupposes the knowledge of the really real in ourselves. But knowing one's self on this level is transforming one's self. Detached observation of one's self is here impossible. And knowing our historical situation on this level transforms our historical situation. Detached observation of our historical situation is here impossible. He who knows in terms of historical realism is he who is creative in himself and in history. Even technological realism has a certain awareness of this situation. Through its educational methods and its public communications it has shaped the forces of intellect and will through which man controls things, scientifically and technically. A psychological type has been created, in Europe as well as in America, which is powerful and empty at the same time and is feared by those Europeans and Asiatics who are still under the influence of some form of mystical realism. The latter, on the other hand, has in connection with the scientific ideals of the Occident produced that type of theoretical detachment from history and of scholarly asceticism which has transformed the scholar into an apparatus for the registration of facts, without critical or creative passion. I do not want to underestimate the heroism of scientific self-surrender in every inquiry, an attitude that corresponds to the immovable, eternal element in all knowledge. But this is only *one* element. The other one is the change, the movement, the here and now. While the elder generation of scholars (e.g., Max Weber) emphasized the ascetic element, thus producing an estrangement from life in the academic world, the scholars of the younger generation have more and more emphasized the active element in knowledge and the need for participation in all sides of life. *The ideal of knowledge in historical realism is the union of scientific objectivity with passionate self-interpretation and self-transformation.*

Contemporaneity in knowing demands not only the penetration into the depth of our personal being but also into the depth of our social being. Mystical realism is far from admitting such an attitude. It uses the cognitive function for the sake of escaping the historical and political reality through an intuition of the immutable truth. All those, therefore, who are directly or indirectly dependent on mystical realism (as is, for instance, recent neoclassicism) disregard the historical constellation to which they are bound, in its significance for knowledge. The situation is different with technological realism. It has always been aware of the connection between technical science and the structure of industrial society. The attitude of the proletariat and its political expression, the socialist movement, toward the scholars and their work is rooted in this awareness. The proletarians look at knowledge as a means of power in the class struggle, in which they find themselves strongly criticized by those members of the intelligentsia who are unable to imagine such a necessity and viciously attacked by those members of the ruling groups who use knowledge as a means of power without any inhibition. It is understandable that in this situation socialism accuses the *bourgeoisie* of producing not ideas which are true but ideologies which idealize and justify the power of the ruling class, and this through concepts and values that belong to the past and have no actuality today. Our scholars have seldom understood the seriousness of this attack. The concept of ideology in its polemical sense is a symbol for the volcano over which our society lives. If an intellectual system is successfully interpreted as a mere ideology, it has lost its formative power. The official representatives of science and religion have not even noticed how far advanced this undermining process has gone, and not only in the proletariat. These people will face the coming catastrophe of their intellectual world as unprepared as they faced the catastrophe of their political world after the first World War. It is pathetic and provoking to see the naïveté with which many highly educated people absolutize their own favored position in society, without realizing the general structure which gives them this position. Although it is the duty of scientific honesty to reject any propagandistic abuse of the search for truth, it is also a duty of honesty to know the power of the social structure to which one belongs, for one cannot escape it. It determines one's cognitive functions as much as the system of values in which one lives. He who wants to know the power of reality in the depth of his historical existence must be in actual contact with the concrete, unrepeatable tensions of the present. *The ideal of knowledge in historical realism is the union of scientific objectivity with a passionate understanding and transformation of the historical situation.*

Historical realism repudiates any attempt to escape the present for the sake of an unreal past or an unreal future. Romanticism which turns toward the past (a past that never did exist) and utopianism which turns toward the future (a future that never will exist) are equally wrong from the point of view of historical realism. Both lose the present and do not reach the really real in the historical existence, for the past can be reached only on the basis of an active participation in the present, and the future can be molded only in concrete decisions about actual historical problems. This does not lead to the so-called *Realpolitik* which was proposed by the imperialistic *bourgeoisie* in the Bismarckian and pre-war epochs and was readily—much too readily— accepted by large sections of the German intelligentsia. *Realpolitik* has nothing to do with historical realism. It is a product of a merely technological realism and derives its goal not from a penetration into the meaning of the present but from the so-called "demands of the moment." Therefore, it is finally self-destructive.

There is no conflict between the principle of contemporaneity and the validity of the ethical norms. "Ethical instinct" can never replace the ethical principles, the criteria of good and evil. Historical realism is not without principles and criteria. It presupposes them on its way to the depth of a historical situation. Without universal criteria of justice, no profound analysis of a historical situation is possible. Without principles of the ideal, the real cannot be interpreted in its depth. But historical realism prevents the principles from becoming abstract. It expresses them in the light of the present and as answers to the questions implied in a historical situation.

IV. HISTORICAL REALISM AND FAITH

The question now arises: What is the relation of historical realism to what we have called "self-transcending realism"? Historical realism strives to grasp the power of reality or the really real in a concrete historical situation. But the really real is not reached until the unconditioned ground of everything real, or the unconditioned power in every power of being, is reached. Historical realism remains on a comparatively unrealistic level if it does not grasp that depth of reality in which its divine foundation and meaning become visible. Everything before this point has preliminary, conditioned reality. Therefore, historical realism has truth to the degree that it reaches the ultimate ground and meaning of a historical situation and, through it, of being as such.

But it is the character of the unconditional that it cannot be grasped; its power includes its unapproachable mystery. If we try to grasp it, it is no longer the unconditional that we have in our hands—even if it has the highest religious or ontological names. Idealism is the philosophy that makes this mistake. It confuses the world of essences and values and their unity with the unconditionally real. It fails to transcend this sphere of pure reason, a sphere that can be transcended only by accepting that which is "before reason," the *Unvordenkliche,* as Schelling has called it ("that before which thinking cannot penetrate"), the originally given, the ground and abyss of everything that is. There was a feeling for this limit in all Greek philosophy. Indeed, pure idealism is not Greek, because the ancient mind could not overcome the belief in the eternally resisting matter, the negative, restricting power of which excludes an unconditional divine power. Genuine idealism is possible only on Christian soil, on the basis of the idea of creation which affirms the essential goodness and unity of the world. Perfect systems like those of the great idealists presuppose the Christian victory over the remnants of religious dualism in Greek thought. But they arise only because the other Christian idea is disregarded, the gap between God and man through finitude and sin.

In this respect positivism is more Christian than idealism. It accepts the limited and fragmentary character of the human situation and tries to remain in the sphere of the conditioned. It shows more humility than idealism in taking the given as it is and rejecting romantic or utopian syntheses which have no reality. But positivism does not see the problem of self-transcendence. It restricts itself to the immanence, not because of the unapproachable mystery of the transcendent, but because of its unwillingness to trespass the limits of the empirically given. Positivism is realism without self-transcendence or faith.

Self-transcending realism is the religious depth of historical realism; therefore, it is opposed to mystical and technological realism. Mysticism is not aware of the unapproachable nature of the divine ground of reality (including the "soul"). It tries to reach the unconditional in conditioned steps, in degrees of elevation to the highest. Mystical self-transcendence is a continuous approximation to the ultimate; it does not realize the infinite gap between the finite and the infinite; it does not realize the paradoxical character of faith and of a realism which is united with faith. This does not mean that mystical realism excludes faith. In every mystical experience an act of self-transcendence or faith is implicit. The complete union with the ultimate is, according to all mystics, a gift to be received and not a perfection to be achieved. Therefore, it is a mistake when Protestant theologians, from Ritschl to Barth, establish an absolute contrast between mysticism and faith. It is true, however, that mysticism tries to transcend faith in the experience of mystical union and that it disregards the historical situation and its power and depth. This is different in a self-transcending, historical realism which experiences the ultimate in and through a concrete historical situation and denies any degrees of approximation to it, knowing that it is always, at the same time, unconditionally near and unconditionally far.

Technological realism is even less capable of becoming self-transcendent. It separates realism and faith. In later Ritschlianism, faith became the means of elevating the ethical personality above nature to moral independence, leaving nature to technical control. The technological interpretation of nature, its complete subjection to human purposes, was accepted but not transcended. And domineering personality used faith as a means for maintaining this position of independence and control. This theology expresses very well the difficulty of combining faith with technological realism. Although the faith of which, for instance, a man like William Hermann speaks, is in itself warm, powerful, and passionate, its function in the context of a technological interpretation of reality is the creation of the personality of the victorious *bourgeoisie*. In English positivism no attempt is made to unite faith and realism. "Faith" is the conventional or serious acceptance of the creeds and institutions of the church. And realism is the technological attitude to nature and society. But there is no union between this kind of faith and this kind of realism. They are two worlds, connected only by a powerful social and intellectual conformism.

Self-transcending realism is based on the consciousness of the "here and now." The ultimate power of being, the ground of reality, appears in a special moment, in a concrete situation, revealing the infinite depth and the eternal significance of the present. But this is possible only in terms of a paradox, i.e., by faith, for, in itself, the present is neither infinite nor eternal. The more it is seen in the light of the ultimate power, the more it appears as questionable and void of lasting significance. So the power of a thing is, at the same time, affirmed and negated when it becomes transparent for the ground of its power, the ultimately real. It is as in a thunderstorm at night, when the lightning throws a blinding clarity over all things, leaving them in complete darkness the next moment. When reality is seen in this way with the eye of a self-transcending realism, it has become something new. Its ground has become visible in an "ecstatic" experience, called "faith." It is no longer merely self-subsistent as it seemed to be before; it has become transparent or, as we could say, "theonomous." This, of course, is not an event in nature, although—as always in spiritual matters—words and pictures have to be used which are taken from the spatial sphere. But it is the whole of the personality, including its conscious center, its freedom and responsibility, which is grasped by the ultimate power that is the ground also of every personal being. We are grasped, in the experience of faith, by the unapproachably holy which is the ground of our being and breaks into our existence and which judges us and heals us. This is "crisis" and "grace" at the same time. Crisis in the theological sense is as much a matter of faith as grace is. To describe the crisis as something immanent, open for everybody at any time, and grace as something transcendent, closed to everybody and to be accepted only by a personal decision, is bad theology. Neither crisis nor grace is in our reach, neither grace nor crisis is beyond a possible experience. The present situation is always full of "critical" elements, of forces of disintegration and self-destruction. But it becomes "crisis" in the religious sense, i.e., judgment, only in unity with the experience of grace. In this way historical realism becomes self-transcendent; historical and self-transcending realism are united.

## V. SELF-TRANSCENDENT REALISM AND THEOLOGY

Every religious word is an interpretation of the tension between the conditionally and the unconditionally real, between "realism" and "self-transcendence." Religious terms are the more adequate, the more they express this paradox in its depth and power. The same is true of theological terms. In the phrase "unconditioned power," for instance, the word "power," which, in connection with being ("power of being"), points to the most general characteristic of everything that "is," is used for that which transcends everything that is. A quite different power of being is meant if we speak of "unconditioned power" in the sense of "almightiness" or "omnipotence." Religious and theological words lose their genuine meaning if they are used as terms to designate finite objects under the control of the categories which constitute the world of objects. If this happens, the religious words express too much and too little at the same time: too much in so far as they elevate *one* object (called "God") above all the others; too little in so far as they do not attribute to God the unconditioned power which makes him God (and not a highest being only). The criterion of all theology is its ability to preserve the absolute tension between the conditional and the unconditional.

Religion tries to surpass the given reality in order to approach the unconditional. The means for achieving this is rapture and ecstasy. Wherever we transcend the limits of our own being, moving toward union with another one, something like ecstasy ("standing outside one's self") occurs. Ecstasy is the act of breaking through the fixed form of our own being. In this sense of the term we must say: Only through ecstasy can the ultimate power of being be experienced in ourselves, in things and persons, and in historical situations. Plato in the *Phaedrus* fights against the soberness and the lack of *eros* in the immanent realism of the Sophists. Even in the feeling of unlimited power over nature in technological realism an enthusiastic element is noticeable. There is ecstasy in love and communion, in the penetration of one's own depths, in the experience of freedom and of the sublime greatness of the categorical imperative. This gives a key to the use of intoxicating foods and drinks in primitive cults, and it makes understandable the ecstasy of asceticism and the "rapture" of mysticism. It cannot be said that all this is the opposite of the attitude of faith as expressed in the Bible. It is hard not to hear the ecstatic element in the words and the attitude of the great prophets; in the radicalism of the words of Jesus and the description of his visionary experiences; in the mystery sermons of the Fourth Gospel; in the "holy legend" as conceived by the Synoptic Gospels; in Paul's witness to the effects of the Spirit (especially in its main effect, love); in the triumphant words of Luther about the victory over law, death, and the devil. And even in some utterances of the "theology of crisis" (which wants to be a theology of faith exclusively) the ecstasy of the paradox and the ascetic self-sacrifice of reason and autonomy are unmistakably present.

He who refuses to see all this and fights against the ecstatic element in religion is motivated by a justified fear. He is afraid of the confusion between genuine ecstasy and artificial self-intoxication, for not every kind of enthusiasm is a participation in the unconditioned power, not everything that calls itself ecstasy is an experience of being grasped by the really real. An ecstasy that drives us away from the reality and the demands of the present is destructive, and, if it pretends to be holy, it is demonic. In true ecstasy we receive ultimate power by the presence of the ultimate; in a false ecstasy one section of our being overwhelms the whole of our personality, emptying it and leaving it in a state of disintegration. Any attempt to force the unconditioned power upon us necessarily creates a false ecstasy, for there is no way to reach the ultimate that we can manipulate. It grasps us when and where it will, for it is always also darkness, judgment, and death for us. Cults, sacramental power, pure doctrines, mystical or moralistic theologies that give us a way by which we seem to grasp what is beyond grasp lead us away from the real power of reality, from the depth of the here and now. They betray us in trying to elevate us. True ecstasy is united with faith, and faith transcends what seems to be real, because it is the presence of the really, the ultimately, real.

False ecstasy can be found in many places, even in a religion that is based on the principle of "faith alone" and that often produces an anti-ecstatic morality, as in Protestantism. This refers to the Protestant cultus, or to what is left of it, and even to what purports to reform and enrich it. Protestant liturgy contains very few elements in which the ecstasy of being grasped unconditionally is expressed. But those elements that it does contain are far removed from the depth of the present. They do not really concern us, and, consequently, they are strange and unreal to most of our contemporaries; it is of no use to introduce the "treasures of the past" into our liturgies if they are not able to express the depth of our present situation.

This is true also of the spoken word, which is abundant in Protestantism, in and outside the cultus. "Word of God" is an ambiguous term. It is often used in the sense of the written word of the Bible. But no biblical word is the word of God for us so long as we have to give up our historical reality in order to understand it. Not even the biblical word can reach us religiously if it does not become contemporaneous. The "Word of God" is every reality through which the ultimate power breaks into our present reality, a person (e.g., the Christ), a thing (e.g., a sacramental object), a written text (e.g., the Bible), a spoken word (e.g., a sermon). It is the greatest emergency of the Protestant churches of today they have not yet found a way of preaching in which contemporaneity and self-transcending power are united. The ecclesiastical, and to a great extent the biblical, terminology is removed from the reality of our historical situation. If it is used, nevertheless, with that attitude of priestly arrogance which repeats the biblical word and leaves it to the listeners to be grasped by it or not, it certainly ceases to be the "Word of God" and is rightly ignored by Protestant people. And the minister who feels himself to be a martyr of "divine" frustration—and even becomes ecstatic about this frustration—is guilty of a lack of contemporaneity.

The noncontemporary interpretation of the Bible is based on a noncontemporary understanding of revelation. Revelation is revelation to me in my concrete situation, in my historical reality. If I am asked to make a leap from my situation into a situation of past history in order to receive revelation, what I receive is no longer revelation *for me,* but a report about revelations received by others, for instance, in A.D. 30–33, by people in Palestine. Either I must become a real contemporary of those people, which is impossible, or something must be in the revelation which they received that can become contemporary with me and with every historical situation. At the same time, the denial of contemporaneity endangers the transcendent element in revelation. The leap from my present to a past situation is the "work" I have to do and am able to do in order to receive revelation. In this way revelation is dependent on me in so far as I have to move out of my concrete historical situation into the situation in which I can meet the "historical Jesus." Historical criticism, however, has shown that this is impossible, even if it were theologically admissible. There is no way of meeting the "historical Jesus" (i.e., the product of historical criticism) because the Jesus of whom we have reports was from the very beginning the "Christ of faith." This result of scientific honesty, religious courage, and an indomitable desire for historical truth agrees entirely with the demands of self-transcendent realism. It prevents theology from confusing the venerating intuition of a character of the past with the manifestation of the unconditional in the present. He who is the Christ is contemporaneous, or he is not the Christ.

Self-transcending realism requires the criticism of all forms of supra-naturalism—supra-naturalism in the sense of a theology that imagines a supra-natural world beside or above the natural one, a world in which the unconditional finds a local habitation, thus making God a transcendent object, the creation an act at the beginning of time, the consummation a future state of things. To criticize such a conditioning of the unconditional, even if it leads to atheistic consequences, is more religious, because it is more aware of the unconditional character of the divine, than a theism that bans God into the supra-natural realm. The man of today, who feels separated by a gulf from the theistic believer, often knows more about the "ultimate" than the self-assured Christian who thinks that through his faith he has God in his possession, at least intellectually. A Christian who unites his supra-naturalistic belief with the continuous denial of his historical situation (and the historical situation of many others for whom he is responsible) is rejected by the principles of a self-transcendent realism that is always also historical realism. This is the Protestant solution of the problem: faith and reality.

# Chapter VI

## PHILOSOPHY AND THEOLOGY[1]

PHILOSOPHICAL theology is the unusual name of the chair I represent. It is a name that suits me better than any other, since the boundary line between philosophy and theology is the center of my thought and work. But has the term "philosophical theology" more than a personal meaning? Has it an objective meaning? Is it a justified combination of words?

Some will give a decidedly negative answer to this question. Theological supra-naturalism of Continental, as well as of American, types will denounce philosophical theology as a contradiction in terms or, even more, as high treason against theology. On the other hand, philosophers and theological humanists may denounce philosophical theology ——although perhaps with less fanaticism than the opposite group—as an impure mixture of two incompatible methods of thought. They may admit the right of dealing philosophically with religion as with any other subject. But philosophy of religion is not philosophical theology. Can our name be defended against this double attack?

The answer is implied in the answer to the old question of the relation between philosophy and theology. After at least two thousand years of thought dedicated to the solution of this problem, it is not easy to offer a new solution. Nevertheless, it must be attempted in every generation as long as theology exists, for the question of the relation of philosophy and theology is the question of the nature of theology itself.

The term "philosophical theology" points to a theology that has a philosophical character. What does this mean? First of all, it implies that there is a theology that has *not* a philosophical but some other character. This, indeed, is the case. As long as theological thought has existed, there have been two types of theology, a philosophical one and —let me call it—a "kerygmatic" one. Kerygmatic is derived from the New Testament word *kerygma*, "message." It is a theology that tries to

1. Address delivered on assuming the chair of Professor of Philosophical Theology at Union Theological Seminary.

83

reproduce the content of the Christian message in an ordered and systematic way, without referring to philosophy. In contrast to it, philosophical theology, although based on the same *kerygma,* tries to explain the contents of the *kerygma* in close interrelation with philosophy. The tension and mutual fertilization between these two types is a main event and a fortunate one in all history of Christian thought. The fight of the traditionalists of the early church against the rising logos-Christology, the struggle between the mystics and dialecticians in the early Middle Ages, between Biblicism and scholasticism in the later Middle Ages, between the Reformers and the Aristotelian scholastics, the attack of the Ritschlians on speculative theology, and of the Barthians on a philosophy of religion—all this and much more was the consequence of the existence of a philosophical and a kerygmatic theology. The duality is natural. It is implied in the very word "theology," the syllable "theo" pointing to the *kerygma,* in which God is revealed, and the syllable "logy" pointing to the endeavor of human reason to receive the message. This implies further that kerygmatic and philosophical theology demand each other and are wrong in the moment in which they become exclusive. No kerygmatic theology ever existed which did not use philosophical terms and methods. And no philosophical theology ever existed—deserving the name "theology"—which did not try to explain the content of the message. Therefore, the theological ideal is the complete unity of both types, an ideal which is reached only by the greatest theologians and even by them only approximately. The fact that every human creativity has its typological limitations makes it desirable that theological faculties should include a representative of kerygmatic and one of philosophical theology, whether the latter is called apologetics, speculative theology, Christian philosophy of religion, or philosophical theology. The church cannot do without this type, just as, of course, it cannot dispense with the kerygmatic type.

It is not my task to enlarge on the nature of kerygmatic theology. The most radical attempt to create a merely kerygmatic theology in our period has been made by Karl Barth. But he, in contrast to some of his fanatical pupils, is honest enough to acknowledge that he cannot avoid philosophical language and methods completely, since even our daily-life language is shaped by philosophical terminology and philosophical ways of thought. Neither is it my task to deal with the difficult question as to whether there is a third type, namely, mystical theology, as has often been suggested; or whether mysticism, as I should prefer to assert, is an element of any religious message and therefore a substantial element in both types of theology.

Now, what is the relation of philosophy and theology and, consequently, the exact meaning of "philosophical theology"? In order to answer this question, as far as it can be answered at all, we must try to traverse some difficult ways of abstract thought for which I must beg your patience.

Philosophy asks the ultimate question that can be asked, namely, the question as to what being, simply being, means. Whatever the object of thought may be, it is always something that *is* and not *not is*. But what does this word "is" mean? What is the meaning of being? Santayana, in a very fine analysis of experience, derives all experience from shocks which we receive and which disturb the smooth flux of our intuition. I think he is right. And his insight should be used not only for the sake of stopping the vague and detrimental use of the word "experience" which we find in popular philosophy and theology but also for a more profound, more Aristotelian description of the experience out of which philosophy is born. It is the philosophical shock, the tremendous impetus of the questions: What is the meaning of being? Why is there being and not not-being? What is the structure in which every being participates? Questions like these may be late in their explicit and rational form, although they underlie the most mythological creations. In any case they are essentially human, for man, as the German philosopher Heidegger says, is that being which asks what being is. This question and the shock with which it takes hold of us is especially human. It is the foundation of humanism and the root of philosophy. For philosophy asks the question concerning being itself. This implies that philosophy primarily does not ask about the special character of the beings, the things and events, the ideas and values, the souls and bodies which share being. Philosophy asks what about this being itself. Therefore, all philosophers have developed a "first philosophy," as Aristotle calls it, namely, an interpretation of being. And from this they go on to the description of the different classes of beings and to the system of their interdependence, the world. It is easy to make a simple division between philosophy and theology, if philosophy deals only with the second realm, with sciences, and attempts to unite their last results in a picture of the world. But philosophy, before attempting a description of the world in unity with all kinds of scientific and nonscientific experience, tries to understand being itself and the categories and structures which are common to all kinds of beings. This makes the division between philosophy and theology impossible, for, whatever the relation of God, world, and man may be, it lies in the frame of being; and any interpretation of the meaning and structure of being as being, unavoidably has consequences for the interpretation of God, man, and the world in their interrelations.

This concept of philosophy may be challenged from different angles. The establishment of a first philosophy may be attacked with the popular argument that it entails a return to old-fashioned metaphysics. The presupposition of this argument is the magic of the syllable "meta" in metaphysics, which, in spite of the testimony of all textbooks and lectures on philosophy that it means the book after the physics in the collection of Aristotelian writings, has received the meaning of something beyond human experience, open to arbitrary imagination. But the question of being, the question of a first or fundamental philosophy, is the question of what is nearer to us than anything else; it is we ourselves as far as we *are* and at the same time as human beings are able to ask what it means that we are. It is time to dismiss this abused and distorted word "metaphysics," the negation of which has become an excuse for a terrific shallowness of thought, in comparison with which primitive mythology was extremely profound.

Another criticism may come from the claim of epistemology to be the true first philosophy. I would admit that this claim is justified to a great extent. Parmenides, the first and greatest of the ontologists, knew that being and the logos of being, that is, the rational word which grasps being, belong together, or, as we should say, that being is always subjective and objective at the same time. Epistemology is wrong only if it pretends to exist without an ontological basis. It cannot do so. And this insight has caused the breakdown of the epistemological period of philosophy in the last decades. You cannot have appearance without a being that appears, or knowledge without a being that is known, or experience without a being that is experienced. Otherwise, appearance or experience become only other words for being, and the problem of being is only stated in different terms.

There is a third criticism which we have to face. It may be said that there is no approach for man to the structure and meaning of being, that what being is, is revealed to us in the manifoldness of beings and in the world in which they all are united and interrelated to one another. It could be said: Look at minerals and flowers, look at animals and men, look at history and the arts, and you will learn what being is, but do not ask for being itself above all of them. To this we must answer: You cannot prohibit man from asking the most human question; no dictator can do so, even if he appears in the gown of humble positivism or modest empiricism. Man is more than an apparatus for registering so-called "facts" and their interdependence. He wants to *know,* to know about himself as thrown into being, to know about the powers and structures controlling this being in himself and in his world. He wants to know the meaning of being because he is man and not only an epistemological subject. Therefore he transcends and always must transcend the "No trespassing" signs cautiously built by skepticism and dogmatically guarded by pragmatism. The meaning of being is his basic concern, it is the really human and philosophical question.

But this statement brings us to the turning-point—to the point, namely, in which philosophy shows a kerygmatic and therefore a theological character, for this is the task of theology: to ask for being as far as it gives us ultimate concern. Theology deals with what concerns us inescapably, ultimately, unconditionally. It deals with it not as far as it *is* but as far as it is *for us.* In no theological statement can the relation *to us* be omitted. Without the element of ultimate concern, no assertion is a theological one. As a theologian you can speak and you must speak about everything between heaven and earth—and beyond heaven and earth. But you speak of it theologically only if you show how it belongs to our final concern, to that which decides about our being or not being in the sense of our eternal, ultimate meaning and destiny. This is the truth in the much misunderstood assertion that theology is a practical discipline. If "practical" is understood in contrast to theoretical, that statement is entirely wrong, since truth is an essential element in what concerns us ultimately. If "practical" means that theology must deal with its subject always as far as it concerns us in the very depth of our being, theology is practical. But since by popular distortion the word "practical" has received an antitheoretical flavor and since the Ritschlian school created that definition of theology in order to cut off theology from philosophy, sacrificing truth to morals, it is more adequate to use another term, for instance, to use with Sören Kierkegaard the word "existential." Existential is what characterizes our real existence in all its concreteness, in all its accidental elements, in its freedom and responsibility, in its failure, and in its separation from its true and essential being. Theology thinks on the basis of this existential situation and in continuous relation to it. Asking for the meaning of being, theology asks for the ultimate ground and power and norm and aim of being, as far as it is *my* being and carries *me* as the abyss and ground of my existence, it asks for the threatening and promising power over *my* existence, for the demanding and judging norm of *my* existence, for the fulfilling and rejecting aim of *my* existence. In other words: In asking for the meaning of being, theology asks for God. In asking for the powers and structures constituting the being of self and the world, their interrelation and their manifoldness, theology asks for the appearance of the ground, power, norm, and aim of being in these realms of being. It asks for the way in which man receives or resists the appearance of his ultimate concern. It asks for the way in which nature reveals or hides what concerns us ultimately. It asks for the relation of what concerns us historically to what concerns us ultimately. In other words, it asks for the divine and demonic powers in ourselves, in our world, in nature, as well as in history. This is existential thinking; this is theology. But now we have again reached a turning-point, this time the point in which theology shows its philosophical character. Dealing with the meaning of being as far as it concerns us ultimately, dealing with man and the world, with nature and history, as far as our ultimate concern appears in them, we must know the meaning of being, we must know the structures and powers controlling the different realms of existence.

We have searched for the object or question of philosophy, and we have discovered that a theological element, an ultimate concern, gives the impulse to philosophy. We have searched for the object or question of theology, and we have discovered that a philosophical element is implied in theology—the question of the meaning and structure of being and its manifestation in the different realms of being. Philosophy and theology are divergent as well as convergent. They are convergent as far as both are existential and theoretical at the same time. They are divergent as far as philosophy is basically theoretical and theology is basically existential. This is the reason that philosophy is able to neglect its existential basis and to deal with being and beings as if they did not concern us at all. And this is the reason that theology is able to neglect its theoretical form and to become mere *kerygma*. But as theology always has created a philosophical theology, so philosophers always have tried to reach existential significance, to give a prophetic message, to found a sect, to start a religious-political movement, or to become mystics. But in doing so they were philosophical theologians and were considered as such by followers and foes. Most creative philosophers have been theological in this sense. Only noncreative philosophy cuts itself off entirely from its existential basis. It has in its hands the shell, not the substance, of philosophy. It is school and not life and therefore not philosophy, but the trading of old philosophical merchandise.

Both philosophy and theology become poor and distorted when they are separated from each other. Philosophy becomes logical positivism prohibiting philosophy from dealing with any problem which concerns us seriously—political, anthropological, religious—a very comfortable flight of philosophical thought from the tremendous realities of our period. Or it becomes mere epistemology, always sharpening the knife of thought but never cutting, because cutting toward a truth that concerns us demands venturing courage and passion. Or it becomes history of philosophy, enumerating one philosophical opinion of the past after the other, keeping itself at a noble distance, faithlessly and cynically— a philosophy without existential basis, without theological ground and power. In the same way theology, denying entirely its philosophical concern, becomes as poor and distorted as philosophy without a theological impulse. Such a theology speaks of God as of a being beside others, subject to the structure of being as all beings are, stars and men and animals, the highest being but not being itself, not the meaning of being and therefore a merciful tyrant limited in power, who may concern us very much, but not ultimately, not unconditionally; whose existence, doubtful as it is, must be argued for as for the existence of a new chemical element or a disputable event in past history. Or such a theology separates man from nature and nature from man, the self from its world and the world from the self to which it belongs. It must do so because it does not know of the powers and structures of being which control man *and* nature, the world *and* the self, subjecting both to tragedy and working in both for fulfilment. The unity of being between man and nature is more basic than their difference in consciousness and freedom. A theology that is unable to understand this necessarily oscillates between moralism and naturalism. But being is more than nature and more than morals.

All this is not supposed to be a challenge to a genuine and consistent kerygmatic theology. It is said only against a theology that is not kerygmatic enough to restrict itself from the use of a shallow popular philosophy or that is not philosophical enough to accept the fundamental concepts of a serious first philosophy.

We have found a convergence and a divergence beween theology and philosophy with respect to the question asked by both of them. There is another convergence and divergence with respect to the way the question is answered by both of them. The meaning of being manifests itself in the logos of being, that is, in the rational word that grasps and embraces being and in which being overcomes its hiddenness, its darkness, and becomes truth and light. Truth in Greek is *aletheia,* "what is not hidden." In the word—the logos—being ceases to be hidden; in the rational form being becomes meaningful and understandable. Being and the word in which it is conceived cannot be separated. Therefore, wherever beings are, there is logos of being, a form and structure in which its meaning is manifest. But, although logos is in every being, it is outspoken only in that being which has the word, the rational word, the worth of truth and light—that is, in man. In man the meaning of being can become manifest because man has the word revealing the hiddenness of being. But, although every man has the word of truth potentially, not every man has it actually and no man has it perfectly. Therefore, philosophy asks for the way in which man can find the revealing word, the logos of being. Only in a vision can a few elect find it, Parmenides answers. Only noble aristocratic souls are able to look into the infinite depth of the soul, Heraclitus indicates. Only he who is guided by a blessed demon can make the right decisions, Socrates confesses. Only for the initiated does the idea appear and the darkness of the cave in which human reason is inclosed disappear, Plato prophesies through the mouth of Diotima. Only those who are free citizens can reach the happiness of pure intuition, Aristotle asserts. Only a few wise men reach the state of reason in which the logos of being can reveal itself, the Stoics pronounce. Only in one man—the Christian philosophers continue—has the logos appeared completely, full of grace and truth. This is the point in which the convergence of philosophy and theology is most powerful. It was a theological impulse that drove all these philosophers to a statement about the concrete situation in which the logos of being can appear. An existential concern is involved in all those limiting assertions. And, on the other hand, it is a philosophical concept in which the theology of logos expresses its unconditional concern about the message of Christ. Therefore, philosophical theology is and must be logos-theology, while an exclusively kerygmatic theology, like that of Barth, denies the logos-doctrine.

I stopped naming philosophers who have asked the question as to the place where the logos of being is manifest. One could continue up to the present. For the medieval philosophers, the Christian church is the only place where the logos appears at its very center. For the mystics from Plotinus to Spinoza and for all mystics in India, it is the mystical and ascetic elevation over all beings in which the logos of being itself appears. For the philosophers of the modern Enlightenment in all European countries, it is the third and final period of history only, in which the educated and well-balanced man has grown mature for reason. For Fichte, only the blessed life and, for Hegel, only the fulfilment of history guarantee truth. For Marx, it is the participation in the proletarian struggle and the victory in this struggle in which mere ideology is overcome by truth. In all these men, especially in Marx, the question of the place in which the logos of being appears is taken seriously. In all of them theological passion, existential asking, is obvious. In face of this cloud of philosophical witnesses, those school—and textbook—philosophers who pretend that philosophy is merely a matter of learning and intelligence vanish into complete insignificance, even if they constitute a larger number than those mentioned. There is no philosophy deserving the name without transformation of the human existence of the philosopher, without his ultimate concern and without his faith in his election for truth in the place to which he belongs.

But here also the divergence must be stated. Philosophy, although knowing the existential presuppositions of truth, does not abide with them. It turns immediately to the content and tries to grasp it directly. In its system it abstracts from the existential situation out of which they are born. It does not acknowledge any bondage to special traditions or authorities. It transcends them in asking for being itself beyond all singular beings, even the highest, even the asker himself. Philosophy asks on the existential basis of the Greek city-state and the religion of

Apollo and Dionysus; but it asks for truth itself and may be persecuted by them. Philosophy asks on the existential and concrete basis of the medieval church and civilization. But it asks for the truth itself and may become martyred. Philosophy asks on the existential and concrete basis of bourgeois or proletarian society and culture. But it asks for truth itself and may be expelled. Philosophy, in spite of its existential and concrete basis, turns directly to the meaning of being. This is its freedom, and this brings it about that a thinker who intentionally subjects himself to ecclesiastical or national or class bondage ceases to be a philosopher.

Quite differently, the theologian is bound to the concrete and existential situation in which he finds himself and which is not only the basis but also the subject of his work. As a theologian he is bound to the appearance of the logos after he has acknowledged its appearance at a special space in a special time. As a theologian he deals with the transformation of existence in man's individual and social existence, he deals with what concerns us ultimately. As a theologian he cannot transcend his existential situation either in a personal or in a social respect. His faith and the faith of his church belong intentionally to his thought. This is true of the philosophical, as well as of the kerygmatic, theologian. But the philosophical theologian, as a Christian, tries to show in his work that the existential situation of the Christian church is, at the same time, the place where the meaning of being has appeared as our ultimate concern. In other words, he tries to show that Jesus as the Christ is the logos.

The methodological way in which this must be done cannot be explained here. It cannot be shown how conflicts between special forms of philosophy and the Christian message might be overcome if they are not rooted in ultimate existential decisions. This is a matter for concrete elaboration. Neither can it be shown why, in a philosophical theology, philosophy must provide the concepts and categories and the problems implied in them, to which theology gives the answers drawn from the substance of the Christian message. I only want to give the following indications: Philosophical theology deals with the concept of reason and the categories belonging to it and leads to the existential problem implied in reason, to which the answer is: revelation. Philosophical theology deals with the concept of being and the categories belonging to it, and it leads to the existential problem implied in being, to which the answer is: God. Philosophical theology deals with the concept of existence and the categories belonging to it and leads to the existential problem implied in existence, to which the answer is: the Christ. Philosophical theology deals with the concept of life and the categories belonging to it and leads to the existential problem implied in life, to which the answer is: the Spirit. Philosophical theology deals with the concept of history and the categories belonging to it and leads to the existential problem implied in history, to which the answer is: the Kingdom of God. This is the task and the way of philosophical theology following from the basic definitions given above. It is a permanent work, going from century to century as philosophy goes on and the life of the church goes on. The end of this kind of philosophical theology would be the end of the universal claim of the Christian church, the end of the message that Jesus is the Christ. What has appeared as our ultimate existential concern has appeared at the same time as the logos of being. This is the fundamental Christian claim and the infinite subject of philosophical theology.

# Chapter VII

## NATURE AND SACRAMENT

NO OTHER question in Protestantism has from the beginning offered so much difficulty as has the question of the sacraments, and no other has received such uncertain answers. This is no mere accident, for the whole protest of the Reformation was in fundamental opposition to the sacramental system of Catholicism. Indeed, all sides of the Protestant criticism may be interpreted as an attack of the Protestant spirit upon the Catholic tendency to a sacramental objectivation and demonization of Christianity. The teachings of the Reformed churches represent the most thoroughgoing application of this principle of Protestantism. The famous answer of the Heidelberg Catechism to the effect that the Mass is "an accursed idolatry" expresses the vigorously antidemonic attitude of the Reformed churches in their battle against the Roman Catholic view of the sacraments. Luther broke with Zwingli, because Zwingli's hostile attitude toward the sacraments was strange to the mystical element in Luther's faith (though Luther did not himself succeed in working out a clear and consistent theory of the sacraments). The situation in the church today reflects the same tensions. Many ministers who are in a position to judge the situation as it really is remark with anxiety the "death of the sacraments." Nor are strong countertendencies visible, not even in theology. Yet the problem of the sacraments is a decisive one if Protestantism is to come to its full realization. A complete disappearance of the sacramental element (not the same thing, be it noted, as the particular sacraments) would lead to the disappearance of the cultus and, finally, to the dissolution of the visible church itself. For this reason Protestantism must deal seriously with the whole sacramental aspect of religion, an aspect that is fundamental for an understanding of the way in which Protestantism can gain a strong historical form. The aspect of the question with which we shall deal here is, in spite of its importance, often neglected. It is the problem of the relation between nature and sacrament. Bearing in mind the concrete situation in which we find ourselves, I should like to begin with an analysis of the two sacraments still alive in Protestantism and of the significance of the word in its relation to them.

### I. THE SACRAMENT OF BAPTISM

We begin with baptism not only because it is the basic sacrament but also because it is the easiest to analyze. The sacrament of baptism has only one element, and this element is a simple element, water. It is through water that baptism becomes a sacrament. Without water there would be no baptism. But, on the other hand: "Without the Word of God, the water is simply water and no baptism." This statement from Luther's Catechism raises a whole series of profound theological and historical problems. Among these problems we must first ask the question as to what is meant by the phrase "simply water." And if water as such is to be described as "simply water," why use water at all? Why is not the "Word of God" sufficient without water, why need there be a sacrament? There are three possible answers to this question, which is the question concerning the natural element in the sacrament.

The first answer gives a symbolic-metaphoric interpretation of the element. It considers water as a symbol, say, for purification or for drowning or for both together and speaks of the dying of the old, the unclean, and the resurrection of the new, the pure. On this interpretation, sprinkling by water or baptism by immersion serves the purpose of setting forth in an understandable picture the idea that is expressed also by the accompanying word. The act of baptism is thus a visible representation of the idea of baptism. Obviously, other pictorial actions could serve as representation of the same idea, such as passing through fire, going down into a cave and the like, as are, in fact, familiar in votive ceremonies or in the mystery religions. The use of water may also have a rational motivation, on the ground that water is easy to use, or it may have some justification in the fact of its traditional use. But neither of these explanations suggests any necessary, intrinsic relationship between water and baptism.

The second answer may be characterized as the "ritualistic" interpretation of the element. Here it is asserted that the relation between water and baptism is merely accidental. The connecting of the two is dependent on a divine command. Because of this command, water acquires its sacramental significance as soon as it is employed in the properly celebrated rite of baptism. A residue of this conception, which is fundamentally nominalistic in character, is evident in the Protestant claim that the sacrament had to be instituted by Christ himself according to the biblical reports. The ritualistic conception does not even hint that there might be an intrinsic relationship between water and baptism.

The third answer gives a realistic interpretation of the element. It explicitly raises the question as to whether there is not a necessary relationship between water and baptism. It questions Luther's view that water is "simply water," although accepting his repudiation of the magical conception of the sacraments. A special character or quality, a power of its own, is attributed to water. By virtue of this natural power, water is suited to become the bearer of a sacral power and thus also to become a sacramental element. A necessary relationship between baptism and water is asserted. This realistic conception seems to me to be adequate to the true nature of the sacrament. It rejects the idea that there is a merely arbitrary connection between the idea and the material element.

## II. THE SACRAMENT OF THE LORD'S SUPPER

The analysis of the Lord's Supper is much more difficult and complicated. To begin with, we have here two perceptible elements, bread and wine. In the second place, neither of these elements is an original natural element; both are rather the result of an artificial changing of natural products. In the third place—and this is the most important point—the two together represent the body of Christ, the basic element of the Lord's Supper. And in the fourth place, whereas the body of Christ as a body belongs to nature, as a transcendent body it is beyond nature.

The meaning of the Lord's Supper as a sacrament is that it is the sacramental appropriation of the exalted body of Christ. The human body is the highest creation of nature, containing within itself all other natural elements and, at the same time, surpassing them all. The eating of a real body is, of course, out of the question. The anthropophagism of a primitive cultus had already been eliminated by the antidemonic struggles of early religious periods. And the body of Jesus Christ, in so far as it existed at a particular time in history, is obviously inaccessible to us.

But it is just this body that becomes accessible to us through the fact that it has become transcendent. It remains a body; it does not become spirit; it becomes rather a "spiritual" body. As such it is accessible. But as such it lacks perceptibility. It lacks the natural element without which a real celebration of the sacrament is impossible. The problem is solved by substituting organic substances for the body, substances that nourish the body and that have the form of artificially prepared means of nourishment. That is, in place of the body we have the elements that nourish the body.

We may now make use of the various interpretations of the sacrament which we have derived from our analysis of baptism. If we apply the results of this analysis to the elements of the Lord's Supper, first, to the basic element of the Supper—the body of Christ—it is evident that the body of Christ can be understood only by means of the third, the realistic interpretation. What is it supposed to symbolize? The spirit of Christ? In that case we should be attempting to symbolize black by white. The body of Christ itself is what is referred to. A natural reality is elevated to transcendent, divine meaning. Participation in the divine power is a participating also in the divine power in nature. It seems to me as if Luther's (logically absurd) theory of the ubiquity of the body of Christ was an attempt to give expression to this idea.

It is a more difficult question if we try to determine the precise significance of the secondary elements, the bread and wine. The Catholic doctrine of transubstantiation is the simplest answer to the question. Through transubstantiation, the bread and the wine—the secondary elements—are in substance annulled and replaced; there remains only one element, the body of Christ, which, by means of the transubstantiation, assumes the bread and wine into its own mode of being. Among Protestants, on the other hand, the independence and separate character of the secondary elements are maintained. Hence the question as to their significance is all the more difficult, and especially the question as to the reason for the choice of just these elements. A ritualistic conception of the sacrament would center attention upon the words of institution, for ostensibly they contain a command of Jesus. The command would be responsible for the linking-together of the primary with the two secondary elements, and thus the association of the body of Christ with bread and wine would be explained as the mere accident of a historical situation. But this interpretation would practically eliminate the primary element of the Lord's Supper, the exalted body of Christ; for neither the pouring and drinking of the wine nor the breaking and eating of the bread have any symbolic relation to the transcendent Christ, although at least the breaking of the bread is a clear and adequate symbol for the event on Golgotha. Beyond this the ritualistic interpretation cannot go. The realistic interpretation, on the other hand, can explain bread and wine as representing the natural powers that nourish the body and support in the human body the highest possibility of nature. They point to the presence of the divine saving power in the natural basis of all spiritual life as well as in the spiritual life itself.

### III. THE WORD AND THE SACRAMENT

The classical combination "word and sacrament" means, in the first place, "the word as well as the sacrament." Next it signifies, "the sacrament through the word." And it has often been used, especially in Protestantism, as "word without sacrament." This variety of implications is inevitable so long as the two concepts are understood as being qualitatively contrasted or, more concretely expressed, so long as it is denied that the word by itself can have a sacramental character. But there is no justification for such a denial. The word is, first of all, a natural phenomenon. As such, it can, like other natural elements, become a part of a ritual act in which it functions as the bearer of a transcendent power: it can become sacramental.

The word as breath, as sound, as something heard, is a natural phenomenon. At the same time, however, a word is the bearer of a meaning. There are two possible ways of understanding the relation between the word as a natural phenomenon and the word as a bearer of meaning. The one possibility is to deprive the word of its intrinsic power and to deny any essential relation between the word and the meaning it bears. The power, the significance, the penetrating force of words is then attributed to the meaning which could be expressed as well by other words. The words are thought of as arbitrarily interchangeable. The other possibility is to consider the sound and the meaning as bound together in such a way that the natural power of words becomes the necessary bearer of its power of meaning, so that the one is not possible without the other. Where this is asserted, words by their natural power are potential bearers of a transcendent power and are suitable for sacramental usage.

Sacramental words that definitely exhibit this character are to be found in Protestantism in connection with the administration of the sacraments and also in the pronouncing of the words of absolution. In these cases the following questions arise: Are the words that are here used only signs that indicate and communicate a meaning? Or are they words in which sound and meaning are so united that the speaking of the words, and therefore the natural process of speaking as such, has a power through which they can become bearers of a transcendent power? If the second question is answered in the affirmative, a realistic interpretation of the sacramental word would be implied, and the ritualistic conception, which traces the words back only to commands, as well as the symbolic-metaphorical interpretation, which makes words only empty tokens, would be precluded.

We have shown in our analysis of the two Protestant sacraments, as well as of the words used in them, that the "realistic" interpretation alone provides an adequate explanation of their nature. We must, however, raise the question as to whether such an interpretation is logical and justifiable and as to what significance its application would have for a theory of the sacraments and for the shaping of the cultus in Protestantism. Above all, we must ask: What conception of nature is implied in such a realism and how can it be shown that such a conception of nature is necessary?

### IV. WAYS OF INTERPRETING NATURE

The concept of nature has a number of very different meanings, depending upon what it is contrasted with. The *formal* concept of nature contrasts the natural with everything nonnatural (the unnatural or the supernatural). It therefore also includes soul and mind as results of natural growth. The *material* concept of nature contrasts the natural with everything in which freedom is involved. The concepts antithetical to the material concept of nature are spirit and history. Theology places a negative value-judgment upon the natural in the formal sense, which is viewed as corrupted, sinful, and fallen, in opposition to the supernatural, which is the redeemed, the restored, the perfected. In this study we are concerned with nature in its material sense as the bearer of sacramental meaning and power.

The conception of nature that we find earliest in history, so far as we have knowledge of it, is the magical-sacramental conception. According to it, everything is filled with a sort of material energy which gives to things and to parts of things, even to the body and the parts of the body, a sacral power. The word "sacral" in this context, however, does not signify something in opposition to the profane. Indeed, at this phase of cultural development the distinction between the sacred and the profane is not a fundamental one. The natural power in things is, at the same time, their sacral power, and any commerce with them is always both ritualistic and utilitarian. One could characterize this primitive view as pan-sacramentalism, but, if this is done, one must remember that what we today call the "sacramental" is not thought of by the primitive mind as a separate or special religious reality. The primitive man holds to a magical interpretation of nature; the technical control of reality is supposed to be effected without reference to what we call "natural law." The control of reality is accomplished through the operations of magical energy without using the circuitous methods of rational manipulation. It should be pointed out, however, that there has never been a merely magical relation to nature. The technical necessities somehow always assert themselves and create certain areas in which rational objectivity prevails.

When this occurs, generally the magical view of nature disappears and is replaced by the rational-objective attitude. Only when the latter view of nature is reached may we speak of "things" in the strict sense, that is, as entities completely conditioned. Mathematical physics and the technical control of nature based on it are the most impressive and the most consistent expressions of this view. Nature is brought under control, objectified, and stripped of its qualities. No sacramental conception can find a root in this soil. Nature cannot become the bearer of a transcendent power, it can at most be an image of it, a witness to it. But the rational-objective view of nature is also never fully applicable. The qualities of things resist any attempt at their complete eradication. Even in the structure of the atom there is something primordial, a Gestalt, an intrinsic power. And the highly complicated machines created by the applied sciences are, in many ways, analogous to the basic organic forms; they can gain a new magical power over the minds of those who serve them.

The technical attitude toward nature and its merely quantitative analysis have been opposed since the times of Greek philosophy by the vitalistic interpretation of nature. Here an immediate power of being is attributed to things. Everything, the whole world-process, is envisaged as an expression of life: *élan vital,* "the vital urge," the "creative power of life," and the like are the characteristic phrases used. The modern Gestalt theory has given unexpected scientific confirmation to these ideas. But vitalistic philosophy goes beyond this justified protest. Even the mind is subjected to the principle of unbroken vitality and is branded as a sort of disease and fought against as a degenerate form of life. In this vitalistic philosophy nature recovers its power again, but it is a power without meaning; and power without meaning is ultimately impotent. Sacramental trends on the basis of the "vitalistic" philosophy of nature can be seen in the attempts of some semipagan movements to re-establish the symbolism of the religions of nature by using elements and forms of the natural world (fire, water, light) as powerful in themselves without relationship to spirit and transcendence.

The symbolic-romantic interpretation of nature attempts to give back to nature its qualitative character, its depth, its meaningfulness, by interpreting nature as a symbol of the spirit. The power of things is the power of soul or spirit in them. It is clear that this provides rich possibilities for the symbolic interpretation of sacraments. In the place of pan-sacramentalism we have here a pan-symbolism. But it should be pointed out that this view is very little aware of the real structure of nature. It gives us the creations of an arbitrary imagination. The quantitative, calculable "nature" of physics is certainly not overcome by it; only subjective imagination has been added. For this reason the symbolic-romantic interpretation of nature cannot provide a solid basis for a new theory of the sacrament.

The unsatisfactory character of all the interpretations of nature mentioned thus far drives us to a view which we may call "new realism," a term in which elements of the medieval and of the modern use of the word "realism" are united. Thinkers like Schelling and Goethe and Rilke in our day, have proposed this way of penetrating into the depth of nature. We must follow them with the means of our present knowledge of nature and man. The power and meaning of nature must be sought within and through its objective physical structures. Power and physical character, meaning and objective structure, are not separated in nature. We cannot accept the word of mathematical science as the last word about nature, although we do not thereby deny that it is the first word.

The power of nature must be found in a sphere prior to the cleavage of our world into subjectivity and objectivity. Life originates on a level which is "deeper" than the Cartesian duality of *cogitatio* and *extensio* ("thought" and "extension"). It was the wish of the vitalistic interpretation of nature to reach this level. But a philosophy of life that denies intellect and spirit has deprived life of its strongest power and its ultimate meaning, as even Nietzsche realized when he said: "Spirit is life which itself cutteth into life." The difficult problem for all attempts to reach the uncleft level of reality is the necessity to penetrate into something "nonsubjective" with categories of a subjective mind and into something "nonobjective" with categories of objective reality. This necessarily falsifies the pictures, which can be corrected only by a strict understanding of the indirect, symbolic character of terms used for the description of the power and meaning of nature.

A realistic interpretation of nature such as we have outlined would be able to provide the foundation of a new Protestant theory of sacraments. But this alone is not sufficient. No sacrament, in Christian thought, can be understood apart from its relation to the new being in Jesus as the Christ; and, consequently, no sacrament can be understood apart from history. Nature, in being adapted to sacramental use in Christianity, and especially in Protestantism, must be understood historically and in the context of the history of salvation. Obviously, there are historical elements in nature. Nature participates in historical time, that is, in the time that proceeds in an unrepeatable and irreversible way. The structure of the cosmos, of atoms, of stars, of the biological substance, is changing in an unknown direction. Although the historical element in nature is balanced with the nonhistorical one (the "circle of genesis and decay," the self-repetition in nature, the circular movement which dominated Greek thinking), Christianity, following old mythological visions in Persia and Israel, decided for the historical element and included nature in the history of salvation.

If nature is interpreted in this realistic and, at the same time, historical way, natural objects can become bearers of transcendent power and meaning, they can become sacramental elements. The Protestant criticism against any direct magical or mythological use of nature as the bearer of the holy is heeded. Nature, by being brought into the context of the history of salvation, is liberated from its ambiguity. Its demonic quality is conquered in the new being in Christ. Nature is not the enemy of salvation; it does not have to be controlled in scientific, technical, and moral terms or be deprived of any inherent power, in order to serve the "Kingdom of God," as Calvinistic thinking is inclined to believe; rather, nature is a bearer and an object of salvation. This is the basis for a Protestant rediscovery of the sacramental sphere.

### V. EXAMPLES OF THE REALISTIC INTERPRETATION OF NATURE

We shall now give some examples of the realistic interpretation of nature. This will be difficult because the apprehension of the inherent powers of nature is not a possible task for rational discourse. Other methods of approach must be employed, and these methods are not conclusive because they permit us to do little more than point to something the acknowledgment of which cannot be forced. Our task is made a little easier, however, because, in spite of all our rationalistic education, certain elements of the realistic interpretation of nature are still present in our minds, consciously and subconsciously.

In all times and even in Christian lands the feeling that certain numbers have a peculiar quality of their own has had an astonishing power. In the first place we must mention the number 3, for the mystical quality of this number has, more than its logical nature, contributed to the idea of trinity from the time of Origen to that of Hegel. We can still understand the quite different significance of the number 4 and the cubic perfection which it has connoted since Greek classicism. We can still sense something of the tension and richness suggested by the number 12. The ambiguity of such intuitions finds expression in the valuation of the number 7, partly as holy, partly as evil. Christianity, of course, cannot accept the valuation of anything natural as evil in itself, because "being as being is good"—an evaluation that Augustine rightly derives from the idea of creation. This refers to numbers as well as to all other natural objects, whether they are, in the present stage of the world, useful or dangerous for men. They become evil in the context into which they may enter and which is dependent on finite freedom. Yet all these intuitions are residues, and any attempt by occult means to recover them in their power can scarcely be successful. Probably the real significance of numbers for us has to do with a quite different aspect of the matter, namely, the mystery of infinite numbers and their relation to the finite.

We are still sensitive to the natural power residing in certain elements in inorganic nature. The four elements of the old philosophy of nature —of which water is particularly significant for us, because of its use in baptism—have always exercised a strong power over men, even when we have made a conscious effort to guard against it. Depth psychology offers a partial explanation for this phenomenon. It points out that water, on the one hand, is a symbol for the origin of life in the womb of the mother, which is a symbol for the creative source of all things, and that, on the other hand, it is a symbol of death—the return to the origin of things.

A residue of former awareness of the powers of nature lies in the idea of the "precious" stone (*Edelstein*); clearly, the word "precious" here is not to be interpreted either in aesthetic terms (beautiful) or in terms of price or technical quality. (Recall the "magic tales" about the power of precious stones and also the use of precious stones in the Apocalypse.)

The metaphysics of light in medieval philosophy shows a surprising unity of physical knowledge and mystical intuition. The "light" in this theory is the forerunner of the modern electrodynamic analysis of matter, and, at the same time, it is the symbol of the divine form, as manifest in all things. The romantic philosophy of nature tried to penetrate into the qualitative power and spiritual meaning of light but was not able to bridge the gap between poetic imagination and scientific research.

Goethe was more successful in this respect in his famous doctrine of colors and in his fight against Newton's quantitative-dynamic theory of light and color. In this controversy (which is not yet decided, even on the level of physics) the quantitative-technical interpretation of nature, represented by Newton, clashed with the qualitative-intuitive attitude toward nature, represented by Goethe. Goethe was passionately interested in what we have called the "power" of colors, their spiritual meaning and effect. Theology should seriously consider this problem. The development of Christianity from the Byzantine through the high medieval to the Protestant epoch is mirrored in the use of colors for pictures and churches. The "gold" of the Byzantine basilicas and of the early Gothic paintings expresses the mystical-transcendent feeling of this period. For "gold" is not a color in the scale of natural colors; it is, so to speak, the transcendence of mere color and therefore the adequate expression for transcendence as such. In contrast to this, the stained windows of the cathedrals let the natural light in, but in a broken way and in the most intensive colors. The metaphysics of light and the stained windows correspond with each other. In the Protestant churches (in so far as they are genuine and not simply Gothic or Byzantine imitations) the light of day streams through unstained windows, adding to the intellectual atmosphere, but this often makes the distinction between school and church difficult to observe.

The myth of Paradise (the Garden of Eden) shows the "power" of vegetative life, represented by the trees and their significance for Adam. They are bearers of divine powers, such as eternal life and the knowledge of the good and evil forces in all things. In the transcendent fulfilment, according to the Apocalypse, there will be the tree of life, by whose leaves the nations will be healed.

The "power" of animals can be seen in a fourfold direction. The animal can become a symbol of intense energy, as, for example, the bull, the lion, and the eagle in religious symbolism. Second, it can become the most vivid symbol for the demonic in nature, as expressed in the serpent and the demonic animal figures and gargoyles of Gothic sculpture. The demonic "power" of animals appears in a shocking way in the experience of the "guardian of the threshold" in occultism, a phenomenon that might be characterized as man's intuition of himself in abhorrent animal forms. In the light of this experience we can easily understand the offensive quality of abusive epithets drawn from the names of animals. The strong reaction against such names may be explained as an unconscious assertion of the validity of the epithet and, at the same time, as a deep inner resistance to this very assertion. Animals—this is the third direction in which their "power" can be seen —are most important for religious sacrifices. They replace and represent the sacrifice of man which the gods or God rightly demand; and so an animal, the lamb, can symbolize the great sacrifice on Golgotha in all Christian art and literature. The fourth point which can be made about the "power" of animals shows the tragic limitations of their power. Mystics and romantics have discovered that something like melancholy is expressed in the face of the animal, a feeling of frustration and bondage in the service of vanity, as Paul has called it. According to such poetic-philosophical vision, nature generally and the animals especially have failed to reach the freedom and spirituality which are the heritage of man.

The sense of the meaning and power of the human body has never been lost, despite the influence of mechanistic biology and medicine. In the human body all the potencies of nature are concentrated, but in such a way that they transcend their lower forms and rise to a level of freedom. In the human body nature enters history. The coming of the Kingdom of Heaven is accompanied by the healing of the human body. The Christ is, as Jesus replies to the Baptist, to be recognized by his power of healing. The disciples receive the gift of healing, because it belongs to the new being. In the body of the Christ nature is united with history. In the "center of history" nature reaches its fulfilment in the body which is the perfect organ and experience of the Spirit. This, of course, is the basis of the Lord's Supper as a sacrament.

The examples given so far deal with the power and meaning of natural objects. No realm of such objects is, in principle, excluded from a sacramental consideration. But, beyond this, power and meaning can be found in situations and configurations of nature. We refer to the old and also to the new belief that such complexes express something which can be "read" out of them. The most famous example of this belief is the astrological interpretation of nature. In our estimate of it we must distinguish two elements: the general presupposition of the interdependence of all parts of the universe and the cosmic determination of the individual being, on the one hand; the method of deciphering and calculating special forms of this dependence, on the other hand. While the latter has no convincing methodological foundation, the former is implied in the very concepts of cosmos or universe and in the philosophical, as well as the theological, presupposition that everything participates in the ground and structure of being and, consequently, can and must be understood in unity with the whole.

The power inherent in natural configurations is also visible in the rhythms of certain recurring events, like day and night, summer and winter, seedtime and harvest, and also in the rhythms of human life, such as birth and puberty, work and rest, maturity and death. The power inherent in these rhythms of nature has in all times given rise to their use as bearers of sacral power. Most rites of initiation or consecration and many of the great festivals have their origin here. An awareness of the power in these rhythms of nature still plays an important role in Jewish and Christian historical thinking and in their idea of a history of salvation. The syncretizing of the pagan with the main Christian festivals has its roots in the historical-realistic interpretation of nature in Christianity.

These examples, which could be augmented almost indefinitely, must suffice. But one natural process—the most important for the Protestant attitude toward nature—must be given considerable attention, namely, the "word." Like all other objects and complexes in nature, the word had originally a magical significance. It had a power in itself as, for instance, the holy word *Om* in India; the incantations and charms all over the world; and the remnants of this basic feeling in the liturgical formulas of the Christian churches. Indeed, the sense of this power has been so great that any suggested change in certain of these words would meet the most fanatical religious resistance. This fact shows that it is not the meaning as such, which could be expressed in different ways, but the inherent magical or quasi-magical power that is decisive. In direct contrast to the magical word we have the "technical" word as it is employed, for instance, in commercial trade-names. We find the best examples of this type in artificial words, such as, for example, "Socony," "A and P," and "C.I.O.," or in the attempt of Esperanto to create a purely utilitarian means of communication. The same meaning could be just as well expressed by some other combination of sounds. Yet it should not be overlooked that a clevely selected commercial trade-name possesses a suggestive force and does eventually acquire a new power.

The word as a device of aesthetics transcends both the magical and the technical word, although it is ultimately rooted in the magical use of words—we still speak of the "magic of poetry." But the magic of a poem is mediated by the aesthetic form in which sound, rhythm, and meaning are united. Since the end of the nineteenth century a struggle has been directed against the banalization of the aesthetic word in poetry and prose. "Banal" is a characterization for words that have lost their original power by daily use and abuse or by the disappearance of an originally powerful meaning embodied in them. Nietzsche, Stefan George, Rainer Maria Rilke, and many others tried to save language from this sort of degeneration. They fought a desperate and not always successful fight against the disintegration of language as a spiritual power in a world of mass communication and of continuous lowering of the spiritual level. Movements of liturgical reform have worked in the same direction in Catholicism as well as in Protestantism. But it is not enough to rediscover and use the language of periods that possessed greater power of spiritual expression than ours does. It is necessary to find expressions adequate to our own situation, words in which the transcendent meaning of reality shines through a completely realistic and concrete language, the language of self-transcending realism. On this ground alone can Protestantism create a new sacramental word.

There are many other realms and elements of nature whose relation to sacramental thinking could be discussed. The examples given so far are offered to show a way in which Protestantism in its cultus, as well as in its ethos, could reach a more affirmative attitude toward nature. The lack of such an attitude has greatly contributed to the rise of an anti-Christian naturalism which has not only scientific but even stronger emotional roots: the religious devaluation of nature has been answered by a naturalistic devaluation of religion.

### VI. SACRAMENTAL OBJECTS

Any object or event is sacramental in which the transcendent is perceived to be present. Sacramental objects are holy objects, laden with divine power. From the point of view of the magical interpretation of nature, any reality whatsoever may be holy. Here the distinction between "the holy" as divine or as demonic, as clean or unclean, is not yet known. At this stage the unclean and the holy can still be looked upon as identical. The significance of prophetic criticism lies in the fact that it dissolves the primitive unity between the holy and the real. To the prophets the holy is primarily a demand. Nothing can be holy apart from the fulfilment of the law. Holiness and purity are brought together. The "unclean" is eliminated from the idea of the holy. To the extent to which this process takes place the original sacramental interpretation of nature disappears. The holy is now transformed into an unconditional demand, transcending any given reality. Nature as such is deprived of its sacred character and becomes profane. Immediate intercourse with nature no longer possesses religious significance. Ritualistic demands are transformed into ethical (and utilitarian) demands. Nevertheless, the sacramental attitude does not lose its power. Indeed, it can never entirely vanish from the consciousness. Unless the holy has some actuality, its character as a demand becomes abstract and impotent. In Hegel's view that the "idea" is not lacking in the power to realize itself we can still discern a residue of the sacramental attitude, in contrast to the antisacramental, critical, and moralistic attitude of the Enlightenment. If this holds true for the secular sphere, it is all the more true for the religious sphere. No church can survive without a sacramental element. However effectively prophetic criticism serves to make impossible an absolute reliance upon the holy as present, however effectively it opposes every fixation and every objectification of the sacrament, it cannot do away with the sacramental background; indeed, prophetic criticism itself is possible only by virtue of this background. Just as Old Testament prophecy in its vehement attack upon the demonic sacramentalism into which the old worship of Yahweh had fallen continued to hold to the sacramental idea of the covenant between God and nation, so the Protestant fight against Roman Catholic sacramentalism remained bound to the Scripture as an expression of the presence of the divine in Jesus Christ. Any sacramental reality within the framework of Christianity and of Protestantism must be related to the new being in Christ. No Protestant criticism would be conceivable in which this foundation was denied.

But if the presence of the holy is the presupposition of any religious reality and any church, including the Protestant churches, then it follows that the interpretation of nature in sacramental terms is also a presupposition of Protestantism, for there is no being that does not have its basis in nature. This holds true also for personality. If the holy is seen as present in a personality, if the personality shows that transparence for the divine which makes the saint a saint, then this is expressed not only in his spiritual life but also in his whole psychological organism, in "soul and body." The pictures and sculptures of the saints would be meaningless without the presupposition that their sainthood is expressed in their bodies and especially in their faces. Sainthood is not moral obedience but "holy being," a substance out of which moral and other consequences follow. The "good tree" precedes the "good fruit." But where the "holy being" is accepted as the "prius" of the holy act, there the basic principle of all sacramental thinking is also accepted: the presence of the divine, its transparence in nature and history.

### VII. PROTESTANTISM AND SACRAMENT

Protestant thinking about sacraments must not revert to a magical sacramentalism, such as has been preserved by Catholicism down to our own time. No relapses to a pre-prophetic or pre-Protestant attitude should occur on Protestant soil.

This means, first of all, that there can be no sacramental object apart from the faith that grasps it. Apart from the correlation between faith and sacrament, there can be no sacrament. From this it follows that a sacrament can never be made into a thing, an object beside other objects. The intrinsic power of nature as such does not create a sacrament. It can only become a *bearer* of sacramental power. Of course, without such a bearer there can be no sacramental power, the holy cannot be felt as present. But the bearer does not in and of itself constitute the sacrament. Moreover, we must remember that for a Christian the idea of a purely natural sacrament is unacceptable. Where nature is not related to the events of the history of salvation its status remains ambiguous. It is only through a relation to the history of salvation that it is liberated from its demonic elements and thus made eligible for a sacrament. However, their relationship does not deprive nature of its power. If it did, that would mean that being itself would be destroyed; for the intrinsic power of things is their power of being, and for them to be without power would mean that they were without being. When the term "being" is employed other than as an abstract category, it means the power to exist. To say that the world has been created is to say that power of being has been given to the world. And the world retains this power, even if it is demonically distorted. It is not because of an alleged powerlessness of nature that Christianity cannot recognize purely natural sacraments; it is rather because of the demonization of nature. In so far, however, as nature participates in the history of salvation, it is liberated from the demonic and made capable of becoming a sacrament.

It could be inferred from this that the Protestant interpretation of nature would attribute sacramental qualities to everything. No finite object or event would be excluded as long as it was the bearer of a transcendent power and integrally related to the history of salvation. This is true in principle, but not in our actual existence. Our existence is determined not only by the omnipresence of the divine but also by our separation from it. If we could see the holy in every reality, we should be in the Kingdom of God. But this is not the case. The holy appears only in special places, in special contexts. The concentration of the sacra·mental in special places, in special rites, is the expression of man's ambiguous situation. The holy is omnipresent in so far as the ground of being is not far from any being; the holy is demonized because of the separation of the infinite ground of being from every finite reality. And, finally, the holy is manifest in its power to overcome the demonic at special places, ultimately at one place, in Jesus as the Christ. The danger of this situation is that the "special places," the peculiar materials, the ritual performances, which are connected with a sacrament claim holiness for themselves. But their holiness is a representation of what essentially is possible in everything and in every place. The bread of the sacrament stands for all bread and ultimately for all nature. This bread in itself is not an object of sacramental experience but that for which it stands. In Protestantism every sacrament has representative character, pointing to the universality of the sacramental principle.

The representative character of sacramental objects and events does not imply, however, that it is possible to create a sacrament arbitrarily or that these objects or events are interchangeable at will. Sacraments originate when the intrinsic power of a natural object becomes for faith a bearer of sacramental power. Sacraments cannot be created arbitrarily; they originate only by virtue of historical fate. All sacramental realities depend upon a tradition which cannot be abandoned arbitrarily or exchanged with some other tradition. But it can be destroyed by prophetic criticism. Most of the sacramental features of the Catholic tradition have been radically questioned by Protestantism; indeed, they have been abandoned on Protestant soil. And the process of reduction has not stopped with this. In the course of its history Protestantism has become so indifferent to sacramental thinking that even the two remaining sacraments have lost their significance, with the result that only the word has retained a genuinely sacramental character. In the revival of Reformation theology in our day, the word plays an immense role, whereas the sacraments play no role whatsoever. It is fairly evident that the Protestant sacraments are disappearing. To be sure, they can still have a long life simply because of the conservative character of all sacral forms. And then, too, renaissances of one sort or another are by no means beyond the range of possibility. But the one thing needful is that the whole Protestant attitude toward the sacraments be changed. Of primary importance for such a development is a new understanding of the intrinsic powers of nature which constitute an essential part of the sacraments. We need also to realize that the word has its basis in nature, and hence that the usual opposition between word and sacrament is no longer tenable. We must recognize the inadequacy of "Protestant personalism" and overcome the tendency to focus attention on the so-called "personality" of Jesus instead of on the new being that he expresses in his person. We must consider the unconscious and subconscious levels of our existence so that our whole being may be grasped and shattered and given a new direction. Otherwise these levels will remain in a state of religious atrophy. The personality will become intellectualistic and will lose touch with its own vital basis. The phenomenal growth of secularism in Protestant countries can be explained partly as a result of the weakening of the sacramental power within Protestantism. For this reason the solution of the problem of "nature and sacrament" is today a task on which the very destiny of Protestantism depends. But this problem can be solved only by an inter-pretation of nature which takes into account the intrinsic powers of nature. If nature loses its power, the sacrament becomes arbitrary and insignificant. Of course, the power of nature alone does not create a Christian sacrament. Nature must be brought into the unity of the history of salvation. It must be delivered from its demonic bondage. And just this happens when nature becomes a sacramental element.

# III. RELIGION AND ETHICS

# Chapter VIII

## THE IDEA AND THE IDEAL OF PERSONALITY

### I. THE CONCEPT OF PERSONALITY

PERSONALITY is that being which has power over itself. Every finite being has a special power, a special vitality, and a meaningful structure. It has a unique form that expresses in a unique way the creative ground of its being as well as of all being. And it has a special higher or lower place in the context of all things, according to the power it represents in the whole of reality. This power of being, of action, reaction, and expression, is given to everything with its very existence. It is its nature, that which makes it what it is—*this* and nothing else. The same is true of that reality out of which personality grows. In spite of the special character of this reality, it is like everything else, something given, a nature with a unique power and form. We call it "person" and attribute to it the capacity of becoming personality. Only on the basis of that kind of being which we acknowledge as a person in our social evaluations can personality develop. "Person" in this sense is not a legal concept (a corporation can be a legal person); it is a moral concept, pointing to a being which we are asked to respect as the bearer of a dignity equal to our own and which we are not permitted to use as a means for a purpose, because it is purpose in itself. This is the basis of personality, the individual human being, the person who alone among all beings has the potentiality of self-determination and, consequently, of personality.

Personality is that being which has the power of self-determination, or which is free; for to be free means to have power over one's self, not to be bound to one's given nature. This is the root of the eternal problem of freedom, that he who is free is so as *this* special individual with his special nature, law, and form to which he is subject, and which he expresses and transcends in every personal act. It is the same reality, the human individual, the person, who is bound to his nature and to

115

the whole of all nature and yet who controls his nature, thus being *in* it and *above* it at the same time. The depth of the problem of freedom is this cleavage in the same being; it exists and yet it is related to its existence by determining it. We can understand this only by a sharp awareness of the way in which we act and determine ourselves. The academic discussions concerning the freedom of the will use concepts that are inappropriate to the act of self-determination as we experience it in every decision. They are inappropriate because, while referring to human beings, they use the pattern of a "thing with qualities." If man is considered an object and nothing more than an object, the question of freedom is answered before it is even asked. And the answer is negative, whether it is expressed in deterministic or in indeterministic terms, for indeterminism is just as far removed from the experience of self-determination as determinism is. Freedom cannot be explained in concepts taken from a reality that is the opposite of freedom. Freedom can be described only in concepts that point to the experience of actual self-determination.

Personality can also be defined as that individual being which is able to reach universality. Freedom is the power of transcending one's own given nature; but it would not be real freedom if the individual merely exchanged its peculiar nature for another one. Freedom is not the power of transmutation, and personality is not the power of a constant change of attitude, as some romanticists have believed. They surrendered the basis of all freedom, the unique person, the incomparable individuality. Through a universal empathy they were apparently able to understand everything, the remotest past and the strangest forms of life. Something of this is still effective in our historical relativism which can appreciate everything and cannot decide for anything. But the result is not freedom, it is emptiness and cynicism. It is not self-determination but loss of one's self. And the final outcome is a yearning for something definite and authoritarian, to which the romantic pseudo-freedom is sacrificed. In earlier romanticism it was the authority of the Catholic church which gave security and content; today it is any strong authoritarian system in which the romanticists of our time take refuge. But personality cannot develop on this basis. The freedom of personality is not freedom from one's individual nature for the sake of another one or none at all; it is freedom for universality on the basis of individuality. Personality is that being in which the individual is transformed by, and united with, the universal structure of being.

If we call "world" the structural unity of an infinite manifoldness, personality and world may be understood as correlative concepts. Man alone has a world, while all living beings, including man, have an environment. But man transcends any given environment in the power of the universal forms and structures of reality which make *him* a person and make the *whole of being* a world, a "cosmos." Confronting a world, man becomes a definite self; and, being a definite self, he can confront a world. This basic correlation describes the structure of the reality in which man lives, it makes him a person and a potential personality. The correlation of macrocosm and microcosm which was so important for the thinking of Greek and Renaissance philosophy expresses this interdependence of personality and the universal structure of being. Through confronting the macrocosm, the personal self becomes aware of its own character as a cosmos, and by being a microcosm the personal self is able to apprehend the macrocosm, the world as world. Human freedom is a function of this structural interdependence of self and world, of microcosm and macrocosm. Man can become a unity and totality in himself, because he faces a world that is a unity and totality. And man has a world that is a unity and totality because he is a unity and totality in himself. But, at the same time, man is a part of his world and the world is a part of him. He is both separated from and connected with his world, free from it and bound to it. As a personality, he is closed in himself, and, as having a world, he is open to everything. This tension between being "closed" and being "open" characterizes the development of every personality. The more the openness prevails, the more the personality is in danger of remaining bound to the "mother-womb" of the cosmic whole. The more the closedness prevails, the more the personality is in danger of losing its creative ground and the fulness of life. It is obvious that the danger of the Protestant humanist development of personality, especially on Calvinistic soil, is that of separation, while Catholicism, especially of the Greek Orthodox type, is in danger of losing, or never reaching, a fully developed personal life. Generally speaking, we can attribute the predominance of "openness" to the mother-type of religion (the sacramental type), while the rise of strongly "closed" personalities is connected with the father-type of religion (the theocratic type).

The description given so far has not taken into consideration a basic element in the development of personality, namely, the unconditional demand addressing itself to every potential personality to become an actual personality. Without this element, personalities would develop in the same way as other natural processes—by accident or by necessity. The result of such a process would not be personality but merely another part of nature. The cosmos would devour its own children. Therefore, it is not left to the arbitrary decision of the individual self whether it wants to become a personality. The individual cannot escape the demand to rise above its natural basis, to be free, to become personality. Any attempt to escape this demand confirms the demand by the disintegration which the escape produces in the person. The unconditional demand to be free does not come from outside man, it is not a strange law to which he is subjected by a tyrannical god or a despotic society or a psychological mechanism; it is the expression of his own being, of the ground and aim of his existence. Personality, the possession of control over one's self, is rooted in the structure of being as being. The depth of reality is freedom, the ultimate power of being is power over itself. And the individual personality is the place within the whole of being where this becomes manifest and actual. The unconditional character of the demand to become personal is the ethical expression of the ontological structure of being itself. This is the religious foundation of the idea of personality. "Vitalistic" philosophy is wrong because it does not penetrate into the level of being in which personality is rooted. It penetrates only into the vital basis of personality but not beyond it. And philosophical "personalism" is wrong because it does not see that personality is not something given but something which has reality only in a free self-realization on the basis of a pre-personal vitality. Only in this latter way is the idea of personality established in its religious sanctity, its ethical dignity, and its ontological profundity. Every religious denial of this idea, every ethical misuse of the personal power in us and others, every ontological dissolution of the wholeness of personal existence, is demonic in its character and destructive in its consequences. The practical and theoretical acknowledgment of personality is an intrinsic element of the Christian message and the Protestant principle.

The experience of the ultimate power and meaning of the personal is expressed in myth and dogma whenever they symbolize the unconditional, the ground and abyss of all beings, in personalistic terms. This kind of symbolism is indispensable and must be maintained against pantheistic, mystical, or naturalistic criticism, lest religion and with it our attitude toward nature, man, and society fall back to the level of a primitive-demonic pre-personalism. The danger of the personal symbol is only that its symbolic character may be forgotten and that a judgment about the depth and meaning of reality may be transformed into a judgment about a special being beside or above us, the existence and nature of which is a matter of proof or disproof. If this takes place, the ground of things itself becomes a thing, a part of the world, and, if it claims absoluteness, it becomes an idol. Facing such an idol, we may revolt and attempt to assume its place, or we may surrender our freedom and dignity as personalities.

Having established and interpreted the idea of personality in its different implications, we now confront a fundamental alternative. It is presupposed that personality is that being which has power over its own being. This leaves two possibilities for any personal life. Either the *power* of being or the power *over* being prevails. In the first case, freedom, autonomy, and self-control are weakened or lost and pre-personal elements try to conquer the personal center; but, at the same time, abundance of life, vitality, connection with all powers of being, and dynamic movement increase. Nothing is finished, nothing is subjected to a strict form, life is kept open. In the second case the fulness of life, its natural strength, is weakened or completely repressed; but, at the same time, concentration, self-control, discipline, stability, and consistency are created. Few creative possibilities remain, no "chaos" is left, life has ceased to be open. Since the second type has been promoted as the "ideal of personality", we can say that the conquest of the contemporary *ideal* of personality in the name of the eternal *idea* of personality is the aim of the following analyses.

From several possible approaches to the problem of personality we choose three basic issues that have special significance in the present cultural situation. They are: the relationship between personality and things, the relationship between personality and community, and the relationship between personality and soul. This third consideration is the most fundamental one, on which the other two are dependent, for "soul" in the sense in which it is used here designates the pre-personal, vital, unconscious, and collective ground out of which the personality grows. In each case we shall try to carry the analysis to the point where the religious question will become pressing—the question of the ultimate meaning of personality and its relation to the different realms of reality. And we shall ask this question with special reference to the solutions that have been offered and that should be offered by Protestantism.

## II. PERSONALITY AND THING

The question of the relationship between personality and thing has been dealt with less frequently and less passionately than has the question of the relationship between personality and community. And yet it is an equally important problem, and it has become increasingly fateful for the man of today.

The primitive magical interpretation of reality is based on an experience of the intrinsic power of things. For the primitive man things have a kind of numinous or sacral quality. This gives them a tremendous significance for his whole existence. He feels them always as forces capable of fulfilling or destroying, of shattering or saving, his life. He approaches them with ritualistic methods. Even when he tries to use them, he is bound to their power, their wilfulness, and their protection. He is a part of them, having a limited power of his own but no superiority in principle. He himself is a smaller or greater power among a system of powers to which he must adapt himself.

All this changes when the system of powers is replaced by the correlation of self and world, of subjectivity and objectivity. Man becomes an epistemological, legal, and moral center, and things become objects of his knowledge, his work, and his use. They become "things" in the proper sense of the word—mere objects, without subjectivity, without power, of their own. They lose their numinous power, their sacral quality. They are no longer able to fulfil and to save, nor are they able to destroy and to pervert. Nothing divine and nothing demonic is left in them. They have become means for the personality and have ceased to be ends in themselves.

The process by which things cease to be powers and become mere things has several sources. The first source to be mentioned is the religion of the Old Testament, especially of the prophets. All things are subjected to the God who is their creator. They have no power of their own; they have no sacral quality in themselves. All the numinous power is transferred to the God who alone is God. And this God is the God of righteousness, demanding of everyone the fulfilment of the law and denying to everyone any sacred power. Things are means for the fulfilment of the divine commandments, or they are mirrors of God's creative power besides which there is no other creativity. From the very beginning of Greek philosophy things are deprived of their sacral power when all power is attributed to the transcendent ground of things. In Plato the inherent power of things is in some way re-established, not in time and space but in the cosmos of eternal essences. The ideal of personality is described in terms of elevation above the real things, in terms of the intuition of their essences. The history of Greek sculpture shows the same development. A continuous process of secularization deprives the gods, men, and things of their divine-demonic substance. They become natural objects presented for aesthetic enjoyment but not for adoration or communion. Lutheran Protestantism has deprived *things* of their inherent power by making the center of the personality the place where God meets man. Things as we encounter them are "ordered by God." We simply have to accept them in obedient fulfilment of our duties and, for secular Protestantism, in using them efficiently. In Luther himself this attitude is somehow balanced by his great intuition of God's irrational acting in nature and history and by his own resistance to anything resembling law. But later, after the victory of a rational interpretation of nature, philosophy as well as theology on Lutheran soil lose this insight. The philosopher Fichte calls nature "the visible medium for the fulfilment of duty." And in the theology of Wilhelm Hermann nature appears only as the obstruction to the development of human personality. Just through its fight against nature the Christian personality becomes what it ought to be, and the belief in God is based on the support that he gives in this struggle. In Calvinism things are made powerless, in order to be subjected to the control of the Kingdom of God. They are supposed to serve its divine-human purposes after they have lost their ecstatic quality, their magic power, and their divine-demonic fascination. Wherever remnants of an "ecstatic" attitude appear, they are considered as idolatry and are looked on with abhorrence. All this has led, on the one hand, to a strong antisacramentalism, to an extreme devaluation of things, and, on the other hand, to a most impressive elevation of domineering personalities, contemptuous of nature and things. The secular consequence of this attitude— though in a somehow moderated form—appears in modern bourgeois society and its valuation of natural science and of technical transformation of nature. Not things as such in their quality, in their hierarchy and intrinsic power, are the objects of knowledge but those elements of reality which can be calculated and used for utilitarian purposes. For the sake of their technical use things are deprived of their inherent meaning. The world as a universal machine is the myth of the modern man, and his ethos is the elevation of the personality to the mastery of this machine. These different ways of depriving things of their power in the name of the ideal of personality have merged in the present stage of industrial society and determine the spiritual outlook of our day.

A conspicuous expression of this attitude toward things is to be seen in the way in which applied art uses them and shapes them. The form given to houses, furniture, and all kinds of objects of our daily use is not derived from their inherent power and practical meaning; rather, it is forced upon them from the outside. First, they exist, and then an alleged beauty is put upon them. The lines and colors of most things used for commercial manufacture do not express the true nature of the material of which they are made, nor do they express the purpose for which they are produced. They do not express anything except the bad taste of a society that is cut off from the meaning and power of things. The streets of our cities and the rooms of our houses give abundant and repulsive evidence of the violation of things in our technical civilization. In every ornament produced by this attitude, in the method of trimming things which are supposed not to be beautiful in their genuine appearance, falsehood, façade, and aesthetic betrayal are manifest. That is the necessary result of the loss of vital contact with things.

The present demand for a "new realism" is directed against this distorted subjectivity. It is significant that this demand was first made by technology, although the technical use of things had deprived them of their inherent power more radically than anything else had. Technical products resist arbitrary shapes to a large degree. The machine piston permits no ornaments. It has its intrinsic beauty in its technical perfection. Many of the spiritual leaders in architecture and the applied arts have realized this situation, and they are trying to rediscover the inherent power and beauty of the materials they use and of the products they create. They want to unite themselves with the things, not in order to exploit them but in an attitude of devotion and in the spirit of *eros*. They are trying to create a new relationship that is based not on violation, wilfulness, and arrogance on the part of man but on his desire for community with the power of things. This trend is not confined to a few leaders. It is a large and strong movement, struggling for aesthetic honesty and a new creative dealing with the subpersonal world. The more this movement has advanced, the more it has been realized that everything has levels that transcend scientific calculability and technical usefulness. No thing, not even iron and concrete, is completely determined by its ability to serve utilitarian purposes. Everything has the power to become a symbol for the "ground of being," which it expresses in its special way. It is not merely a "thing" but a part of the universal life which, at no point, is completely deprived of freedom, of that freedom which in the personal life comes to its own.

The distortion of the relationship between personality and thing appears not only in the subjection of things to personality but also in the subjection of personality to things. Man who transforms the world into a universal machine serving his purposes has to adapt himself to the laws of the machine. The mechanized world of things draws man into itself and makes him a cog, driven by the mechanical necessities of the whole. The personality that deprives nature of its power in order to elevate itself above it becomes a powerless part of its own creation. This is not an accusation of the machine in the sense of reactionary romanticism; for the machine, like everything that participates in being, is not without an element of individual form, as its most passionate servants often say. They view and feel it sometimes as a living being, with which they have some kind of community and for which they are ready to sacrifice much—and not for merely utilitarian purposes. A new conception of the relation between man and tool, even in large-scale production, an interpretation of the meaning of man's control of things within a larger religious framework—all this could reduce the slavery of man to the immense machine of mass production and mass consumption. But this possibility is today prevented from realization by forces outside the relation between personality and thing. While the machine takes from the manual worker and upon itself all purely mechanical phases of production, this achievement is largely offset by economic tendencies that are dependent on the possessors of economic power (see the later discussion of the relationship between personality and community).

Personality and thing are united in the "work" in which the power of the thing is discovered and affirmed by the personality and in which the power of the personality is imprinted on the thing. This mutual reception of the personality by the thing and of the thing by the personality means the "fulfilment" of both of them. In creative work the actual freedom of personality and the potential freedom of nature are united. The personal power of self-determination and the determined power of things meet in the form of our work. This is the ethical justification of a full devotion to work, even if it implies the surrender of a fully developed cultural personality. But a sacrifice is also demanded of things: for the sake of a higher unity in which they are forced to enter, they must be restricted in their own natural power. This sacrifice laid upon things in every human dealing with them corresponds to the sacrifice laid upon the personality in every creative work. Both have to give up some of their potential power in order to reach a higher, actual power by entering a new creation. Such considerations are especially significant for our dealing with those living beings, which, although excluded from personal existence, show in their spontaneous reactions an analogy to human self-determination. Here especially is valid what must be said generally about the relationship between personality and thing—that it is, in principle, a mutual service. The true work is a mutual fulfilment, the false work, a mutual violation of personality and thing. The "ideal of personality" in the sense in which we have to conquer it, leads to the exploitation of things and the mechanization of personality; the "idea of personality," as we have to claim it, leads to mutual fulfilment of thing and personality.

### III. PERSONALITY AND COMMUNITY

Subpersonal beings can be subjected and appropriated by the personality without an absolute resistance from their side. But personality cannot be appropriated at all. It is either destroyed as personality, namely, in its power of self-determination, or it is acknowledged and made a member of a community. The permanent resistance of every personality against any attempt to make it a thing, to appropriate it and deprive it of its self-determination, is the presupposition for the rise of personality as such. Without this resistance of the "thou" to the "ego," without the unconditional demand embodied in every person to be acknowledged as a person in theory and practice, no personal life would be possible. A person becomes aware of his own character as a person only when he is confronted by another person. Only in the community of the I and the thou can personality arise.

Community, however, transcends personality. Community has a special quality, a power of being of its own, which is more than the mere aggregate of all the personalities in the community. It has a life of its own, which can sustain personality but which can also do violence to it. Because of this, a situation arises within the community which corresponds to the relationship between personality and things. In the primitive ritualistic conception of social life, the social groupings, like family, rank, neighborhood, tribe, and ritual community, have a sacral power by which the individual is absolutely subordinated to the community and by which his self-determination is swallowed up in the all-embracing unity of the group. His development into a personality is restricted and often destroyed by the community; yet the community, at the same time, gives to him its life, its fulness and depth, its meaning and content. It is not the individual but rather the tradition—the stream of life that runs through the generations, the sacred custom, the sacral law—that creates and sustains the community. The individual is protected, but only in so far as he is a member of the community. The purpose of the community is not to foster the welfare of the individual but rather to maintain and to strengthen the life of the group, including present and future. The individual is a means, and only as a part of the whole is he an end.

The rise of personality to conscious self-determination occurs when the individual transcends his social ties and subordinations. This can happen in a variety of ways—through the unconditional demand of a religion of law that holds every individual responsible; through the rational criticism of old social structures and the rise of an autonomous culture; through the nominalistic dissolution of social and spiritual unities; through the Protestant appeal to the individual in matters of conscience; through the Calvinistic belief in individual predestination; through the democratic attempt to form a society on the basis of individual reason. In these ways personality becomes the bearer and goal of social life. It subjects the social realities to its own purposes, precisely as it does with the world of things. The sacral powers which had united the society are now secularized and deprived of their meaning. The social groups lose their power to crush and to mutilate personality, but they also lose their power to create and protect it.

A process of social disintegration starts, in which first the community and then the personality is deprived of its spiritual substance. But, since there is no vacuum in social life any more than in nature, other powers enter the space left by the disintegration of the original social unity, especially economic factors, psychological mechanisms, sociological constellations. The personality, after having undermined the community, is undermined itself, even though it be legally recognized and even though it is aware of ethical demands. The present situation gives abundant evidence of this statement.

Every community is founded on a hierarchy of social powers. According to the sacral interpretation of communal life, the socially powerful personality is the representative of the power inherent in the community itself. The power of this personality does not originate with him as an individual. It is determined by the function he performs for the whole group. This is the original meaning of the idea of the divine vocation of kings. Personal brilliance is not decisive (though it is not excluded if it does not endanger the sacred structure of the whole). The representative of power, even if not especially fitted to wield it, is protected by the "place"—in a certain sense the "sacred" place—that he keeps. The power does not have a private character, it is not created by successful competition between isolated individuals, and consequently it does not produce the opposition of other isolated individuals. Power obtained by birth or sacred succession is silently acknowledged and symbolically expressed. (This, of course, is a structural analysis, not an empirical description. Actually there are always deviations and disturbing trends.)

The rise of personality—in the different ways mentioned above—undermines the sacred degrees of power. Person is equal to person with respect to the most significant "power," namely, that of being a person and consequently a potential personality. This implies the demand for equality in law and for the abolition of sacred privileges. Freedom in the sense of social and spiritual self-determination is fought for. Not the group but the personality is the goal of the group life. Each individual is supposed to have the same opportunity for personal development. But social power does not cease to exist; it belongs to every political structure. And, if it is not a matter of sacred hierarchies, it tends to become a matter of individual will to power. But a domination based on the struggle of strong individuals is lacking in objective responsibility and representative symbolism. The mass of people who are naturally (though not legally) excluded from any serious competition become mere objects of this kind of domination. They are subjected to it, but they do not acknowledge it inwardly. They do not feel that it represents the whole to which they belong. Such a type of social power has a private, profane, naturalistic character, but it is equally coercive for those who are dominated and for those who dominate by subjecting themselves to the rules of the power game. This form of private, objectively irresponsible domination (though exercised often by very responsible personalities) has prevailed in the latest period of Western civilization, above all in the economic field. From the economic field this form of power conquered the political realm by the increasingly powerful apparatus of public communications in press, radio, movies, etc.

This situation places a heavy compulsion upon the ruling economic group. It forces them to stake their whole personal existence on the struggle for economic survival in the universal competition, in obedience either to the laws of the market or to the monopolistic control of the market. They become parts of a dynamic natural force that drives them with or against their will and deprives them of a full human development in their personal life. The poverty of mind and spirit of many of the great economic leaders stands in a surprising contrast to the immense power that is concentrated in their hands.

Sometimes this lack of personal growth is the result of a conscious sacrifice; usually it is the consequence of a mixture between social compulsion and personal will to power.

For those who are mere objects of domination this situation means the complete loss of self-determination, it means for them the bondage to the inescapable laws of the business cycle, the horror of permanent insecurity—the other side of the freedom of contract, a spiritual emptiness produced by concentration on the needs of the daily life and by the ever present demon of anxiety. The most significant implication of this development is the fact that labor becomes a commodity which can be bought at will and for any purpose. The relation between man and work, as described earlier, is destroyed. The work ceases to be a meaningful part of life, although it determines the whole life of the worker. The technical mechanization is especially meaningless and depressing for anyone who has not even the consciousness that he contributes to the well-being of the whole group. He cannot have this awareness under normal circumstances, since he must produce for the profit of those who are in power and since his own share in the goods produced is determined by the laws of the market or by the restrictive activity of the monopolies.

The situation in the economic and political realms has strict analogies in the educational and cultural realms. In a social structure of hierarchical character the spiritual form which the individual receives depends upon the degree of social power that he represents. Education shapes the personality in a concrete but limited way, according to the social place in which the individual finds himself through birth and tradition. The purpose of education in this stage of social development is to introduce the new generation into the meaning and reality of the group, its life and its symbols. The ideals determining the education are the traditional ideals of the community, and there is no attempt to go beyond to universal ideals. Autonomous personalities are not permitted to grow. It is the spirit of the group that provides form and meaning, on the one hand, limits and exclusiveness, on the other.

In the degree to which personalities rise over and against this structure of society, new cultural forms are created with a quite different character. They are no longer the expression of a concrete spiritual substance, but they try to express the human as such. They strive toward universality according to the correlation of personality and world. In comparison with the concreteness and exclusiveness of the more collectivistic stages, the humanistic culture is abstract, even when embracing all the concreteness of the past.

There are two elements in the rise of the humanistic personality which demand consideration, the personality as such, on the one hand, and its spiritual content, on the other. The rise of personality has in itself a tremendous significance for the history of culture. It is the way in which mankind realizes the unconditional meaning and value of personality. The humanistic ideal of personality contains as its depth and permanent truth the acknowledgment of the eternal idea of personality. This is its greatness and its indestructible validity. Therefore, theology should be more careful than it usually is in its manner of confronting Christianity with humanism. This applies especially to recent revivals of the struggle between Luther and Erasmus by the neo-orthodox theology. But Luther's assertion that man's will is in bondage to demonic structures is meaningful only if man, in his essential nature, is free. Luther's (as well as Paul's and Augustine's and Aquinas') statement loses its profundity and its paradoxical character if it is identified with philosophical determinism. Only a being that has the power of self-determination can have a *servum arbitrium,* a "will in bondage," because a being without the power of self-determination has no *arbitrium* ("capacity of decision") at all. Humanism, of course, if it is nothing more than humanism, does not understand the paradox of the classical Christian doctrine (as much Catholic and Protestant teaching does not either). It does not understand that the Christian doctrine of the bondage and the liberation of man (of sin and grace) speaks of a level of experience which is not even touched by the philosophical statement of man's essential freedom. In so far as humanism has fought for *this* freedom, which makes man man and gives him the dignity of being the image of God and the microcosm, humanism is an indispensable element of Christianity.

This leads to the question of the content of the spiritual life of the autonomous personality. What are the principles of its self-determination? What content is to be received in the unity of the humanist personality? The answer can only be: the world as the universe of meaningful forms, for the self-determining personality confronts the world in its infinite possibilities of creative interrelationship. Thus the humanistic ideal of the completely formed personality arises. Humanism has created the ideal of a personality in which, on the basis of a definite individuality, all potentialities of man's spiritual being are actualized as much as possible. And this ideal controls modern ethics, culture, and education. It has created most impressive personalities in the European Renaissance, in German classicism, in Anglo-Saxon religious humanism. But it has also developed dangerous consequences, not by accident but by its very nature. The humanistic ideal of personality tends to cut the individual off from his existential roots, from the social group, its traditions and symbols. It tends to make him abstract-universal and detached from any concrete concern: everything interests, nothing affects. There is no unconditional concern, demanding, directing, and promising; there is no ultimate meaning, no spiritual center. This, of course, is the result of a long development in which the latent religious power of humanism has evaporated by secularization and naturalistic reduction.

The most disintegrating consequence of the victory of the humanistic ideal of personality is the fact that the latter can be appropriated only by a social class that has the external prerequisites for such an abstract universalism. And even within the class that is able to receive and to mediate this humanistic education, only a small élite use it for a development of their personalities, while the majority adopts the ideal only as a condition for their belonging to the ruling class and not for the sake of giving form to their personalities. But even worse is the consequence of the humanistic "ideal of personality" for the large masses of people. They participate in it only by receiving unconnected pieces of the humanistic culture through the all-powerful means of public communication and as a matter of detached interest or subjective thrill. Even this kind of adult indoctrination is not without some value. It liberates people from all kinds of narrow provincialism and opens world horizons. But, on the other hand, it tends to destroy the sources of concrete experiences and individual formations. It produces a general level of normality and mediocrity above which even more intelligent and creative people rise only with great difficulty. This situation is the opposite of what the humanistic ideal of personality intended. And out of this situation the contemporary reaction against not only the ideal but also the idea of personality has grown, namely, the passionate desire for a return to the primitive level. But now it appears in naturalistic terms as the Fascist ideal of a new tribal existence. The rise of the personality above the community is followed by a fall of the personality below the community.

Many movements revolt against this situation, for instance, socialism, the youth movement, romantic nationalism. They all fight for a new community. Indeed, "community" (the German word *Gemeinschaft* has richer connotations) has become a program and catch-word for the longing of a whole generation. But a continuous frustration of all these attempts proves the power of the structure against which they struggle: the ideal of personality, the reality of mechanized masses, the emptiness and deformation of innumerable individuals, the dominance of a universal economic machine which is the fate of the masses as well as of every single person. Some of these opposing movements were themselves too much infected by the spirit of their enemy, as was the case with socialism and political nationalism. Or they did not see the power and world-historical significance of the period the end of which they demanded and prophesied, as was the case with the youth movement and all forms of romanticism, religious and secular. The few who try to find the depth and meaning of life within and through the actual structure of our society and culture do so silently and with the consciousness of the preliminary character of everything they are doing. They are looking for a period in which the personality will again be a part of a community with a spiritual center and new powerful symbols.

### IV. PERSONALITY AND SOUL

We shall define "soul" in this context as the vital and emotional ground from which the self-conscious center of personality arises. The body, of course, is included in this definition in so far as the body is the immediate expression and the form of the self-realization of the soul. The relation of the conscious center to the psychic foundation of the personality corresponds to the interrelation of the personality with things and community. Wherever the ideal of personality prevails, the soul is gradually deprived of its power and subjected to a rationalized and intellectualized consciousness. The vengeance of the soul for this repression is the chaotic and destructive outbreak of the repressed forces that revolt against the dictatorship of an overburdened and overvaluated self-consciousness. Both the history of Protestantism and the history of idealism give abundant evidence of this statement.

In the pre-Reformation period all aspects of the psychic life are considered and acted upon in their relationship to the divine. A subtle psychology analyzes the hidden impulses of the human soul *sub specie aeternitatis* ("from the point of view of the eternal"). The doctrine of grace, or, more exactly, of the different graces, gives to every psychological type a special ultimate meaning and moral power. The idea that every grade in the clerical and secular hierarchy has a special indispensable function for the whole removes the danger of an isolation of individuals, groups, and psychic functions. All sides of human existence are drawn into the spiritual life of the whole. It could not, however, be avoided that the quantitative degrees and the refined system of relativities in the relationship to the ultimate should obscure the unconditional, qualitative demand of a personal, central, and total responsibility and devotion. Hence the question of the salvation of the individual remained without an unambiguous answer. In contrast to the Catholic system of psychic and social degrees, the Reformation appeals to the conscious center of the personality, to conscience and decision. It sweeps away the "graces" for the sake of the one grace, the re-establishment of the relation to God; it is not interested in mystical and ecclesiastical psychology; it does not admit the representation of one person by another in relation to God and it destroys the sacral degrees. It makes everything dependent on personal decision and faith. The more inclusive aspects of the psychic and bodily life lose their religious significance and are left to secularization.

The great spiritual revolution which occurred in Luther was the fruit of a century-long discipline of introspection and self-examination. Only on the basis of this "culture of the soul" could Luther's experience of God grow to such an explosive power. It was the same basis that made the heroic and inspired personalities of the Reformation period possible. With the vanishing of the spiritual substance of the past, moral and intellectual law replaced the original experience of the Reformers and the powerful paradox of their message.

The heroic type of personality of the Reformation period was followed by the rational type in the period of the Enlightenment, by the romantic type in the beginning of the nineteenth century, and by the naturalistic type of personality since the middle of the last century. Within the Protestant, and especially in the Lutheran, churches, Luther's genuine experience was imposed as a law on every listener in every sermon and in every hour of religious instruction. But since Luther's presupposition—the late medieval situation—no longer existed, the repetition of Luther's experience became increasingly impossible, and the doctrine of justification, which represents a breaking-through of every law, became a law itself as unrealizable as the laws of the Catholic church. This law with its moral and intellectual implications was imposed on the people. Church and society were united in enforcing it, in demanding the radicalism of the heroic age of Protestantism as the permanent attitude of everybody. This created a repression of vital forces which was very successful in the beginning. But the repression was always partly opposed, and it became more and more untenable until it finally broke down in the first decades of the twentieth century. The disintegration of the consciousness-centered personality is now proceeding on a terrifying scale. The immediate expression of it is the increase in mental diseases, especially in Protestant countries. Nietzsche and the great novelists of the later part of the nineteenth century and, following them, the Freudian and the other schools of depth psychology brought to light the mechanisms of repression in the bourgeois Protestant personality and the explosive re-emergence of the vital (unconscious) forces. They were prophets of things to come in the twentieth century. Through all this it became manifest that repression is not self-determination and, consequently, not a solid ground for the rise of personality. Repression produces a psychic "underground," which either drives toward dishonesty or to hardening and inflexibility or to safety valves, allowed by bourgeois society, such as unrestricted economic acquisitiveness, or, finally, to the revolutionary struggle against the repressive psychic and social systems themselves.

It was to be expected that this explosive reaction against the bourgeois conventions would lead to a large-scale disintegration, in comparison with which the former stage would seem highly desirable. This transitional period is unavoidable. But it should be regretted only if it does not lead to a new form of personal life. The new form cannot, of course, be imposed from the outside as another law. It must grow; and the power of spiritual growth is "grace." Grace in the sense in which it is used here has a larger meaning than the "forgiveness of sins" in Protestant theology. Not that a return to the half-magical idea of grace in Roman Catholicism is advocated. The Protestant principle and its criticism of sacramental demonry cannot be weakened. But "grace" must include—as it does in the New Testament—all sides of the personal life, its vital foundation, its psychic dynamics, its individual uniqueness, and its conscious center. In depth-psychology there is frequently more awareness of the meaning of grace and, consequently, more effective "care of souls" than in the ministry of the church. The ideal of personality, in the way in which it has developed in modern Protestantism and secularism, is based on an illusion, on the illusion of "pure consciousness." There is no such thing. Unconscious psychic forces continuously break into our conscious center and direct it just when we believe ourselves to be completely free. The dark ground of pre-personal being, which contains elements of the universal process of life as well as the life-process of the individual, is effective in every moment of our conscious existence. Whether it is repressed or not, it is real and powerful, and its manifestations show the limits of personal freedom. One of these manifestations is the stage that is called "possession," in which the personal center is "split" (the original sense of "schizophrenia") or, more exactly, the consciousness is conquered by a "destructive structure" originating in the "dark ground" of the personality—the unconscious. Under the name of "demoniacs" the possessed were well known to the New Testament and the early church. But Jesus and his disciples and followers did not overcome the stage of possession by proclaiming the ideal of personality but by embodying a "constructive structure," originating in the divine ground, that is, in grace. Grace is, so to speak, the "possession from above," overcoming the possession from below. While the latter destroys the personal center through the invasion of "darkness," the former re-establishes it by elevating the creative power of the ground into the unity of a personal life. Every personality stands between possession and grace, susceptible to both. Personality is the open arena of the struggle between them. The "ideal of personality" is a heroic attempt to overcome this situation, to create an autonomy of the personal life in which the demonic is excluded (the word as well as the reality) and in which the divine is not needed. But this attempt was doomed to fail. It was an illusion, as classical Christianity and present-day realism have recognized.

What, then, about the concept of "religious personality"? The term can be used if it is not meant to signify anything more than a man of religious devotion. But this has nothing to do with the ideal of personality, not even when the man's life is strongly determined by religion or when he belongs to the founders and leaders of religion or among the saints. None of these is a "religious personality." Nor should this term be applied to Jesus or Paul, Augustine or Luther. A "religious personality" in the modern sense of the word is a personality in whom religion plays an outsanding role in the building of the personality structure. Religion is thus considered as an important means for the growth of personality. The end is the development of personality, one of the means is religion. In order to "use" religion in this way, its ecstatic, transcending, divine-demonic character must be removed. Religion must be confined within the limits of pure reason or mere humanity. Possession and grace must be denied. The "religious personality" tries to determine its own relation to the unconditional. But, with respect to the unconditional, we can never in any way gain power over ourselves, because we cannot gain power over the unconditional. Religious self-determination is the negation of religion, for the unconditional determines us. This is the decisive criticism of the "ideal of personality."

# Chapter IX

## THE TRANSMORAL CONSCIENCE

THE famous theologian, Richard Rothe, in his *Christian Ethics* has made the suggestion that the word "conscience" should be excluded from all scientific treatment of ethics, since its connotations are so manifold and contradictory that the term cannot be saved for a useful definition. If we look not only at the popular use of the word, with its complete lack of clarity, but also at its confused history, this desperate advice is understandable. But, though understandable, it should not be followed, for the word "conscience" points to a definite reality which, in spite of its complexity, can and must be described adequately; and the history of the idea of conscience, in spite of the bewildering variety of interpretations that it has produced, shows some clear types and definite trends. The complexity of the phenomenon called "conscience" becomes manifest as soon as we look at the manifold problems it has given to human thought; man shows always and everywhere something like a conscience, but its contents are subject to a continuous change. What is the relation between the form and the content of conscience? Conscience points to an objective structure of demands, making themselves perceivable through it, and represents, at the same time, the most subjective self-interpretation of personal life. What is the relation between the objective and the subjective sides of conscience? Conscience is an ethical concept, but it has a basic significance for religion. What is the relation between the ethical and the religious meaning of conscience? Conscience has many different functions: it is good or bad, commanding or warning, elevating or condemning, fighting or indifferent. Which of these functions are basic, which derived? These questions refer only to the description of the phenomenon, not to its explanation or valuation. They show its complex character and the reason for its confused history.

### I. THE RISE OF CONSCIENCE

The concept of conscience is a creation of the Greek and Roman spirit. Wherever this spirit has become influential, notably in Christianity, conscience is a significant notion. The basic Greek word, *syneidenai* ("knowing with," namely, with one's self; "being witness of one's self"), was used in the popular language long before the philosophers got hold of it. It described the act of observing one's self, often as judging one's self. In philosophical terminology it received the meaning of "self-consciousness" (for instance, in Stoicism in the derived substantives *syneidesis, synesis*). Philo of Alexandria, under the influence of the Old Testament, stresses the ethical self-observation in *syneidesis* and attributes to it the function of *elenchos,* that is, accusation and conviction. The Roman language, following the popular Greek usage, unites the theoretical and practical emphasis in the word *conscientia,* while philosophers like Cicero and Seneca admit it to the ethical sphere and interpret it as the trial of one's self, in accusation as well as in defense. In modern languages the theoretical and the practical side are usually expressed by different words. English distinguishes *consciousness* from *conscience,* German *Bewusstsein* from *Gewissen,* French *connaissance* from *conscience*—though the latter word is also used for the theoretical side.

The development of the reality as well as of the concept of conscience is connected with the breakdown of primitive conformism in a situation in which the individual is thrown upon himself. In the sphere of an unbroken we-consciousness, no individual conscience can appear. Events like the Greek tragedy with its emphasis on personal guilt and personal purification, or like the stress upon personal responsibility before God in later Judaism, prepare for the rise of conscience by creating a definite ego-consciousness. The self, says a modern philosopher, has been discovered by sin. The merely logical self-consciousness does not have such a power. Without practical knowledge about one's self, produced by the experience of law and guilt, no practical self-consciousness and no conscience could have developed. Predominantly theoretical types of mentality lack a mature self. Even Nietzsche, who attacks more passionately than anyone else the judging conscience, derives the birth of the "inner man" from its appearance. In pointing to the subpersonal character of guilt and punishment in primitive cultures, he praises the discovery of the conscience as the elevation of mankind to a higher level. The fact that self and conscience are dependent on the experience of personal guilt explains the prevalence of the "bad conscience" in reality, literature, and theory. It gives evidence to the assertion that the uneasy, accusing, and judging conscience is the original phenomenon; that the good conscience is only the absence of the bad conscience; and that the demanding and warning conscience is only the anticipation of it. Since ego-self and conscience grow in mutual dependence and since the self discovers itself in the experience of a split between what it is and what it ought to be, the basic character of the conscience—the consciousness of guilt—is obvious.

Shakespeare, in *King Richard III,* gives a classic expression to the connection of individual self-consciousness, guilt, and conscience:

> O coward conscience, how dost thou afflict me!....
> What! do I fear myself? There's none else by.
> Richard loves Richard; that is, *I am I.*
> Is there a murderer here? No. Yes, I am.
> Then fly. What, from myself? Great reason why,
> Lest I revenge. What, *myself upon myself?*
> Alack, I love myself. Wherefore? For any good
> That I myself have done unto myself?
> O, no! alas, I rather hate myself.....
> My conscience hath a thousand several tongues,
> ....crying all, Guilty! guilty.

In the next moment, however, Richard immerges into the we-consciousness of the battle, dismissing self and conscience:

> ....conscience is a word that cowards use.....
> Our strong arms be our conscience, swords our law.
> March on, *join* bravely, let us to't pell-mell;
> If not to heaven, then *hand in hand* to hell.[1]

### II. CONSCIENCE IN THE BIBLICAL LITERATURE

While the Old Testament has the experience but not the notion of conscience (Adam, Cain, David, Job), the New Testament, especially Paul, has the word and the reality. Through the influence of Paul—who in this, as in other cases, introduced elements of Hellenistic ethics into Christianity—conscience has become a common concept of the Christian nations, in their religious, as well as in their secular, periods.

Conscience, in the New Testament, has religious significance only indirectly. It has a primarily ethical meaning. The acceptance of the gospel, for instance, is not a demand of the conscience. It does not give laws, but it accuses and condemns him who has not fulfilled the law.

1. *King Richard III,* Act V, scene 3.

Consequently, it is considered to be not a special quality of Christians but an element of human nature generally. In Rom. 2:14-15 Paul expresses this very strongly: "When Gentiles who have no law obey instinctively the Law's requirements, they are a law to themselves, even though they have no law; they exhibit the effect of the Law written on their hearts, their conscience bears them witness, as their moral convictions accuse or, it may be, defend them" (Moffatt). According to these words, the conscience witnesses to the law (either the Mosaic or the natural law) but it does not contain the law. Therefore its judgment can be wrong. Paul speaks of a "weak conscience," describing the narrow and timid attitude of Christians who are afraid to buy meat in the market because it might have been used for sacrifices in pagan cults. Paul criticizes such an attitude; but he emphasizes that even an erring conscience must be obeyed, and he warns those who are strong in their conscience not to induce by their example those who are weak to do things which would give them an uneasy conscience. No higher estimation of the conscience as guide is possible. Paul does not say that we must follow it because it is right but because disobedience to it means the loss of salvation (Romans, chap. 14). You can lose your salvation if you do something that is objectively right, with an uneasy conscience. The unity and consistency of the moral personality are more important than its subjection to a truth which endangers this unity. In principle, Christianity has always maintained the unconditional moral responsibility of the individual person in the Pauline doctrine of conscience. Aquinas and Luther agree on this point. Aquinas states that he must disobey the command of a superior to whom he has made a vow of obedience, if the superior asks something against his conscience. And Luther's famous words before the emperor in Worms, insisting that it is not right to do something against the conscience—namely, to recant a theological insight—are based on the traditional Christian doctrine of conscience. But neither in Paul nor in Aquinas nor in Luther is the conscience a religious source. They all keep the authority of conscience within the ethical sphere. Luther's refusal to recant his doctrine of justification is an expression of his conscientiousness as a doctor of theology. He declares that he would recant if he were refuted by arguments taken from Scripture or reason, the positive source and the negative criterion of theology. But he does *not* say—as often has been stated by liberal Protestants—that his conscience is the *source* of his doctrine. There is no "religion of conscience" either in the New Testament or in classical Christianity before the sectarian movements of the Reformation period.

In the New Testament the relation of the moral conscience to faith as the foundation of the religious life is dealt with in only two connections. In Heb. 9:9 the ritual religion is criticized because "gifts and sacrifices . . . . cannot possibly make the conscience of the worshipper perfect." Therefore, the writer continues, "let us draw near with a true heart, in absolute assurance of faith, our hearts sprinkled clean from a bad conscience." Only perfect salvation can give the moral status from which a good conscience follows. But the "assurance of faith" is not a matter of conscience. The other link between faith and conscience is given in the criticism of heresy. Heresy entails an unclean conscience because it is connected with a moral distortion. In I Tim. 1:19 and 4:2 libertinists and ascetics, both representatives of pagan dualistic morals, are rejected. Against them the writer says: "Hold to faith and a good conscience. Certain individuals have scouted the good conscience and thus come to grief over their faith." They are "seared in conscience." The judgment that one cannot be a heretic with a good conscience has been accepted by the church. The moral implications of heresy were always emphasized, though not always rightly. Heresy is not an error in judgment or a difference in experience but a demonic possession, splitting the moral self and producing a bad conscience. On this basis the church waged its fight against the heretics in all periods.

### III. THE INTERPRETATION OF CONSCIENCE IN MEDIEVAL AND SECTARIAN THEOLOGY

Scholasticism raised the question: According to what norms does the conscience judge, and how are these norms recognized by it? The answer was given in terms of the artificial (or distorted) word, *synteresis,* i.e., a perfection of our reason which leads us toward the recognition of the good. It has immediate and infallible evidence, being a spark of the divine light in us: the uncreated light in the depth of the soul, as the Franciscans asserted; the created light of our intuitive intellect, as the Dominicans said. The basic principles given by the *synteresis* are: (1) The good must be done; the evil must be avoided. (2) Every being must live according to nature. (3) Every being strives toward happiness. Conscience is the practical judgment, which applies these principles to the concrete situation. It is *syllogismus practicus*. We are obliged to follow our conscience whether the *syllogismus* is correct or not. We are, of course, responsible for not knowing the good. But we are not allowed to act against our conscience, even if it were objectively correct to do so. Man has an infallible knowledge of the moral principles, the natural law, through synteresis; but he has a conscience, which is able to fall into error in every concrete decision. In order to prevent dangerous errors, the authorities of the church give advice to the Christian, especially in connection with the confession in the sacrament of penance. *Summae de casibus conscientiae* (collections concerning cases of conscience) were given to the priests. In this way the conscience became more and more dependent on the authority of the church. The immediate knowledge of the good was denied to the layman. The Jesuits removed the synteresis and with it any direct contact between God and man, replacing it by the ecclesiastical, especially the Jesuitic, adviser. But the adviser has the choice from among different authorities, since the opinion of each of them is equally probable. Heteronomy and probabilism destroy the autonomous, self-assured conscience.

In spite of these distortions, the medieval development has performed a tremendous task in educating and refining the conscience of the European people generally and the monastic and half-monastic groups especially. The depth and breadth of the bad conscience in the later Middle Ages is the result of this education and the soil for new interpretations of the meaning and functions of conscience.

Turning to the "sectarian" understanding of conscience, we find the Franciscan idea of the immediate knowledge of the natural law in the depth of the human soul. But two new elements supported and transformed this tradition—the so-called "German mysticism," with its emphasis on the divine spark in the human soul, and the "spiritual enthusiasm" awakened by the Reformation, with its emphasis on the individual possession of the Spirit. Thomas Muenzer and all his sectarian followers taught that the divine Spirit speaks to us out of the depth of our own soul. Not *we* are speaking to ourselves, but God within us. "Out of the abyss of the heart which is from the living God" (Muenzer) we receive the truth if we are opened to it by suffering. Since the enthusiasts understood this divine voice within us in a very concrete sense, they identified it with the conscience. In this way conscience became a source of religious insight and not simply a judge of moral actions. The conscience as the expression of the inner light has a revealing character.

But the question arose immediately: What is the content of such a revelation through conscience? Luther asked Muenzer, and Cromwell asked Fox: What is the difference between practical reason and the inner light? Both of them could answer: the ecstatic character of the divine Spirit! But they could be asked again: What bearing has the ecstatic form of revelation on its content? And then the answer was difficult. Muenzer refers to practical decisions in his daily life, made under the inspiration of the Spirit; and Fox develops an ethics of unconditional honesty, bourgeois righteousness, and pacifism. It was easy to ask again whether reasonableness and obedience to the natural moral law could not produce the same results. The "revealing conscience" is a union of mysticism with moral rationality. But it does not reveal anything beyond biblical and genuine Christian tradition. An important result arising from this transformation of the concept of conscience is the idea of tolerance and its victory in the liberal era. The quest for "freedom of conscience" does not refer to the concrete ethical decision, but it refers to the religious authority of the "inner light" which expresses itself through the individual conscience. And since the inner light could hardly be distinguished from practical reason, freedom of conscience meant, actually, the freedom to follow one's autonomous reason, not only in ethics, but also in religion. The "religion of conscience" and the consequent idea of tolerance are not a result of the Reformation but of sectarian spiritualism and mysticism.

IV. MODERN PHILOSOPHICAL DOCTRINES OF THE CONSCIENCE

The modern philosophical interpretation of conscience follows three main lines: an emotional-aesthetic line, an abstract-formalistic line, and a rational-idealistic line. Secularizing the sectarian belief in the revealing power of conscience, Shaftesbury interprets it as the emotional reaction to the harmony between self-relatedness and relatedness to others, in all beings and in the universe as a whole. The principle of ethical action is the balance between the effects of benevolence and the effects of selfishness as indicated by conscience. The conscience works better and more accurately, the more the taste for the universe and its harmony is developed. The educated conscience has a perfect ethical taste. Not harmony with the universe but sympathy with the other man is the basis of conscience, according to Hume and Adam Smith; we identify ourselves with the other one and receive his approval or disapproval of our action as our own judgment. This, of course, presupposes a hidden harmony between the individuals and the possibility of a mutual feeling of identification. It presupposes a universal principle of harmony in which the individuals participate and which reveals itself to the conscience.

The emotional-harmonistic interpretation of conscience has often led to a replacement of ethical by aesthetic principles. The attitude of late aristocracy, high *bourgeoisie,* and bohemianism at the end of the last century was characterized by the elevation of good taste to be the ultimate judge in moral affairs, corresponding to the replacement of religion by the arts in these groups. It was an attempt to reach a transmoral conscience, but it did not reach even a moral one, and it was swept away by the revolutionary morality and immorality of the twentieth century.

The second method of interpreting conscience philosophically is the abstract-formalistic one. It was most clearly stated by Kant, and it was introduced into theology by Ritschl. Kant wanted to maintain the unconditional character of the moral demand against all emotional relativism, against fear and pleasure motives, as well as against divine and human authorities. But in doing so he was driven to a complete formalism. Conscience is the consciousness of the "categorical (unconditional) imperative," but it is not the consciousness of a special content of this imperative. "Conscience is a consciousness which itself is a duty." It is a duty to have a conscience, to be conscientious. The content, according to Ritschl, is dependent on the special vocation, a special historical time and space. Only conscientiousness is always demanded. This corresponds to the Protestant, especially the Lutheran, valuation of work. It is the expression of the activistic element of the *bourgeoisie* and is identical with bourgeois adaptation to the technical and psychological demands of the economic system. Duty is what serves bourgeois production. This is the hidden meaning even of the philosophy of the "absolute ego" in Fichte, who describes conscience as the certainty of the pure duty which is independent of anything besides its transcendent freedom. In the moment in which the transcendent freedom comes down to action it is transformed into obedience to a well-calculated system of economic services. It is understandable that this loss of a concrete direction of conscientiousness paved the way for very immoral contents in the moment in which they were ordered, for instance, by a totalitarian state.

Against the aesthetic-emotional as well as the authoritarian form of determining the conscience, attempts were made in modern philosophy to have rationality and contents united. The most influential of these attempts is the common-sense theory of Thomas Reid and the Scottish school, i.e., the moral sense is common to everybody, being a natural endowment of human nature (like the synteresis of the scholastics). Decisive for practical ethics is the sense of benevolence toward others (Hutcheson). This theory expresses adequately the reality of the British (and to a degree, American) conformism and the natural benevolence in a society in which the converging tendencies still prevail over the diverging ones, and in which a secularized Christian morality is still dominant. Another attempt to find rational contents for the conscience has been made by Hegel. He distinguishes the formal and the true conscience. About the first he says: "Conscience is the infinite formal certainty of oneself—it expresses the absolute right of the subjective self-consciousness, namely, to know within and out of itself what law and duty are, and to acknowledge nothing except what it knows in this way as the good." But this subjectivity is fallible and may turn into error and guilt. Therefore, it needs content, in order to become the true conscience. This content is the reality of family, society, and state. With the state (as the organization of historical reason) the formal conscience is transformed into the true conscience. It is a historical misjudgment to link these ideas to the totalitarian use of the state and the pagan distortion of conscience by national socialism. Hegel was a rationalist, not a positivist. His idea of the state unites Christian-conservative and bourgeois-liberal elements. His famous, though rarely understood, idea of the state as the "god on earth" is based on the identification of the state with the church as the "body of Christ," expressed in secular terms. The conscience which is determined by the state in this sense is determined not by bureaucratic orders but by the life of a half-religious, half-secular organism—the counterpart to the Christian-rationalistic common sense of the Anglo-

Saxon society. While the Scottish solution is largely dependent on the social attitude of Western Christianity and Hegel's solution on Lutheran Protestantism, the spirit of Catholicism has received a new philosophical expression in recent philosophical developments of which I take Max Scheler as a representative. In his doctrine of conscience Scheler opposes the popular conception of conscience as the "voice of God." He calls this, as well as the quest for "freedom of conscience," a principle of chaos. Instead of freedom of conscience, he demands subjection to authority as the only way of experiencing the intuitive evidence of the moral principles. It is impossible to reach such evidence without personal experience, and it is impossible to have such an experience without acting under the guidance of an authority which is based on former experience. In this respect, ethical (we could say "existential") experience is different from theoretical (i.e., "detached") experience. Although this fits completely the situation of the Catholic, it is not meant as the establishment of external authority. "All authority is concerned only with the good which is universally evident, never with that which is individually evident." Ethical authority is based on general ethical evidence. But does such a general ethical evidence exist? Or is philosophical ethics bound to be either general and abstract or to be concrete and dependent on changing historical conditions? And if this is the alternative, can the problem of conscience be answered at all in terms of *moral* conscience?

### V. THE IDEA OF A TRANSMORAL CONSCIENCE

A conscience may be called "transmoral" which judges not in obedience to a moral law but according to the participation in a reality which transcends the sphere of moral commands. A transmoral conscience does not deny the moral realm, but it is driven beyond it by the unbearable tensions of the sphere of law.

It is Luther who derives a new concept of conscience from the experience of justification through faith; neither Paul nor Augustine did so. Luther's experience grew out of the monastic scrutiny of conscience and the threat of the ultimate judgment, which he felt in its full depth and horror. Experiences like these he called *Anfechtungen,* that is, "tempting attacks," stemming from Satan as the tool of the divine wrath. These attacks are the most terrible thing a human being may experience. They create an incredible *Angst* ("dread"), a feeling of being inclosed in a narrow place from which there is no escape. (*Angst,* he rightly points out, is derived from *angustiae,* "narrows.") "Thou drivest me from the surface of the earth," he says to God in despair and even hate. Luther describes this situation in many different ways. He compares the horrified conscience, which tries to flee and cannot escape, with a goose which, pursued by the wolf, does not use its wings, as ordinarily, but its feet and is caught. Or he tells us how the moving of dry leaves frightens him as the expression of the wrath of God. His conscience confirms the divine wrath and judgment. God says to him: "Thou canst not judge differently about thyself." Such experiences are not dependent on special sins. The self, as such, is sinful before any act; it is separated from God, unwilling to love him.

If in this way the bad conscience is deepened into a state of absolute despair, it can be conquered only by the acceptance of God's self-sacrificing love as visible in the picture of Jesus as the Christ. God, so to speak, subjects himself to the consequences of his wrath, taking them upon himself, thus re-establishing unity with us. The sinner is accepted as just in spite of his sinfulness. The wrath of God does not frighten us any longer; a joyful conscience arises as much *above* the moral realm as the desperate conscience was *below* the moral realm. "Justification by grace," in Luther's sense, means the creation of a "transmoral" conscience. While God is the accuser in the *Anfechtung* and our heart tries to excuse itself, in the "justification" our heart accuses us and God defends us against ourselves. In psychological terms this means: in so far as we look at ourselves, we must get a desperate conscience; in so far as we look at the power of a new creation beyond ourselves we can reach a joyful conscience. Not because of our moral perfection but in spite of our moral imperfection we are fighting and triumphing on the side of God, as in the famous picture of Duerer, "Knight, Death, and Devil," the knight goes through the narrows in the attitude of a victorious defiance of dread and temptation.

An analogy to this "triumphant conscience," as developed by Luther personally as well as theologically, has appeared in the enthusiastic philosophy of Giordano Bruno. The moral conscience is overcome by the "heroic affect" toward the universe and the surrender to its infinity and inexhaustible creativity. Participation in the creativity of life universal liberates from the moral conscience, the bad as well as the good. Man, standing in the center of being, is bound to transform life as it is into higher life. He takes upon himself the tragic consequences, connected with the destructive side of finite creativity, and must not try to escape them for the sake of a good moral conscience.

While in Bruno the transmoral conscience is based on a mystical naturalism, Nietzsche's transmoralism is a consequence of his dramatic-tragic naturalism. Nietzsche belongs to those empiricists who have tried to analyze the genesis of the moral conscience in such a way that its autonomy is destroyed: Hobbes and Helvetius, on the ground of a materialistic metaphysics; Mandeville and Bentham, on the ground of a utilitarian psychology; Darwin and Freud, on the ground of an evolutionary naturalism—all have denied any objective validity to the voice of conscience, according to their rejection of any universal natural (rational) law. Nietzsche has carried these ideas further, as the title and the content of his *Genealogy of Morals* show. He says: "The bad conscience is a sickness, but it is a sickness as pregnancy is one." It is a creative sickness. Mankind had to be domesticated, and this has been done by its conquerors and ruling classes. It was in the interest of these classes to suppress by severe punishments the natural instincts of aggressiveness, will to power, destruction, cruelty, revolution. They succeeded in suppressing these trends. But they did not succeed in eradicating them. So the aggressive instincts became internalized and transformed into self-destructive tendencies. Man has turned against himself in self-punishment; he is separated from his animal past from which he had derived strength, joy, and creativity. But he cannot prevent his instincts from remaining alive. They require permanent acts of suppression, the result of which is the bad conscience, a great thing in man's evolution, an ugly thing if compared with man's real aim. Nietzsche describes this aim in terms which remind one of Luther's descriptions of the transmoral conscience: "Once in a stronger period than our morbid, desperate present, he must appear, the man of the great love and the great contempt, the creative spirit who does not allow his driving strength to be turned to a transcendent world." Nietzsche calls him the man "who is strong through wars and victories, who needs conquest, adventure, danger, even pain." This man is "beyond good and evil" in the moral sense. At the same time, he is good in the metaphysical (or mystical) sense that he is in unity with life universal. He has a transmoral conscience, not on the basis of a paradoxical unity with God (such as Luther has), but on the basis of an enthusiastic unity with life in its creative and destructive power.

Recent "existential" philosophy has developed a doctrine of the transmoral conscience which follows the general lines of Luther, Bruno, and Nietzsche. Heidegger, the main representative of existential philosophy, says: "The call of conscience has the character of the demand that man in his finitude actualize his genuine potentialities, and this means an appeal to become guilty." Conscience summons us to ourselves, calling us back from the talk of the market and the conventional behavior of the masses. It has no special demands; it speaks to us in the "mode of silence." It tells us only to act and to become guilty by acting, for every action is unscrupulous. He who acts experiences the call of conscience and—at the same time—has the experience of contradicting his conscience, of being guilty. "Existence as such is guilty." Only self-deception can give a good moral conscience, since it is impossible *not* to act and since every action implies guilt. We *must* act, and the attitude in which we *can* act is "resoluteness." Resoluteness transcends the moral conscience, its arguments and prohibitions. It determines a situation instead of being determined by it. *The good, transmoral conscience consists in the acceptance of the bad, moral conscience,* which is unavoidable wherever decisions are made and acts are performed. The way from Luther's to Heidegger's idea of a transmoral conscience was a dangerous one. "Transmoral" can mean the re-establishment of morality from a point above morality, or it can mean the destruction of morality from a point below morality. The empiricists from Hobbes to Freud have analyzed the moral conscience, but they have not destroyed it. Either they were dependent in their concrete ethics on Anglo-Saxon common sense; or they identified utility with the social conventions of a well-established *bourgeoisie;* or they cultivated a high sense of conscientiousness, in scientific honesty as well as in the fulfilment of duties; or they did not dare, unconsciously or consciously, to draw the radical moral consequences of their dissolution of the conscience. In Nietzsche and Heidegger none of these inhibitions is left. But it is not without *some* justification that these names are connected with the antimoral movements of fascism or national socialism. Even Luther has been linked with them, as have Machiavelli and Bruno. This raises the question: Is the idea of a transmoral conscience tenable? Or is it so dangerous that it cannot be maintained? But if the idea had to be dismissed, religion as well as analytic psychotherapy would have to be dismissed also; for in both of them the moral conscience is transcendent—in religion by the acceptance of the divine grace which breaks through the realm of law and creates a joyful conscience; in depth psychology by the acceptance of one's own conflicts when looking at them and suffering under their ugliness without an attempt to suppress them and to hide them from one's self. Indeed, it is impossible *not* to transcend the moral conscience because it is impossible to unite a *sensitive* and a *good* conscience. Those who have a sensitive conscience cannot escape the question of the transmoral conscience. The moral conscience drives beyond the sphere in which it is valid to the sphere from which it must receive its conditional validity.

# Chapter X

## ETHICS IN A CHANGING WORLD

"CHANGING world" in the title of this chapter does not mean the general change implied in everything that exists; neither does it mean the continuous change connected more fundamentally with history than with nature; but it points to the fact that we are living in a historical period, characterized by a radical and revolutionary transformation of one historical era into another one. Nobody can doubt this fact seriously, and nobody who has even a minimum of historical understanding would do so after what has occurred during recent years. We are in the midst of a world revolution affecting every section of human existence, forcing upon us a new interpretation of life and the world. What about ethics in this connection? Does it represent a realm above change? Is it suprahistorical in its foundation, its values, and its commands? Or does it follow the stream of historical becoming, and will it be transformed as rapidly as the other realms of life are transformed in our days? If the latter be the case, what authority, what power of shaping human life, is left to it? Can the unconditional claim with which every moral demand imposes itself on human conscience be maintained if the contents of the demand are different in every period of history? But if the former be the case—if ethics constitutes a realm above history, immovable and unconcerned by historical change—how can it influence man, living in history and transformed by history? Would it not remain a strange body within the context of human experience, separated from it in untouchable remoteness, perhaps worthy of awe but without actual influence on the life-process? In order to answer these questions and to refer them to our present situation, I intend to deal, first, with some solutions appearing in the history of human thought which are still of tremendous actual importance; second, I want to give my own solution; and, third, I will try to apply this solution to the present world situation by giving some practical examples.

I

There are three great types of life and thought representing three different solutions of the problem of ethics in historical change: first, the static supra-naturalistic solution, represented by the Roman Catholic church and expressed in the ethics of Thomas Aquinas. Second, the dynamic-naturalistic solution, represented by the National Socialist movement and expressed in the ethics of the philosophers of life. Third, the rationalistic-progressive solution, represented by Anglo-Saxon common sense and expressed in the ethics of the philosophers of reason. With tremendous psychological power the static supra-naturalistic solution maintains the eternal and immovable character of the ethical norms and commands. Philosophy and theology co-operate in this direction. The world is conceived as a system of eternal structures, preformed in the divine mind, which are substance and essence of everything and which establish the norms and laws for man's personal and social practice. Philosophy discovers these structures and laws, revelation confirms and amends them. And revelation adds some superstructures of its own that are new and higher laws but equally eternal and immovable. Both the natural and the supra-natural structures together form a hierarchy of powers and values which control nature and are supposed to control human activities. The church, itself a hierarchical system, teaches this system, educates for it, fights for its political realization, defends it against new systems. But in doing so the church cannot disregard the actual situation and the historical changes. The church must adapt its ethical system to new problems and new demands. The Catholic church has been able to do so in an admirable way for centuries, and the living authority of the pope is still a marvelous instrument for achieving adaptations without losing its immovable basis. Nevertheless, it is obvious that the Catholic church did not fully succeed in dealing with the presuppositions and demands of the bourgeois era. Protestantism and the Enlightenment created new systems of ethics standing in opposition to the supposedly eternal system of the medieval church. And when the church tried to go with the stream of the rising *bourgeoisie,* as, for instance, in the moral preachings of seventeenth- and eighteenth-century Jesuitism and in the teachings of nineteenth-century modernism, either it lost its seriousness and authority, or it gave the bad impression of a fight of retreat in which every position was defended as long as possible and then surrendered. And the important utterances of the Holy See during the nineteenth century concerning social and political problems presuppose, in order to be applicable, the unbroken unity and authority of the Christian church, which no longer exist. Therefore, they did not influence at all the spirit of modern ethics and the direction of bourgeois society. The price paid by the static supra-naturalistic answer to our question has been the loss of a determining influence on the changing world of the last centuries.

The opposite solution, represented by national socialism, was prepared for in two main ways—by the Continental vitalistic philosophy and by Anglo-American positivism and pragmatism, the latter being only a different form of the vitalistic philosophy. National socialism has used and abused the philosophical motives of the Continental philosophy of life, especially of Nietzsche, Pareto, and Sorel. Philosophy must express life in its changing forms and trends. Truth, according to Nietzsche, is that lie which is useful for a particular species of beings. Values are produced and withdrawn in the dynamic process of life—biologically speaking, by the strongest kind of living beings; sociologically speaking, by the new élite; politically speaking, by the eruptive violence of a revolutionary group. Change, being the main character of life, is also the main character of ethics. There are no independent norms above life, no criteria by which power could be judged, no standards for a good life. Good life is strong life or violent life or the life of a ruling aristocracy or the life of a conquering race. This implies that the individual, instead of being guided by the ethical norms which are manifest in his conscience, is obliged to merge his conscience into the group conscience. He must co-ordinate his standards with the group standards as represented by the leaders of the group. The dynamic-naturalistic type of answer to the question of ethics in a changing world has a primitive-tribal character. It is, historically speaking, at the same time the most recent and the most ancient of all solutions of the ethical problem.

I have mentioned Anglo-Saxon positivism and pragmatism in this connection. It is an important task of this paper to make it clear that pragmatism and vitalistic philosophy belong to the same type of ethical dynamism. When pragmatism speaks of experience, it surrenders the criteria of truth and the good no less than does vitalistic philosophy.

There are for it no norms above the dynamic process of experience, namely, of experienced life. The question of what kind of life creates ethical experience and what the standards of a true ethical experience are is not answered and cannot be answered within the context of pragmatic thought. Therefore, the pragmatists and the positivists take their refuge in an ethical instinct, which is supposed to lead to an ethical common sense. This refuge is secure as long as there is a society with a strong common belief and conventional morals maintained by the leading groups of society. Such was the situation in the acme of the bourgeois development, for instance, in the Victorian era. But it no longer worked when the harmony of a satisfied society slowly disappeared and dissatisfied groups, masses, and nations asked for a new order of life. The ethical instinct of those groups was much different from the ethical instincts of the ascendant Victorian *bourgeoisie,* and the refuge in ethical instinct and common sense became ineffective. Pragmatism and positivism were unable to face this threat because in their basic ideas they agree with the principles of the philosophy of life. The intellectual defense of Anglo-Saxon civilization against Fascist ideologies is extremely weak. Common-sense philosophy and pragmatism are not able to provide criteria against the dynamic irrationalism of the new movements; and they are not able to awaken the moral power of resistance, which is needed for the maintenance of the humanistic values embodied in Western and Anglo-Saxon civilization. It is not positivism and pragmatism but the remnants of the rationalistic-progressive solution of the ethical problem on which the future of that civilization is based. The solution is the most natural one for an undisturbed bourgeois thought and is still deeply rooted in the subconscious of contemporary philosophers as well as of laymen. There are, according to this point of view, some eternal principles, the natural law of morals—but without the supra-natural sanction claimed for it in the Catholic system. These principles, as embodied in the Bill of Rights, are like stars which always remain far remote from every human realization but which, like stars, show the direction in which mankind must go. Once discovered, they cannot disappear again, although their theoretical and practical realization is always in a process toward a higher perfection. In this way they are adaptable to every human situation.

Is this the solution of the problem of ethics in a changing world? In some ways it is, in some ways not. It indicates the direction in which the solution must be sought. There must be something immovable in the ethical principle, the criterion and standard of all ethical change. And there must be a power of change within the ethical principle itself; and both must be united. But the rationalistic-progressive solution is far from reaching this unity. It establishes some principles, such as freedom and equality, in the name of the absolute natural law, to be found in nature and human reason at any time and in any place. Mankind is supposed to realize these principles, theoretically and practically, in a process of approximation. It is the same natural law, the same principles which always are more or less known, more or less received in reality. "More or less" points to a quantitative difference, not to a qualitative change, not to new creations in the ethical realm. Ethics in a changing world changes only quantitatively, namely, as far as progress or regression with respect to their realization is concerned. More or less freedom and more or less equality are admitted, but not a new freedom or a new equality. But the principles on which the progressive-rationalistic solution is based represent a special pattern, a special type of freedom and equality, that of the later ancient or that of the modern bourgeois period. They do not represent principles comprehensive enough to embrace all periods and creative enough to bring new embodiments of themselves. They are not eternal enough to be ultimate principles and not temporal enough to fit a changing world. Therefore, as the Catholic system was not able to adapt itself seriously to the modern period of bourgeois growth, so the bourgeois-progressive rationalism was not able to face the breakdown of the bourgeois world. Supra-natural and rational absolutism in ethics both proved to be unable to adapt themselves to a fundamental change in the historical situation.

## II

Is there a possible solution beyond the alternative of an absolutism that breaks down in every radical change of history and a relativism that makes change itself the ultimate principle? I think there is, and I think it is implied in the basis of Christian ethics, namely, in the principle of love, in the sense of the Greek word *agape*. This is not said in an apologetic interest for Christianity, but it is said under the urge of the actual problem in our present world situation. Love, *agape*, offers a principle of ethics which maintains an eternal, unchangeable element but makes its realization dependent on continuous acts of a creative intuition. Love is above law, also above the natural law in Stoicism and the supra-natural law in Catholicism. You *can* express it as a law, you can say as Jesus and the apostles did: "Thou shalt love"; but in doing so you know that this is a paradoxical way of speaking, indicating that the ultimate principle of ethics, which, on the one hand, is an unconditional command, is, on the other hand, the power breaking through all commands. And just this ambiguous character of love enables it to be the solution of the question of ethics in a changing world. If you look at the principles of natural law as embodied in the Bill of Rights, you will find that, taken as the concrete embodiments of the principle of love in a special situation, they are great and true and powerful; they represent love by establishing freedom and equal rights against wilfulness and suppression and against the destruction of the dignity of human beings. But, taken as eternal laws and applied legalistically to different situations, for instance, to the early Middle Ages or the decay and transformation of economic capitalism, these principles become bad ideologies used for the maintenance of decaying institutions and powers. This is the reason for the extremely profound struggle of Paul and Luther against the "Law" and for their insistence on the mortifying consequences of the law and the vivifying power of love. *Love alone can transform itself according to the concrete demands of every individual and social situation without losing its eternity and dignity and unconditional validity.* Love can adapt itself to every phase of a changing world.

I like to introduce at this place another Greek word, namely, *kairos,* "the right time." This word, used in common Greek, has received an emphatic meaning in the language of the New Testament, designating the fulfilment of time in the appearance of the Christ. It has been reinterpreted by German religious socialism in the sense of a special gift and a special task, breaking from eternity into history at a special time. "Kairos" in this sense is the historical moment in which something new, eternally important, manifests itself in temporal forms, in the potentialities and tasks of a special period. It is the power of the prophetic spirit in all periods of history to pronounce the coming of such a kairos, to discover its meaning, to express the criticism of what is given and the hope for what is to come. All great changes in history are accompanied by a strong consciousness of a kairos at hand. Therefore, ethics in a changing world must be understood as ethics of the kairos. The answer to the demand for ethics in a changing world is ethics determined by the kairos; but only love is able to appear in every kairos. Law is not able because law is the attempt to impose something which belonged to a special time on all times. An ideal which has appeared at the right time and is valid for this time is considered to be the ideal for history as a whole, as that form of life in which history shall find its end. The outcome of this attitude necessarily is disillusionment and the rise of ethical libertinism and relativism. This is the point in which the dynamic-naturalistic solution, in spite of its destructive consequences, was right and still is right against Catholic and bourgeois ethics. Or, expressed in terms of church history, this is the point in which Luther is right against Thomas and Calvin. Love, realizing itself from kairos to kairos, creates an ethics which is beyond the alternative of absolute and relative ethics.

## III

This solution may be explained and made more concrete by some examples.

As a first example let us consider the idea of equality, one of the foundations of rationalistic-progressive ethics. In the light of the principle of love and in the perspective of the idea of kairos, the following can be said: Love implies equality in some respect. He who loves and he who is loved are equal for each other as far as they are worthy of love, the one for the other. But nothing else than just this principle of equality is implied—essentially implied—in love. Everything else is a historical embodiment of that principle in different situations, with love and the distortion of love at the same time. Looking at a Greek city-state, we discover that there is a political equality between the individuals within a special group and, to a certain extent, between all those who are free; but there is an absolute inequality between the free and the slaves. Love is not manifest as *the* principle; but, since it potentially is the principle, it is effective even in the religion and culture of Apollo and Dionysus. It is effective in the kind of equality that the city-state gives to those who belong to it, excluding slaves and barbarians. Love is effective even in this restricted equality, but it is a restricted, distorted love—love within the boundaries of national pride and racial discrimination. The central kairos in which love has become manifest as what it really is had not yet appeared. Nor had it appeared when Stoicism in the period of the universal Roman Empire extended equality to all human beings—men and women, children and slaves. In these ideas the principle of love breaks through the limitations of national and social arrogance, but it does so as universal, rational law and not as love. The Stoic equality is universal but cool and abstract, without the warmth and the communal element of the limited equality in the city-state. At its best it is participation in Roman citizenship and in the possibility of becoming a wise man. In the Christian event, love has become manifest in its universality but, at the same time, in its concreteness: the "neighbor" is the immediate object of love, and everybody can become "neighbor." All inequalities between men are overcome in so far as men are potential children of God. But this did not lead Christianity to the Stoic idea of equality. Not even the inequality between lord and slave was attacked, except in the realm of faith and love. Later, not the totalitarian, but the hierarchical, principle was supported by the Christian church according to the late ancient and medieval situation. The social and psychological inequalities of the feudal order did not seem to contradict the element of equality implied in the principle of love. On the contrary, the mutual interdependence of all the degrees of the hierarchy, the solidarity of all the members of a medieval city, and the patriarchalistic care of the feudal lords for their "people" were considered as the highest form of equality demanded by the principle of love. In bourgeois liberalism, equality was again interpreted in terms of the general natural law, the law of reason and humanity. Equality became equality before the law and the demand for equal economic chances. This was in accordance with the principle of love over against the tyranny and injustice into which the older system had developed. But in the measure in which the equal chance of everybody became a mere ideology to cover the exclusive chance for a few, the liberal idea of equality became a contradiction of love. A new idea of equality has risen, the meaning of which is the equal security of everyone, even if much political equality must be sacrificed. One must not condemn the collectivistic and authoritarian forms of equality only because they are the negation of its liberal and democratic forms. Love may demand a transformation in our kairos. A new creative realization of the element of equality as implied in the principle of love may be brought about in our period. It will be good, as far as it is in better accord with the demands of love in our special situation than the liberal and feudal forms were. It will be bad, as far as it is a distortion and contradiction of love; for love is eternal, although it creates something new in each kairos.

I could refer to many other ethical problems in order to show their double dependence on the principle of love, on the one hand, and on the changing kairos, on the other hand. For instance, I could point to the valuation of work and activism in the different periods of history and their relation to leisure and meditation. It is obvious that the coming collectivism will reduce the emphasis on work and activism considerably by restraining the principle of competition. As the struggle against some forms of feudal and ecclesiastical leisure and meditative life was a demand of love in the period of the decaying Middle Ages and in the moment in which mankind started its control over nature, so it is now a demand of love and of our kairos that leisure and meditation return on the basis of a new collectivistic structure of society over against a self-destructive adoration of work and activism.

Other examples are the problems of asceticism and worldliness, of self-control and self-expression, of discipline and creativity, in their relation to each other. Both sides of these contrasts follow from the principle of love. The negation of the first side would prevent the self-surrender implied in love; the negation of the second side would destroy any subject worth being loved. It depends on the kairos as to which of these sides, in which form, and in which balance with the other side, is emphasized. For our present situation neither the supra-natural ascetism of the Catholic system nor the rational self-control of bourgeois society nor the naturalistic war- and state-discipline of fascism can give the solution. And the same is true of feudal eroticism, of bourgeois aestheticism, and of Fascist adoration of vitality; another solution is demanded by love and by our kairos. Some elements of the solution are provided by psychoanalysis, although mere psychotherapeutic psychology is not able to create by itself a new system of ethics. Other elements of the solution are brought about by the rediscovery of the classical meaning of *eros* and by the different attempts to relate it to *agape*. The educational movements and the criticism of the bourgeois ideal of the family have contributed a great deal. But everything is in motion, and the criterion of the final solution is the measure in which *eros,* on the one hand, and self-control, on the other hand, are shaped by love.

A final question must be answered. If love is the principle of ethics and if kairos is the way of its embodiment in concrete contents, how can a permanent uncertainty, a continuous criticism which destroys the seriousness of the ethical demand, be avoided? Is not law and are not institutions necessary in order to maintain the actual ethical process? Indeed, law and institutions are demanded. They are demanded by love itself; for every individual, even the most creative, needs given structures that embody the experience and wisdom of the past, that liberate him from the necessity of innumerable decisions of his own, and that show him a meaningful way of acting in most cases. In this point Catholicism was superior in love both to Protestantism and to liberalism; and this is the reason why the younger generation in many countries eagerly demand laws and institutions able to relieve them from the unbearable burden of continuous ultimate decisions of their own. No ethics ever can become an actual power without laws and institutions. Luther, in his great emphasis on the creativity of love, forgot this need. This is one of the reasons why the moral education of the German masses is less thorough than that in the Calvinistic countries. On the other hand, there is more readiness for a kairos in Germany than there is in the highly educated and normalized Western nations. Love demands laws and institutions, but love is always able to break through them in a new kairos and to create new laws and new systems of ethics.

I have not mentioned the word "justice." It would be misleading in the present discussion because it is generally understood in the sense of the abstract natural law of Stoicism and rationalism. As such it is either empty or it is the concrete law of a special period and is thus without universal validity. If justice is taken concretely, it means the laws and institutions in which love is embodied in a special situation. The Platonic ideal of justice was the concrete harmony of the city-state; in Israel, justice was the pious obedience to the commands of God; in medieval feudalism it was the form of mutual responsibility of all degrees of the hierarchy to each other; in liberalism it was the laws abolishing formal privileges and introducing legal equality. In the more collectivistic society of the future, justice will be the system of laws and forms by which a sufficient security of the whole and of all members will be maintained and developed. From this it follows that justice is the secondary and derived principle, while **love,** actualized from kairos to kairos, is the creative and basic principle.

I have given no definition of love. This is impossible because there is no higher principle by which it could be defined. It is life itself in its actual unity. The forms and structures in which love embodies itself are the forms and structures in which life is possible, in which life overcomes its self-destructive forces. And this is the meaning of ethics: to express the ways in which love embodies itself and life is maintained and saved.

# Chapter XI

## THE PROTESTANT PRINCIPLE AND THE
## PROLETARIAN SITUATION

### I. INTRODUCTION

FROM many points of view it would seem that Protestantism and the proletarian situation have nothing to do with each other. The facts support this view almost indisputably. Consider, for instance, the intense struggle of nearly a hundred years between the spokesmen of Protestantism and those who have made the proletarian situation the basis of their thinking; the sociological connection of the Protestant churches in central Europe with the *petite bourgeoisie* and feudalism, and in western Europe and America with big business and the successful entrepreneurs; the inner opposition of the proletarian masses to the type of life and ideas characteristic of Protestantism; the political alliance of the proletarian parties with the Catholic party and the opposition of the parties supported by Protestant circles to the political representatives of the working classes. A fundamental difference becomes evident in all this. The proletarian situation, in so far as it represents the fate of the masses, is impervious to a Protestantism which in its message confronts the individual personality with the necessity of making a religious decision and which leaves him to his own resources in the social and political sphere, viewing the dominating forces of society as being ordered by God.

This opposition seems to be irreconcilable from the point of view of history, as well as from that of principle. Nor can one overcome the difficulty by distinguishing between socialism and the proletarian situation and then asserting that, although the interpretation and shaping of the proletarian situation was actually accomplished by socialism (though with false means), it could have been better and more successfully dealt with by Protestantism. Such a view leaves unexplained the fact that Protestantism has not actually done this, and that, in its stead, socialist theory and practice have become the fate of the proletariat while Protestantism has remained aloof from it. Socialism and the proletarian situation cannot be separated. They have formed each other. But one thing must be conceded: socialism is not identical with the proletarian situation. The proletarian situation *could* have been shaped by some other historical force. The relation between socialism and the proletarian situation is one of great tension. But it is not, therefore, a less binding and less fateful relation.

But if it is not possible to separate socialism and the proletarian situation, the dangerous consequence for Protestantism seems to result that there remains *one* human situation impervious to it. The unconditional and universal character of its message would thus be given up; instead of being a prophetic message for man as man, it would become a religious possibility for only certain groups of men. The fact that almost the entire literature and agitation of socialism reflect this very conviction needs no proof. If this view were correct, the end of Protestantism would be at hand, even if the Protestant churches should actually obtain a temporary increase in power through the intellectual and political energies of the antilabor groups supporting them sociologically. Hence the question concerning Protestantism and the proletarian situation is the most pressing aspect of the more comprehensive question concerning Protestantism and socialism. In so far as socialism is a world view, Protestantism may enter into a more or less fruitful apologetic discussion with it. But in so far as socialism is the expression of the proletarian situation, it poses for Protestantism the question concerning the meaning and the validity of its own unconditional and universal claim.

In view of the strangeness of the proletarian situation to present-day Protestantism, a positive answer to this question can be given only if it is possible for Protestantism to extricate itself from its present status without losing its own inherent character. Only if it is Protestant to give up that sort of Protestantism to which the proletarian situation remains inaccessible can the unconditional and universal character of the Protestant message be maintained. This possibility does, however, exist. It is the possibility that makes Protestantism "Protestant." What makes Protestantism Protestant is the fact that it transcends its own religious and confessional character, that it cannot be identified wholly with any of its particular historical forms. Thus, if there is an incongruity between Protestantism in its present status and the situation of the proletariat, it does not follow that the incongruity belongs in essence to Protestantism. Protestantism has a principle that stands beyond all its realizations. It is the critical and dynamic source of all Protestant realizations, but it is not identical with any of them. It cannot be confined by a definition. It is not exhausted by any historical religion; it is not identical with the structure of the Reformation or of early Christianity or even with a religious form at all. It transcends them as it transcends any cultural form. On the other hand, it can appear in all of them; it is a living, moving, restless power in them; and this is what it is supposed to be in a special way in historical Protestantism. The Protestant principle, in name derived from the protest of the "protestants" against decisions of the Catholic majority, contains the divine and human protest against any absolute claim made for a relative reality, even if this claim is made by a Protestant church. The Protestant principle is the judge of every religious and cultural reality, including the religion and culture which calls itself "Protestant."

The Protestant principle, the source and judge of Protestantism, is not to be confused with the "Absolute" of German idealism or with the "Being" of ancient and recent philosophy. It is not the highest ontological concept derived from an analysis of the whole of being; it is the theological expression of the true relation between the unconditional and the conditioned or, religiously speaking, between God and man. As such, it is concerned with what theology calls "faith," namely, the state of mind in which we are grasped by the power of something unconditional which manifests itself to us as the ground and judge of our existence. The power grasping us in the state of faith is not a being beside others, not even the highest; it is not an object among objects, not even the greatest; but it is a quality of all beings and objects, the quality of pointing beyond themselves and their finite existence to the infinite, inexhaustible, and unapproachable depth of their being and meaning. The Protestant principle is the expression of this relationship. It is the guardian against the attempts of the finite and conditioned to usurp the place of the unconditional in thinking and acting. It is the prophetic judgment against religious pride, ecclesiastical arrogance, and secular self-sufficiency and their destructive consequences. The Protestant principle in this sense is not strange to the situation of the proletariat in modern society. It is, on the contrary, the exact expression of its religious significance as an

outstanding example of man's situation. The inadequacy of Protestantism in the face of the proletarian situation is, accordingly, the result
of the contradiction between the Protestant principle and Protestantism
as it actually is. Hence we may divide our discussion into two parts:
(1) the vindication of the Protestant principle in the proletarian situation and (2) the failure of historical Protestantism in face of the
proletarian situation.

The demands for Protestant action which arise out of the Protestant
principle and the proletarian situation will come out of the discussion
itself and thus will require only a summing-up in a few concluding
remarks.

In the foregoing analysis the definition of the concept of "the proletarian situation" has been presupposed. But a more precise definition
of it is necessary before we can approach our subject. The proletarian
situation is not to be understood as the situation in which all members
of the proletariat live. This would be both too narrow and too broad
a conception—too narrow, because not *only* the proletariat, and too
broad because not *all* of the proletariat, are in the proletarian situation.
What is meant by the term "the proletarian situation" is rather the
typical situation of a certain group in capitalistic society. It is taken
for granted that the proletarian type is seldom, if ever, wholly realized;
that it is, as circumstances change, subject to modifications which alter
the type; and that it is undergoing changes along with capitalism,
which is itself in process of development. But these restrictions which
are valid for the definition of any sociological concept, do not preclude
the setting-up of such concepts; they determine only their methodological character. The proletarian situation is thus to be understood as
the situation of that class within the capitalist system whose members
are dependent exclusively upon the "free" sale of their physical ability
to work and whose social destiny is wholly dependent upon the turn
of the market. This definition presupposes a thoroughly capitalistic
system, an exclusive dependence upon the sale of labor, and a complete
dependence upon the chances of the market. If these criteria are strictly
applied, the merely typical character of what we have called the "proletarian situation" becomes evident, for there is nowhere a fully developed capitalist system. Without taking into account the various
periods of capitalism itself, certain precapitalist and postcapitalist conditions always prevent the full development of the system. Further-

more, exclusive dependence upon the sale of physical labor is by no means the most prevalent situation. Either it has not yet developed (even though there is a tendency for the system to develop more and more in this direction), as among those members of the middle class and of the white-collar group who are not fully proletarianized; or it is no longer real, as is the case with highly skilled workers and with labor leaders. Moreover, the full dependence upon the oscillation of the market is not yet reached when a remnant of feudal safeguards is operative, or it is no longer real when labor legislation has created new safeguards. From a logical point of view the concept of the proletarian situation is an evidence of the fact that concepts derived from history are concepts of a representative and typological character. From the point of view of the actual, human situation, however, no justification is needed for using this concept in a time when the fate of millions of unemployed who cannot sell their labor becomes increasingly the fate of a nation and even of a cultural epoch.

## II. THE VINDICATION OF THE PROTESTANT PRINCIPLE
### IN THE PROLETARIAN SITUATION

The Protestant principle implies a judgment about the human situation, namely, that it is basically distorted. The difficult concept of "original sin" denotes an original self-contradiction in human existence, coincident with human history itself. This cleavage in human nature is not to be interpreted, and thereby justified, as a necessary consequence of the finiteness of creaturely existence. The fateful character of the human situation is not due to finitude as such; nor does finitude provide the basis for guilt and its tragic consequences. Both the fateful character and the guilt of human existence are due rather to the self-assertiveness of the finite being in its pride, concupiscence, and separation from its ground. Not finitude, then, but this perversion of human nature is the fateful element in the human situation. Man alone is in this situation because in him life rises to the level where it is able to determine itself. Man's power of self-determination carries with it the possibility of a perverted, destructive self-determination. But the possibility of perversion does not explain its reality. For the possibility of self-contradiction is rooted in the *self*-determination of man, the direction of which cannot be determined beforehand. This basic, underivable cleavage in human existence underlies all human history and makes history what it is.

Such an aspect of the Protestant principle, when seen in the light of the proletarian situation, finds a complete vindication, and, conversely, the proletarian situation becomes ultimately explicable only by means of that element of the Protestant principle just referred to. In the proletarian situation the perversion of man's nature shows its reality in the social realm. This assertion can be theologically denied only by those who conceive of the relation between God and the world as exclusively a relation between God and the soul. But this is not consistent with either the prophetic message or the Protestant principle. The perversion of human existence is real in social, just as strongly as in individual, distortions and with even more primitive force; and collective guilt is just as real and perceptible as individual guilt; neither can be separated from the other.

From the beginning, the proletarian consciousness has been aware of the perversion and inner contradiction of a society that permits such a thing to exist as a proletarian situation and the breaking-up of society into classes. In this negative moral judgment about man's actual existence, the socialistic evaluation of the proletarian situation and the Protestant understanding of the universal human situation agree. The universally human reveals itself in the proletarian situation. This involves the theological recognition of the fact that there are situations in which the perversion of man's essential nature is manifest primarily as a *social* perversion and as *social* guilt; and it involves the philosophical recognition of the fact that the proletarian situation, far from being merely a historical accident, represents a distortion of essential human nature and a demonic splitting-up of humanity in general. So the judgments derived from the Protestant principle and from the proletarian situation complete each other. The Protestant judgment becomes concrete, actual, and urgent in its application to the class situation of today; and the socialist judgment becomes universal, profound, and religiously significant if put in the frame of man's general situation.

The Protestant principle relates its judgment of the human situation to the whole man. It does not interpret the inner contradiction of human nature in terms of a dualism between spirit and body but rather passes its judgment in the same way upon the spiritual as upon the physical existence of man. The body is no "prison" but rather a "temple," and it is not the body that struggles against the spirit but rather "the flesh"—a term that signifies the pride of the spirit as well as the lusts of the body. From this it follows that the whole man is the subject of the religious demand and promise and that the help of man to man must involve the whole man, body and spirit together. The Protestant principle, which exempts no aspect of human existence from the judgment that it is involved in contradiction with itself, considers the whole man, man as a unity of body and soul, in his relationship with the transcendent. This biblical idea was rediscovered by the Reformation in its opposition to the dualistic elements of the Catholic system. But in Protestantism itself this idea has become only partially effective for individual ethics and not at all for social ethics.

The proletarian situation confirms the biblical doctrine; for in this situation there is a unity of both bodily and spiritual distortion of man's true nature, in the face of which every attempt to save the soul and leave the body to perdition must appear to be frivolous. "Body" is to be understood here as representing the whole vital sphere. The exclusion of it from salvation in some types of Christianity is in itself perversion and guilt.

The distorted character of the vital existence of millions and millions of proletarians in city and country is too obvious to need much description. It is worse in some nations than in others and in some sections of a country than in others. It is worst in periods of unemployment, and it is intolerable—leading to mass explosions—in times of protracted mass unemployment. In view of these facts, it is dishonest to use the instinctively materialistic reaction of the proletariat to its fate as an excuse for discrediting the proletarian struggle. Much so-called "idealism" has its roots in the social and economic security of the upper classes; and Protestantism has just as little reason to praise this bourgeois idealism as it has to condemn proletarian materialism. The philosophical expression of the materialistic reality of the proletarian situation is of only secondary importance. The thing of primary importance is the imposed materialism in the actual life of the proletariat. This actual materialism in the objective proletarian situation is to be taken very seriously; the theory of materialism, however, is to be taken seriously only in so far as it reflects this actual situation. The Protestant principle can interpret this actual materialism inherent in the life of the proletariat just because Protestantism is not in principle allied with bourgeois idealism.

The basic distortion of the human situation involves all men. It is the negative side of the idea of a unified humanity. No one can withdraw himself from this situation. Everyone is bound to it in spite of man's essential freedom. Of course, self-determination belongs to man as man. It distinguishes him from nature. But in the power of his freedom he can contradict himself, he can estrange himself from himself. And this is not only an individual possibility but also a universal reality. Mankind universally is in the bondage of self-estrangement. Man's freedom is superseded by his servitude. This is what the Reformation emphasized against the optimistic individualism of humanists like Erasmus. It is a basic element of the prophetic and the biblical message. It is constitutive for the Protestant principle. But this realistic interpretation of human existence as a whole did not prevent the early Christians or the Reformers from attacking every concrete manifestation of the universal evil, individual as well as social. The category of "the universally human" did not lead away from the particular human problem of a definite social situation. The "universal" and "the concretely historical" do not contradict each other. So primitive Christianity challenged the Roman state as a demonic power having the ambiguity of the demonic to be creative and destructive at the same time, establishing order and compelling men to the worship of itself. So Luther saw in the papacy in Rome the "Antichrist" dominating Christendom and attacked it with all his prophetic wrath, although he knew he risked the unity of Christendom.

The proletarian situation compels Protestantism to take a similar attitude, for the proletarian situation is an inescapable consequence of the demonic structure of capitalism. No men in our time, regardless of whether they belong to the bourgeois or the proletarian group, can escape the permanent and essential contradictions of the capitalist system. The most obvious and basic of these contradictions is the class struggle that is going on at every moment, both from above and from below. No one can avoid having a part in it, since in capitalism it necessarily produces the struggle for existence. This does not mean that anyone should or could accept the class struggle as desirable. It is the symptom of a disease, or, symbolically speaking, it is the symptom of a demonic possession in the grip of which modern society lives.

Therefore, although the proletariat and its leaders urge the fight against the ruling classes, they do not favor the class struggle—which goes on anyway—they try to encourage the fight for the existence of the proletarians. And they try to do something else; they try to overcome the system as such which, by its very structure, produces the class struggle. This gives the proletarian fight both its universal significance and its dangerous dialectics. Protestantism, in the light of its own principle, should be able to understand this situation, to see its demonic implications and its divine promises.

The Reformation struggled against two ideologies, that is, against two ways of concealing the true human situation, namely, the Catholic and the humanistic ideology. Catholicism claims to offer a secure way of overcoming the separation of man from his divine ground through sacramental graces and ascetic exercises, the efficacy of which is guaranteed by the hierarchy and its sacramental powers. Humanism denies the perverted character of the human situation and tries to achieve essential humanity on the basis of human self-determination. Over against these two ideologies—the religious and the secular—Protestantism must insist upon the unveiled and realistic recognition of the perennial situation of man. Historical Protestantism, however, has not escaped the ideologizing of its own principle. Protestant orthodoxy and Protestant idealism represent the sacramental and the humanistic forms of the old ideologies. In both forms a "man-made God" has been substituted for the true God, a God that is either inclosed in a set of doctrines or is believed to be accessible through morals and education.

In the power of the Protestant principle, Protestantism must fight not only against other ideologies but also against its own. It must reveal the "false consciousness" wherever it hides. It must show how the "man-made God" of Catholicism was in the interest of the feudal order, of which the medieval church was a part; how the ideology of Lutheranism was in the interest of the patriarchal order, with which Lutheran orthodoxy was associated; how the idealistic religion of humanistic Protestantism is in the interest of a victorious *bourgeoisie*. The creation of these ideologies—religiously speaking, idols—representing man's will to power, occurs unconsciously. It is not a conscious falsification or a political lie. If this were the case, ideologies would not be very dangerous. But they are dangerous precisely because they are unconscious and are therefore objects of belief and fanaticism. To reveal these concrete ideologies is one of the most important functions of the Protestant principle, just at it was one of the main points in the attack of the prophets on the religious and social order of their time. Theology, of course, must provide general insight into human nature, into its distorted character and its proneness to create ideologies. But this is not enough. A religious analysis of the concrete situation must unveil concrete ideologies, as Luther and the Reformers did when they unveiled the all-powerful Roman ideology.

The proletarian situation is, objectively, an outstanding instance of an ideology-unveiling situation. Subjectively, this is not always the case. Being a man, the proletarian is not exempt from the human tendency to erect an ideological superstructure over his own interests. He always does it; and, likewise, socialist theory and propaganda, in order to justify the struggle of the proletariat, tend to build up a questionable ideological superstructure. Over against this, however, stands the objective proletarian situation upon which the ideology must suffer shipwreck. The needs of man, of a sociologically homogeneous mass of men, tear away the ideological mask. They provide the criterion for distinguishing what is real from what is merely ideological. Anything that cannot rescue the proletariat from the perversion of existence in the capitalistic order is rejected. This refers to romantic-conservative as well as to progressive-idealistic ideas. This fear of ideological camouflage is the reason for the influence upon socialism of Feuerbach's criticism of religion. It is on this basis that the churches and their theoretical and practical symbols are criticized. In so far as they ignore the proletarian situation, they are looked upon as ideologies. And so also is a theology that remains aloof from the concrete proletarian struggle. The proletarian situation, in forcing Protestantism to bring to the fore the critical element of its own principle, creates the constant suspicion that Protestantism has itself become an ideology, the worship of a man-made God. For this reason, the proletarian situation provides a fundamental vindication of the Protestant principle and the most serious judgment of historical Protestantism.

The Protestant principle took form in Luther's fight for justification by grace and through faith alone. "Justification" in this sense is the paradox that man, the sinner, is justified; that man the unrighteous is righteous; that man the unholy is holy, namely, in the judgment of God, which is not based on any human achievements but only on the divine, self-surrendering grace. Where this paradox of the divine-human relationship is understood and accepted, all ideologies are destroyed. Man does not have to deceive himself about himself, because he is accepted as he is, in the total perversion of his existence. But being accepted by God means also being transformed by God—not in terms of a tangible change but in terms of "anticipation." Anticipation is neither having nor not-having. With respect to the empirical objects of the world, one can say that to anticipate something is simply not to have it; it is an anticipation of it in the merely ideal form of an image. But the object of religious anticipation is not an empirical object. It never and nowhere can be possessed in an empirical way. The *only* way of possessing it is by anticipation. This idea of anticipation received its classic expression in the word of Jesus: The Kingdom of God is at hand. It is here and yet it is not here. The metaphor "at hand" has the same double meaning as the metaphor "anticipation"— the former from the objective, the latter from the subjective, side. The paradox inherent in these concepts indicates the character of the relation of the infinite and the finite in the light of the Protestant principle and the idea of justification: possessing and not possessing at the same time. Anticipation without possession is religiously as impossible as nearness without presence; for nobody can anticipate the ultimate without being touched by it, and nobody can pronounce that the Kingdom of God is at hand who is not already drawn into it. On the other hand, nobody can have the ultimate, nothing conditioned can possess the unconditional. And nobody can localize the divine that transcends space and time.

It is significant that the proletarian situation, just because it is so emphatically anti-ideological, is characterized by a pronounced form of anticipation. It is through anticipation that the proletariat experiences the meaning of its existence. It is through anticipation that the inner contradiction of our epoch becomes evident, just as the anticipation of the early Christians made them aware of the demonic powers which ruled their world. When the proletariat awoke from its stupor under early capitalism and became conscious of itself as proletariat, a new anticipation was thereby brought to birth. Indeed, the one did not happen without the other. The anticipation of the proletariat, in the religious sense of the word, expresses both the nonpossession of what is anticipated, the living in the proletarian situation, and the anticipatory possession of what is hoped for, the creative tension in which the present is potentially overcome. Just because of his anticipation the proletarian is no longer *only* a proletarian. He becomes aware of the impossibility of his existence, and this consciousness of the evil is a factor in the process of overcoming it. That is the fundamental difference to be seen in the situation of the proletarian before and after it was interpreted and molded by Marxism: whereas previously the perversion of his existence was only objective in character, afterward, because of awareness and anticipation, it became also subjective, and by that very fact its objective power was broken.

The Protestant principle provides the possibility for understanding the paradoxical character of anticipation as it is found in the proletariat, and, besides this, it has the power to guard against a distortion that threatens all anticipation, i.e., utopianism. The attitude of anticipation develops into utopianism if it is allowed to lose its essential dialectical character and is held as a precise and literal intellectual anticipation—an anticipation that at some time in the future is to be replaced by a tangible, objective possession. The thing ultimately referred to in all genuine anticipation remains transcendent; it transcends any concrete fulfilment of human destiny; it transcends the otherworldly utopias of religious fantasy as well as the this-worldly utopias of secular speculation. And yet this transcendence does not mean that distorted reality should be left unchanged; rather it looks forward to a continuous revolutionary shattering and transforming of the existing situation. Thus proletarian anticipation involves a·real change in proletarian existence, a real shattering and overcoming of capitalism. But it does not and cannot involve the bringing-about of a situation that is exempt from the threat that always confronts human existence.

Christianity interprets the divine action in history and personal life through the ideas of providence and predestination. In the power of these ideas, human destiny is elevated above the uncertainties of human freedom and self-determination to a level of "transcendent necessity." Since man is in the bondage of existential self-contradiction, he is, according to Christian and Protestant teaching, unable to overcome this situation by himself. The bondage to "demonic structures" can be released only by a bondage to "divine structures." But this bondage, this "transcendent" necessity, is not causal, and even less is it mechanical necessity. It is a dependence which, far from abolishing human freedom, re-establishes it in its essential integrity. Man remains man, whether he is "possessed" or in the state of grace. He never becomes a "thing," a mere object, deprived of his psychological freedom. The unity of these two elements—empirical freedom and transcendent necessity—characterizes all symbols, indicating the relation of the unconditional to the conditioned. Neither determinism nor indeterminism is an adequate description of this relation, which is a matter of basic experience in all great representatives of religion (Isaiah, Paul, Augustine, Luther, Calvin, Mohammed). Their actual behavior and that of their followers show that the seeming contradiction between empirical freedom and transcendent necessity is not a real contradiction. Those who have emphasized most (and often in a deterministic distortion) the "unconditional dependence" on the divine, as Calvin and the Puritans did, have created the most activistic type of men in all history.

The same tension appears in the attitude of the proletariat toward its own movement. It combines the certainty that the anticipated event is coming with the feeling of responsibility for its coming. Marx's dialectic has expressed it, but it springs from deeper roots than he knew. It is operative in every great revolutionary movement: the certainty that success is destined to come stimulates the highest degree of activity. Marx gave this original impulse a conceptual form, following Hegel, who, in his philosophy of history, attempted to interpret the arbitrary acts of human self-determination as the bearers of an all-embracing meaningful necessity. This was a philosophical rationalization of the idea of providence. Even in the Marxian dialectic something of the faith in providence is left, a joining-together of universal necessity and historical responsibility. The course of the historical process leads with dialectical (not mechanical) necessity to the emergence of the *bourgeoisie* and the proletariat, to the victory of the proletariat over the *bourgeoisie,* and thence to the abolition of the class society. This necessity does not, however, give to the proletariat the right merely to watch the process but rather makes the demand that the dialectical necessity be materialized by means of revolutionary effort.

The "calling" of the proletariat to overcome the class society is something that the proletariat is always in danger of losing. It must stand the test of struggle. Indeed, according to Marx, the failure of the proletariat and the consequent social chaos are always a possibility. But this possibility of failure does not represent something that invalidates the all-embracing dialectical necessity. The dialectic of history moves on relentlessly to bring to an end the class-conflict phase of human development. Hence, if the proletariat fails in its "calling," mankind must begin again. Even if the proletariat should be replaced by some other instrument of destiny, the fundamental dialectic of history will remain unchanged in character. In Judaism and Christianity the idea of "calling" is very important as an element in the larger concept of predestination. Israel is called, so are the disciples, so is every generation of Christians, so is every special church, so is Protestantism. But he who is called might be rejected if he does not fulfil his calling. Protestantism might miss its calling and be rejected by the judgment of its own principle. And if the proletariat should no longer maintain its role of overcoming the demonic structure of capitalism, it would necessarily be "rejected" by virtue of its own "calling." But the admission of these possibilities does not imply the rejection of either the Protestant principle or the anticapitalistic principle. These principles will arouse new fighters. If Protestantism had had a deeper insight into these aspects of human history, it would have found an approach to the proletarian situation, and it would have been possible for it to give a better interpretation of the proletarian struggle than the socialists, with their hopeless mixture of mechanistic calculation of historical necessities and petty tactics, have provided.

The Protestant principle overcomes the gap between the sacred and the secular spheres, between priesthood and laity. Protestantism demands a radical laicism. There are in Protestantism only laymen; the minister is a layman with a special function within the congregation; and, in addition to possessing certain personal requisites, he is qualified for the fulfilment of this function by a carefully regulated professional training. He is a nonlayman solely by virtue of this training. Just as there is no priest having a special religious function, for everybody is a layman and every layman is potentially a priest, so there is no religion as a special spiritual sphere. Everything is secular and every secular thing is potentially religious. The relation to the unconditional permeates every moment of the daily life and makes it holy. The "holy" is not one value beside others but a qualification, appearing in all values and in the whole of being. Protestantism has not always measured up to the greatness and the radicalism of this idea. On Protestant soil, very soon after Luther's pronouncement of the universal priesthood of all Christians, a quasi-priesthood of the orthodox doctrine arose, as arrogant as the sacramental priesthood of the Roman church. And often Protestant laymen not only have supported this claim but have also acted as the guardians of obsolete traditions, by defending with pseudo-priestly or pseudo-theological fanaticism, elements of the past which already had been rejected by prophetic or honest theological criticism. This is certainly not the proper function of the Protestant layman. He is supposed to challenge any conscious or unconscious attempt of ministers or theologians to set up a religious sphere as separate from his "secular" life and his "secular" work. He is supposed to tear down this boundary.

The proletarian situation has a completely secular character. Not only does the proletariat lack any priestly group in itself, but in its most radical circles it has also separated itself from every connection with the church. For this reason the representatives of most of the Christian churches have challenged socialism, as anti-Christian, anti-religious, and atheistic. Political alliances between socialist and, for instance, Catholic parties cannot bridge the deep gap between the Catholic system and the socialist movements. This is true also of some Protestant churches—for instance, German Lutheranism. But Protestantism must raise the question as to whether the absence of an expressly religious attitude and the manifestations of an outspoken secularism mean the lack of "religion" in the sense of the Protestant principle. Protestantism must ask whether, under the disguise of a secular theory and practice, socialism does not represent a special religious type, namely, the type that originates in Jewish prophetism and transcends the given world in the expectation of a "new earth"—symbolized as classless society, or a stage of justice and peace, or an era of perfect rationality, etc. It must also be asked, in the light of the Protestant principle, whether the proletarian movement does not represent a kind of lay movement, which, although remote from every theological self-expression, bears witness to the human situation, its distortion and its promise. This is especially worth asking in view of the quasi-religious enthusiasm, the willingness to make every sacrifice, the tremendous forming and uniting power of the early proletarian movements. In any case, Protestantism should ask these questions and should consider an affirmative answer as a possibility. It should be open for the prophetic message which is hidden under proletarian secularism, even under its ardent attacks on the Christian churches generally and on Protestantism especially. Protestantism has the power to accept these attacks, to turn them against itself, and to transform itself according to the standard of its own principle.

These are the main respects in which the Protestant principle can find a vindication in the proletarian situation and the proletarian situation can be viewed in a new way and understood in its importance for Protestantism.

### III. THE FAILURE OF HISTORICAL PROTESTANTISM IN THE FACE OF THE PROLETARIAN SITUATION

It is the historical fate of Protestantism that it has been driven in a direction which, although understandable in the frame of world history, does not express the possibilities of the Protestant principle and may prove ultimately disastrous. This is especially true of the contact between Protestantism and the proletarian situation. We shall not analyze all the causes of this development but shall rather point out those aspects in which the antiproletarian tendency in Protestantism is most evident.

In the first place we should mention the hardening into dogma which the Protestant principle has undergone in the orthodox period, whereby it has been petrified into a system of doctrine that raises an unconditioned claim to truth. The effect of this development upon the religion and theology of Protestantism is familiar and has been the subject of extensive research. From the point of view of the Protestant principle, it is clear that in this trend a basic element of the principle has been abandoned. It was claimed that man has objective possession of a truth that is identical with the content and letter of an inspired Scripture. The Scripture is in the hands of the church and its theological experts, and it can be used like an untouchable, unfailing, and completely sufficient document of what is true. The critical power of the Protestant principle against any papal authority, be it that of a living man or that of a written paper, was forgotten. A quasi-sacramental dignity was attributed not only to the biblical text but also to the "pure doctrine" as expressed in the Protestant creeds and the official teaching of the church. A truth beyond the biblical truth—for instance, philosophy—is not wanted. The Protestant doctrine is not subjected to the criticism of the Protestant principle.

As a result of this, the Protestant message in its orthodox form is wholly unsuited to reach the proletariat. Even the middle classes have become inwardly estranged from the teaching of the church—in some cases radically so, in others in a compromising way. But, owing to their educational advantages and their familiarity with history, they have had and still have at least the possibility of understanding it or of sympathetic insight into it, and in many cases even of taking it up again. They have often had a real or a feigned respect for the achievements of the past. But it is quite otherwise with the proletarian masses. They have no sense of a historical background; they have neither the capacity nor the desire to understand the achievements of the past or to acquire a sympathetic insight into them; they stand in the most dire need and in the expectation of something new; and they have access only to those concepts that are rooted in the modern industrial world and to those ideas which interpret their needs and justify their anticipations. But, since Protestantism, as a result of its orthodox seclusion, has been unable to interpret these needs and anticipations, its message has remained unintelligible to the masses, even in its most simple and reduced form. A change is possible only if Protestantism, rediscovering its own principle, recognizes that truth transcends all human fixation, even the letters of a sacred book.

Pietism is another factor that is of great significance for the understanding of the relation between Protestantism and the proletariat. Religion as an affair of the purely inner life isolates the individual and limits the relation between God and the world to the relation between God and the soul. The result of this is that the problems of worldly activity do not come within the scope of religion. The inner life, rather than the social sphere, is the place where God and man may enter into relation with each other. There is, so to speak, a direct line reaching upward from every individual. The Kingdom of God is the heavenly realm which the individual soul hopes to reach. Thus the forward-looking eschatological fervor of primitive Christianity is paralyzed, and the world-transforming aspect of the idea of the Kingdom of God disappears. The social sphere is viewed as a place of probation for the individual, but activity in the world as such does not have an intrinsic significance for the ultimate goal. It is obvious that this attitude could only intensify the gap between Protestantism and the proletariat; for it is characteristic of the proletariat that its fervor is directed forward, creating a will to change the world. This is by no means an accidental, capricious tendency. It is rather a necessity inextricably bound up with the class struggle. In the face of the social situation of the proletariat, individual piety has only relative significance and even becomes unimportant. This holds even for questions like those of individual destiny, individual guilt, and even individual death. However effective the presentation of such questions may be, it is very hard to turn the eyes of the proletariat from the forward to the upward direction. Every attempt of this kind is felt as an attempt to divert attention from the political fight and as such is resisted.

The liberal interpretation of the Protestant principle is in accord with the proletarian outlook in so far as it is based on the autonomous attitude which is natural for proletarian thinking. The rigor of the scientific method in its historical research assures to theological liberalism the interest of educated humanists as well as the esteem of the proletariat (in so far as the latter comes into touch with these questions at all).

And yet this type of Protestantism has not become an effective way of bringing together Protestantism and the proletariat. So long as liberalism remains bound to the humanistic ideal of personality, it cannot influence the masses. The ideal of the religious personality is unsuited for the thinking of the proletariat. Protestantism in all its forms has emphasized the conscious religious personality, his intellectual understanding and his moral decisions. It has become a "theology of consciousness" in analogy to the Cartesian philosophy of consciousness. Even religious feeling, as emphasized by pietism and romanticism, remained in the sphere of consciousness. This had a double consequence. The personality was cut off from the vital basis of its existence. Religion was reserved for the conscious center of man. The subconscious levels remained untouched, empty, or suppressed, while the conscious side was overburdened with the continuous ultimate decisions it had to make. It is not by chance that in Protestant countries the breakdown of the conscious personality has occurred on such a large scale that the psychoanalytic return to the unconscious became a social necessity. A religion that does not appeal to the subconscious basis of all decisions is untenable in the long run and can never become a religion for the masses. The other consequence of the emphasis on the "religious personality" is the isolation of the religious individual. It was especially the Calvinistic type of Protestantism that worked in this direction, alienating the masses who need supra-individual symbols and institutions. Catholicism was much more able to satisfy this need and, consequently, to keep proletarian masses under its sway. But more successful than both the Christian churches was Marxism, whose most important function was to give the despairing, chaotic, empty masses of early capitalism symbols that grasped their unconscious as well as their consciousness, institutions that conquered the atomistic solitude of the individual within the mass, and a myth that created faith, hope, and a fighting community. Protestantism, in order to continue this trend in the future mass society, must transform itself in this point more than in any other one.

With the disappearance of the Catholic hierarchy, Protestantism had to depend upon worldly "hierarchies" for its realization. Luther's decision in connection with the Peasants' Revolt made it a permanent necessity for Lutheranism to depend upon absolutism and to repudiate democratic revolutionary tendencies. Among the Calvinists matters developed quite differently. Very early there came about an alliance of Protestantism, which was fighting for its existence, with the middle classes, who were struggling for their economic independence. In this way there arose, on Lutheran soil, the connection of Protestantism with the patriarchal form of social life and on Reformed soil its connection with the capitalist-liberal form of society. The former is more characteristic of central Europe and the latter of western Europe and America. But in both forms it produced an antagonism to the proletariat. This was due to the fact that after the breakdown of the episcopal power the churches of the Reformation became dependent either on the absolute state and the political groups that controlled it or on the dominant forces in the bourgeois society. This was unavoidable, but it made an appreciation of the revolutionary proletariat by the Protestant churches practically impossible.

It is extremely difficult for most of the exponents of the Protestant churches to detect this sociological conditioning. They imagine that official or private declarations of neutrality will be sufficient to make the church and the groups supporting the church really neutral; they fail to recognize the power of those social realities that exercise an influence quite contrary to what people may think or wish; these social realities, consciously or unconsciously, condition action as well as thought. The old claim, for example, that the churches have taken a neutral attitude toward the farm-labor problem was pure ideology, a definitely "false consciousness." Every aspect of the farm laborer's life showed him that this claim was not true and that the church was on the side of the landowners. It was, therefore, only a short step to the complete estrangement of the farm laborers from the church after they became an urban proletariat. The opportunity that arose for German Protestantism after World War I to become detached from the state has not been utilized up to the present. Lutheranism has maintained its old connection with the groups that were in control in the pre-war monarchy. The church has even supported the conservative opposition to a state in which the proletariat had gained certain positions of power. The only change that has occurred is the rise of religious socialism, which, on the whole, has been tolerated by the Protestant churches, albeit with more or less hostility. The religious socialists have set for themselves the goal of freeing Protestantism from the sociological attachments resulting from its antiproletarian past.

Connected with all this is Protestantism's almost complete surrender to the nationalistic ideology. Only when the pagan basis of nationalism was openly expressed by various groups in recent years did a slight reaction against "the myth of the nation" appear. Yet the old bonds between church and national state are still so strong that Protestantism mostly sides with those groups that have made the name "nationalist" into a party slogan. Only rarely has it been recognized by Protestant leaders to what an extent the name "national" has become an ideology, that is, a conscious or unconscious concealment of the drive for power of certain economic and political pressure groups. This almost unqualified support of the "nationalist" ideology by the Protestant churches obstructs the coming-together of the church and the proletariat.

One basic demand upon Protestantism arises from what has been said above. Protestantism under the stress of the proletarian situation must decide for the Protestant principle as against historical Protestantism. The demand should not be made that Protestants subscribe unconditionally to socialism; rather the demand should be that Protestantism subject all its decisions and activities to the criterion of the Protestant principle in the face of the disturbing and transforming reality of the proletarian situation. Protestantism should take socialism seriously as an expression of the proletarian situation. Not that every individual Protestant should become a socialist, but the individual Protestant should realize that against his will he transforms Protestantism, Christianity, and religion into an ideology; that he serves the "man-made God" of his social group, class, or nation, when he does not take seriously the reality of the proletarian situation as decisive for the future development of Protestantism. The proletarian situation is not something optional to which attention may or may not be given. It is rather the point at which history itself has posed the question to Protestantism, whether it will identify itself with the traditional forms in which it has been realized, or whether it will accept the challenge that confronts it in the situation of the proletarian masses and that calls in question a large part of its present-day life and thought.

# IV. PROTESTANTISM

# Chapter XII

## THE WORD OF RELIGION

### I

IF RELIGION had no word for us in this time, it would have no word at all worth listening to. And if religion had only the word everybody has—every newspaper, every radio, every speaker—if religion simply followed the general trend of public opinion, it would have no word at all worth listening to. If religion gave only a little more enthusiasm, a little more certainty, a little more dignity to something that would be done anyhow, with or without religion, then religion would have no significance at all for the present situation or for any other situation. If religion ceased to be the spiritual sword, cutting through all human enthusiasms and certainties and dignities, judging them, transforming them, transcending them—then religion would be swallowed up by the general process of civilization and should disappear as soon as possible as a useless and disturbing nuisance.

Religion has very often been nothing more than the superfluous consecration of some situation or action which was neither judged nor transformed by this consecration. Religion has consecrated the feudal order and its own participation in it without transcending it. Religion has consecrated nationalism without transforming it. Religion has consecrated democracy without judging it. Religion has consecrated war and the arms of war without using its spiritual arms against war. Religion has consecrated peace and the security of peace without disturbing this security with its spiritual threat. Religion has consecrated the bourgeois ideal of family and property without judging it and has consecrated systems of exploitation of men by men without transcending them; on the contrary, it has used them for its own benefit.

The first word, therefore, to be spoken by religion to the people of our time must be a word spoken against religion. It is the word the old Jewish prophets spoke against the priestly and royal and pseudo-prophetic guardians of their national religion, who consecrated distorted institutions and distorted politics without judging them. The same word must be spoken today about our religious institutions and politics. Will religion in this country, in this moment of history, simply follow the trend of events, the way public opinion runs, the direction in which the makers of public opinion want us to move? Will religion, after it has consecrated a self-complacent and egoistic enthusiasm for peace, consecrate a self-intoxication with war? Will religion in our situation transcend our situation or not?

A word can be spoken by religion to the people of our time only if it is a transcending and therefore a judging and transforming word. Otherwise, religion would become another contributor to what is accepted anyhow, another servant of public opinion, which in some cases is a tyrant as terrorizing as any personal tyrant. If our religion is able to transcend all this, in which direction must it do so?

There are two lines by which the meaning of human existence can be symbolized: the vertical and the horizontal, the first one pointing to the eternal meaning as such, the second to the temporal realization of the eternal meaning. Every religion necessarily has both directions, although different religions overemphasize the one or the other. The mystical element which belongs to all religion is symbolized by the vertical line; the active element which also belongs to all religion is symbolized by the horizontal line. If religion is to speak a transcending, judging, and transforming word to the people of our time, it must do so in both directions, the vertical as well as the horizontal, and this in mutual interdependence.

The first line, the vertical one, symbolizes the attitude of "in spite of" and points to what we may call the "religious reservation." While the second line, the horizontal one, symbolizes the attitude of "because of" and points to what we may call the "religious obligation." In both directions religion has important things to say with respect to the present situation.

## II

History is the sphere in which man *determines himself* in freedom. And history, at the same time, is the sphere in which man *is determined* by fate against his freedom. Very often the creations of his freedom are the tools used by fate against him; as, for instance, today the technical powers created by him turn against him with irresistible force. There are periods in history in which the element of freedom is predominant;

and there are periods in which fate and necessity prevail. The latter is true of our day. In the moment in which (with the wilful help of the ruling classes in all countries) the power of the dictators was firmly established and the decisive step in the catastrophic self-destruction of the liberal system of life was taken, a period of prevailing necessity began.

In a period like this, in which individual destiny no longer counts, in which the value of human life is as low as it was three hundred years ago in the religious wars of self-destruction; in a period like this in which, in practically all countries of the world, insecurity has become as predominant as it was in the most primitive stages of human development and in which the feeling of meaninglessness in millions of people brings about social and personal insanity in ever increasing amount; in a period like this, in which the law of tragedy turns the attempts to strengthen the good into a strengthening of the evil (as we have experienced with respect to the struggle against war in the Anglo-Saxon countries or with respect to nationalism in the dictatorial countries)—in such a period, the emphasis on the horizontal line, on what we could do and should do, has lost its power because everybody feels that whatever we do, however good it may be, will directly or indirectly confirm a historical destiny which shows us its destructive side and hides from us its constructive power.

But, even if the creative possibilities in the catastrophes of our day were more apparent than they are, they would not concern the victims of these catastrophes in their immediate existence, in their quest for happiness, in their longing for meaning and fulfilment. The people of our day must be enabled to say "in spite of," they must be taught to find for themselves the religious reservation which cannot be conquered by the tragedy of history. It is hard to find it, but it must be found if cynicism and despair are not to prevail as they do now, driving the masses into the hands of agitators, driving the strong to the glorification of heroic self-destruction and the weak to the loss of all meaning of life and to suicide.

The human soul cannot maintain itself without the vertical line, the knowledge of an eternal meaning, however this may be expressed in mythological or theological terms. If the people of our day are no longer able to say "in spite of," they will not resist the terrible impact of the historical catastrophe on their minds. If we no longer understand the words of the psalmist, that the loss of body and life and of earth and heaven cannot deprive him of the ultimate meaning of his life—or if we no longer feel what the poet means when he says that all our running, all our striving, is eternal rest in God the Lord—if all this has become strange and unreal to us, then we have lost the power of facing reality without cynicism and despair.

But are the churches and religious groups prepared to speak this word of the vertical line, the "in spite of," the religious reservation, to the people of our time? Or have they forgotten the vertical line entirely? Looking at the prevailing type of the religious life in this country, we might assume that this is the case, that there is no more pointing to the religious reservation but only moral demand, humanitarian activity, and political partisanship. However this may be—and certainly it is not entirely this way—religion's demand on man stands: namely, that man be not only *in* history but also *above* history. And, since this demand is valid and represents the first word that religion must say to the people of our time, it may transform the methods and institutions of our religious life in a very radical way. The sooner this happens, the better. This country is still in a preliminary stage with respect to our historic tragedy. It still has time. The horizontal line has still much of its splendor and attractiveness. The quest for a religious reservation has not yet force enough to reshape our religious consciousness.

But religious leaders should foresee the coming and prepare themselves for it. *The usual question, "What shall we do?" must be answered with the unusual question, "Whence can we receive?"* People must understand again that one cannot do much without having received much. Religion is, first, an open hand to receive a gift and, second, an acting hand to distribute gifts. Without coming from the religious reservation, carrying with us something eternal, we are of no use in working for the religious obligation to transform the temporal.


### III

Of course we are not asked to enter the religious reservation in order to stay in it. The vertical line must become dynamic and actual in the horizontal line; the attitude of "in spite of" must become the driving power in an attitude of "because of." What is the word of religion to the people of our time in this respect? Must it say a word at all? Or is the tremendous trend of activism in the attitude of America today a sufficient guaranty for the fulfilment of the religious obligation? Obviously, after everything I have said, the answer must be "No." Activism as such cannot overcome the law of tragedy, and especially not if it has the character of escapism, the attempt, namely, to escape the feeling of meaninglessness and emptiness with respect to the eternal. And no keen observer of American religious and secular life can overlook this hidden element of flight from one's self implied in all kinds of humanitarian and political activities. The horizontal line becomes empty and distorted if it is not united continuously with the vertical line. This is manifested in two ways of dealing with the religious obligation toward history: one is a shortsighted opportunism, the other a self-deceiving utopianism. Against both these attitudes religion must speak its word to the people of our time. The present situation provides abundant examples of both attitudes.

Let us start with a very recent instance of what I have called "opportunism." I mean the opportunism of the ruling classes in the democratic countries which made the rise of the dictators possible, kept them in power, sacrificed to them first the democratic minorities in their own countries and then one country after the other, including the struggling democracy in Spain. Everybody knows this today, and it was terribly disturbing when the Englishman, Norman Angell, told us that in the very hour in which he was speaking his countrymen were digging the corpses of their children out of the wreckage of their London houses because they had not cared at all about the corpses of the Chinese children in their wreckages a year earlier. Religious obligation, first of all, includes the practical acknowledgment of the unity of all men, expressed in oriental wisdom by the assertion that the other is thou.

But the point I want to make above all—and the one I think religion must make today in this country—is that America, if she takes responsibility for the present world catastrophe, must take it completely and with the full knowledge of what it means. It does not mean defending America against the dictators, it does not mean defeating Hitler, it does not mean conquering Germany a second time: it means accepting her share of responsibility for the future structure of Europe and consequently for the whole world. Whatever happens during the later years of the war, any victory will be won on the physical and moral ruins of Europe. It would be a cynical opportunism if America helped to augment those ruins without being ready and able to build something radically new on them. If this country will not look beyond the day of victory, that day will become the birthday of another defeat of all human values and noble aims.

The word that religion has to speak to this nation and to all those who fight with her is the grave question: Are you willing, are you able, to take upon you the full weight of the task before you? If not, keep away from it; do not follow the cause of an easy opportunism, the twin-sister of an easy utopianism. Overcome both of them before you act. Otherwise, the action of this country will increase the destruction of Europe and lead finally to self-destruction. Religion can overcome opportunism because it can overcome utopianism.

The amount of utopianism in this country, as in most countries after the first World War, is even greater than the amount of opportunism. In the crusading slogans of 1917, in the progressive mood of the 1920's, in the humanism and pacifism of the last decades, a disturbing number of illusions were cultivated and destroyed. Religion, perhaps, could have prevented these illusions and disillusionments about human nature and the nature of history. But religion itself had been driven into an illusory attitude.

It had nearly forgotten the religious reservation, the vertical line, and had dedicated its force to the religious obligation, the horizontal line alone. It had consecrated progressivistic utopianism instead of judging and transcending it. Now the time has come when people would despise religion if it had nothing more to say to them than a word of praise and glorification of the greatness and divinity of man and history. They would call it ideology or lie and turn away toward cynicism and despair. This is already true of a large group in the younger generation, and it is the greatest danger for religion as well as for civilization.

Religion must teach youth something they cannot hear anywhere else —to give themselves with an absolute seriousness and a complete devotion to an aim that in itself is fragmentary and ambiguous. Everything we do in history has this fragmentary and ambiguous character; everything is subject to the law of historical tragedy. But religion, although knowing this, does not retire from history; religion, although pronouncing the tragic destiny of all human truth and goodness, works with unrestricted devotion to the good and the true. Such a message is not simple, but, on the other hand, it is not illusory. It is realistic but not pessimistic; it is knowing but not despairing. It breaks utopianism, but it does not break hope. Hope is the opposite of utopianism. Utopianism necessarily will be destroyed. Hope never dies, because it is the application of the venturing "in spite of" to the tragedy of historical action. Hope unites the vertical and the horizontal lines, the religious reservation and the religious obligation. Therefore, the ultimate word that religion must say to the people of our time is the word of hope.

I do not make concrete suggestions about possible political actions in the name of religion. This is impossible, and it never should be tried. Religion as such could not say whether this country should go into war, and religion as such cannot suggest war aims or social reforms. Religion can give and must give the basis of such decisions; it can give and must give the ultimate criteria of such decisions. The word of religion to the people of our time is not the word of political or economic experts, but it is, if it is a religious word, the word of those who know something about man and history; who know the tragedy and the hope involved in the temporal because they know about the eternal; who know the character and the limits of the religious obligations because they come to it in the power and the wisdom of the religious reservation.

# Chapter XIII

## THE PROTESTANT MESSAGE AND THE
## MAN OF TODAY

### I. THE MAN OF TODAY

THE man of today, with whom this discussion is concerned, is not simply the man who happens to be a member of our generation but rather the man whose whole outlook is molded by the present cultural situation and who, in turn, determines, preserves, or transforms it. If we wish to characterize him in a very general way, we may describe him as the man who, on a Christian background that has been qualified by Protestantism, has built an autonomous culture and lives in it, influencing it and being influenced by it. He is the man who consciously carries within himself humanism and the Renaissance, idealism and romanticism, realism and expressionism, as elements of his own intellectual character. This man is, even if he may by actual count be in the minority, the decisive spiritual type of our day. The tensions of his life represent a creative energy that is active in all the spheres of life.

If we look closer to determine his particular characteristics, we must say: *he is the autonomous man who has become insecure in his autonomy.* A symptom of this insecurity is that the man of today no longer possesses a world view in the sense of a body of assured convictions about God, the world, and himself. The feeling of security in a system of theoretical and practical ideas about the meaning of his life and of life in general has gone. Even as recently as two decades ago, our literature was full of discussions concerning the modern world view or dealing with the conflicts between the various tendencies within it. Nothing more of this is to be seen. Only the pieces of former world views are to be found now. Idealism, for instance, concentrates on questions concerning education and has become embodied in movements like neohumanism. But none of the neohumanists has developed a philosophy which, in comparison with German classical idealism, could be called an integrated world view or even a convincing in-

192

terpretation of human life. Neohumanism has remained a quest without fulfilment. While neither Marx himself nor the main representatives of Marxism accepted metaphysical materialism (Marx attacked it in his *Theses against Feuerbach* as a bourgeois ideology), popular Marxism has largely confused the so-called "historical materialism" with a materialistic world view. But nobody who would deserve to be called a "man of today" accepts such a metaphysics.

It would be inadequate to call certain other attempts to penetrate into the riddle of existence "world views." I refer to the so-called "philosophy of life" whose most brilliant representative was Nietzsche and which has a large group of adherents in Germany and France; or to the philosophy of the unconscious, initiated by Freud, whose influence is growing daily; or to the philosophical and theological movements determined by the rediscovery of Kierkegaard. They all contribute to the destruction of the old world views more than to the building of a new one. They are powerful just because they are not world views. Modern man is without a world view, and just because of this he has the feeling of having come closer to reality and of having confronted the problematic aspects of his existence more profoundly than is possible for the man who conceals these problematic aspects of life by means of a world view.

Obviously, the man of today takes the same attitude toward the message of the churches as he takes toward the autonomous philosophies. He opposes it though not as the representative of one world view attempting to overcome another one; he sees in it problems and solutions that are in part outmoded but in part significant even for our day. He treats the religious doctrines neither worse nor better than he does the interpretations of the world and life from which he takes his spiritual descent and which he has left behind him—perhaps rather better than worse, for he finds in them more recognition of the mystery of life than he does in much autonomous philosophy. But he is not yet ready to abandon autonomy. He still stands in the autonomous tradition of recent centuries. But his situation is different from that of former generations in that he no longer possesses an autonomy in which he is self-assured and creative; rather he possesses one that leaves him disturbed, frustrated, and often in despair. It is understandable that some churches have used this situation for an appeal to the people of today to return to the authority and the tradition of the churches. This is especially true of the Roman Catholic church; in this view the last act of autonomy should be self-surrender to heteronomy.

## II. THE CATHOLIC CHURCH AND THE MAN OF TODAY

In such a situation the Catholic church is naturally in a favored position, for it alone is consistently heteronomous. It alone has an unbroken tradition and authority. Consequently, the Catholic church has a great attraction for the man of our day; and it has also a strong sense of triumph in the face of his broken autonomy. This is due not only to the fact that autonomy is shattered but also to a sense of the spiritual "substance" resident in tradition and authority. When the individual possesses free decision concerning things and occurrences around him, he loses his immediate connection with their meaning. The gift of freedom, including religious freedom, is paid for by a loss in living substance. The loss of spiritual substance since the end of the Middle Ages, both intellectual and religious, has been tremendous; and some day the substance might become completely exhausted. Few are the springs of life that are left and that are uncontested. The springs of the past are almost exhausted—the substance has almost wasted away.

The Catholic church, however, has manifestly been able to preserve a genuine substance that continues to exist, although it is encased within an ever hardening crust. But whenever the hardness and crust are broken through and the substance becomes visible, it exercises a peculiar fascination; then we see what was once the life-substance and inheritance of us all and what we have now lost, and a deep yearning awakens in us for the departed youth of our culture.

It is not surprising that the Catholic church exercises a powerful influence upon the modern man, since it both provides an emancipation from the burden of autonomous responsibility and offers to the man of today the age-old life-substance that was once his. Much more striking is the fact that this influence is not *more* powerful, that the church's sense of triumph is not more clearly borne out by the facts, and that, instead, the number of conversions to Protestantism is always on the increase rather than on the decrease. It is especially surprising that the spokesmen for modern man, on the whole withstand so well the temptation to sacrifice an autonomy that has become feeble and hollow. One cannot dismiss this situation with the explanation that the petrifying of the Catholic church and the mechanizing of her hierarchical apparatus obstruct access to her. But, if these structures were recognized as valuable and necessary, they would be an inducement to men of creative power to break away the crust. Nor does the explanation suffice that the strongly Latin coloration of Catholicism weakens its appeal to the Anglo-Saxon, Teutonic north. In Latin countries the opposition to it is usually stronger than in the northern countries. The situation is rather that the man who enjoys autonomy—however feeble and empty it may be—has experienced something that he cannot easily surrender even if he wished to respond to the appeal of the Catholic church. This "something" which unites the Protestants and those who live in secular autonomy must be examined and understood. Upon it depends the religious and also the intellectual integrity of our day.

### III. THE HUMAN "BOUNDARY-SITUATION"

It is the awareness of the human "boundary-situation" or of the ultimate threat to human existence that prevents the modern man from surrendering to heteronomy. The first element in Protestantism is and must always be the proclaiming of the human boundary-situation, of the ultimate threat confronting human existence. And the modern man is ready, in the brokenness of his autonomy, to give heed to this message and to reaffirm it in the face of the temptation of many offers of religious or nonreligious safety.

In speaking here of the Protestant element in Protestantism we mean to imply that this is not the only element in Protestantism. Protestantism is not *only* Protestantism, it is also—and first of all—Christianity. It is also and above all the bearer and mediator of the "New Being" manifest in Jesus as the Christ. It is also imbued with a spiritual substance, discernible by everyone who knows genuine Protestant piety and unbroken Protestant Christianity. It is a reality that flows through the veins of all the peoples nurtured by Protestantism, although it is mixed with much other blood. Even if the idea of a church that actually determines the morals and world view of the whole nation is only a hope (or an empty claim), this influence is present and working among the Protestant peoples, and it ought not to be overlooked, as it so often is. Almost all creations of modern autonomous culture show traces of the Protestant spirit. As we have said,

Protestantism is, above all, Christianity. It has never wished to be any-thing else, and (in Germany) the Protestant churches prefer to call themselves "Evangelical" rather than Protestant. But the name "Prot-estantism" has, nevertheless, remained and has been transformed from a political into a religious concept. It represents the characteristic element of this manifestation of the Christian substance.

The Protestant element in Protestantism is the radical proclamation of the human border-situation and the protest against all attempts, through religious expedients, to evade it, even though this evasion be accomplished with the aid of all the richness and depth and breadth of mystical and sacramental piety.

Protestantism was born out of the struggle for the doctrine of justi-fication by faith. This idea is strange to the man of today and even to Protestant people in the churches; indeed, as I have over and over again had the opportunity to learn, it is so strange to the modern man that there is scarcely any way of making it intelligible to him. And yet this doctrine of justification by faith has divided the old unity of Christendom; has torn asunder Europe, and especially Germany; has made innumerable martyrs; has kindled the bloodiest and most ter-rible wars of the past; and has deeply affected European history and with it the history of humanity. This whole complex of ideas which for more than a century—not so very long ago—was discussed in every household and workshop, in every market and country inn of Germany, is now scarcely understandable even to our most intelligent scholars. We have here a breaking-down of tradition that has few parallels. And we should not imagine that it will be possible in some simple fashion to leap over this gulf and resume our connection with the Reformation again. It seems to me that the theological attempts which have been made in this direction and which we may subsume un-der the slogan "the Luther Renaissance," have more significance in their academic aspects than in their effect upon the contemporary religious situation. There is in the educated groups a complete alienation from Luther and in the proletariat a determined hostility to him. Hence, what we should do is to discover anew the reality which was appre-hended in that earlier day and which is the same today, and then present it in new terms to the man of today. For this reason, then, we speak of the boundary-situation of man and assert that those struggles which at one time split a continent in two, so far from being struggles about backwoods problems, as Nietzsche says of Luther's ef-forts, were struggles bearing upon the human problem in general, the problem of the human boundary-situation.

The human boundary-situation is encountered when human possi-bility reaches its limit, when human existence is confronted by an ultimate threat. This is not the case in death. Death may, to be sure, point toward the boundary-situation; but it does not do so necessarily, and death is not itself the boundary-situation. This is the reason that we feel death cannot give release from despair. The spiritual cleavage that is experienced in despair is not eliminated with the cessation of bodily existence. The boundary-situation that is encountered in de-spair, threatens man on another level than that of bodily existence. Anyone who knows the threat that lurks in the roots of his own being knows that the idea of death brings no relief. He knows that he may, so to speak, take despair into death with him. This is true, regardless of how he thinks about "after death" or regardless of whether he thinks of it at all.

The border-situation of man is possible because he is not identical with his vital existence. It is possible because man as man stands above his vital existence, because he has in a sense broken away from his vital existence. To be a man involves this transcending of vital existence, the freedom from himself, the freedom to say "Yes" or "No" to his vital existence. This freedom, which is an essential part of him and from which he cannot escape, carries with it the fact that he is radically threatened. Man is in a genuine sense the threatened creature because he is not bound to his vital existence, because he can say "Yes" and "No" to it. This is manifest in the fact that man can raise the question of the true and that he can demand the fulfilment of the good. Anyone who raises a question about *true* reality is in some way separated from reality; whoever makes a demand upon reality presupposes that it is not at hand. Man *must* raise the question, however, and *must* make the de-mand; he cannot escape this fate, that is, the fate of being man. If he did not wish to raise the question, his not doing it would itself be an answer to the question. If he did not choose to make a demand, his not making it would be obedience to a demand. Man always acts, even when inaction is the content of his action. And man always makes his decisions in the exercise of his freedom, even when the escape from freedom is the content of his decision. This inevitability of freedom, of having to make decisions, creates the deep restlessness of our existence; through it our existence is threatened.

The inescapable element in freedom would not be a threat to us if it ultimately made no difference for our existence which way we decide. To live in freedom, however, means that it is not a matter of indifference; it means that we must accept the unconditional demand to realize the true and to actualize the good. If this demand is not fulfilled—and it is not—our existence is driven into discord, into the hidden agony that infects all life, and even death cannot free us from it. Wherever this situation is experienced in its unconditional and inescapable character, the human border-situation is encountered. The point at which not-being in the ultimate sense threatens us is the boundary line of all human possibility, the human border-situation.

The seriousness of the human situation can, to be sure, be covered over or weakened by our relying upon truth that we have already achieved or upon demands already fulfilled, thus evading the unconditional threat. This is a possibility that is always present; in one way or another all of us try to make this escape. Absolute seriousness can be attributed only to the man who scorns this possibility of escape, who views his whole existence from the point of view of the border-situation, and who knows, therefore, that his existence can at no time and in no way be made secure, neither through his submerging himself in the vital life-process, through intellectual or spiritual activity, through sacraments, through mysticism and asceticism, through right belief or strenuous piety, nor through anything that belongs to the mundane substance of religion. The seriousness and force of Old Protestantism is evident from the fact that it did not try through priests and church and sacraments to evade the ultimate threat of the border-situation. In contrast to this, mystical-sacramental religion easily gives the impression of lacking seriousness, of presuming to possess a human guaranty against the ultimate threat to everything human. The lesser importance which the Protestant attributes to the church, to the service of worship, and to the religious sphere in general is at bottom bound up with this awareness of living on the boundary, a boundary that involves the limit not only of secular but also of all religious possibilities. Because religion and the church are in themselves no guaranty to the Protestant and must not be allowed to become such, he confronts them with the same independence with which

he confronts every other human possibility, not with the proud independence of one who makes himself superior to everything else but
rather with the independence of one who finds himself in a situation
in which he shares the lot of everything human to be subject to the
ultimate threat of not-being. It is not a question of convictions or of
the opposition between individual and common conviction; it is rather
a question of being and not-being on the deepest level of man's existence. Perhaps Catholicism is right in thinking that the religious
substance is better preserved in an authoritarian community. But certainly Catholicism is wrong in thinking that Protestantism is to be
explained as an attempt of the individual to become himself the bearer
of the religious substance. It is rather the boundary-situation that is
involved, a situation in which the religious substance with all its
richness and depth and traditional wisdom is recognized as inadequate
if it is supposed to provide security in face of the ultimate threat. On
this plane alone is the opposition between the two Christian confessions to be understood, not on the basis of the clash between subjectivism and ecclesiastical allegiance. The choice lies between either the
radical acceptance of the boundary-situation or the attempt by means
of church and sacrament to secure man against the unconditioned
threat.

IV. THE PROTESTANT CHURCH AND THE HUMAN BOUNDARY-SITUATION

It is clear that a church that stands in this place, or rather at this
border line of any and every place, must be something quite different
from the churches that refuse to be disturbed in their spiritual possession. Such a church must subject itself to a radical criticism and eliminate everything that diminishes the weight of the border-situation—
the sacrament that works magically and thus circumvents the ultimate threat; the mysticism that is supposed to effect immediate unity
with the unconditional and thus escape the ultimate threat; the priest-
craft that purports to transmit a spiritual guaranty that is not subject
to the insecurity of man's existence; the ecclesiastical authority that
claims to be in possession of a truth that no longer stands under the
threat of error; the cultus that gives ecstatic fulfilment and veils over
the unfulfilled character of the divine demand. It is clear that a
church that stands in this position, where not an inch of self-provided
security remains, should inevitably tend to become empty of substance,

impotent in its social reality, secular because of its surrender of all places, things, men, and actions supposed to be holy in themselves. It is clear that such a church has the tendency in itself to become nothing more than an almost amorphous group of men, of secular men without sacramental quality, through whom from generation to generation the consciousness of the human boundary-situation is transmitted. It is clear that such a church would abandon its own character if it should imitate the sacramental type of churches either in cultus or in priestly authority, in doctrine or in spiritual direction. Where it yields to this temptation, it becomes only a weak imitation of those powerful creations. Its power lies elsewhere. It is the power whose symbol has in the past been the cross, for in the cross humanity experienced the human boundary-situation as never before and never after. In this power—indeed, in this impotence and poverty—the Protestant church will stand so long as it is aware of the meaning of its own existence.

The Protestant church is always in danger of forgetting its meaning. Its greatest downfall has been its claim that it has, by virtue of "pure doctrine," become the invulnerable possessor of the truth. It has not understood that to stand at the boundary means to stand not only in unrighteousness but also in error. It has imagined that it held the truth as though it were a possession encased in the letter of Scripture and properly dispensed in the doctrine of the church. In claiming unambiguously to possess the truth and the pure doctrine, it has denied the boundary-situation and thereby its own meaning and power. And then it came about that, just when it no longer questioned itself, it was questioned from the outside radically and destructively. The autonomous culture has, piece by piece, broken down the assumedly untouchable possession of the church, and the church has been forced into a movement of retreat, in which everything that had seemed to be certain has had to be surrendered. The present situation of the church is such that no part of its old possession is any longer secure. But in this very situation some people in the church have come to realize that its task is not the defense of a religious domain but the proclamation of the boundary-situation in which every secular and religious domain is put in question. The attitude of defense has been abandoned. Attack takes the place of defense; but not with the aim of winning back the lost possession, not in the attitude of a hierarchical will to power (as the talk about "the century of the church" suggests), but rather with the aim of driving to the boundary-situation everything that makes an ultimate claim, cultures as well as religions. The Protestant church does not have the mission to fight in the arena of struggling world views. It must fight from above this level to bring everything under judgment and promise.

If what we have said at the outset is true, namely, that the man of today has an understanding of the ultimate threat to the human situation, he should be able to comprehend the message of the Protestant church, provided that it is presented with reference to this situation. This obviously forbids that the message should be set forth in the terminology of the Reformation or in the ways prevailing in the Protestant church today.

Indeed, the biblical terminology itself, including the term "justification," may become more understandable out of the experience of the boundary-situation. "Righteousness" was the Old Testament word that Paul, and after him Luther, used in order to express the unconditional demand that stands over man as man. Righteousness is something that everyone who has stood in the boundary-situation knows he does not have. He knows that human freedom inescapably involves him in human ambiguity, in that mixture of truth and falsehood, of righteousness and unrighteousness, which all human life exhibits. Luther, the young monk, stood in the depth of this boundary-situation and dared to reject all safeguards that piety and the church wished to extend to him. He remained in it and learned in it that just this and only this is the situation in which the divine "Yes" over the whole of human existence can be received; for this "Yes" is not founded on any human achievement, it is an unconditional and free sovereign judgment from above human possibilities.

This experience of the boundary-situation has been expressed with the help of rabbinical, Roman, and scholastic concepts. The "justification of the unrighteous or of the unbeliever," the "pardon of the guilty," "the absolution of the condemned," "justification without works through faith alone"—these are metaphors, partly questionable and partly no longer intelligible. As more or less adequate terms they do not concern us. But the thing itself which they referred to and which is always real does concern us: the threat to human existence and the "Yes" over it where this threat is recognized.

The man of today is aware of the human ambiguity of which we have spoken. He is aware of the confusion of his inner life, the cleavage in his behavior, the demonic forces in his psychic and social existence. And he senses that not only his being but also his knowing is thrown into confusion, that he lacks ultimate truth, and that he faces, especially in the social life of our day, a conscious, almost demonic, distortion of truth. In this situation in which most of the traditional values and forms of life are disintegrating, he often is driven to the abyss of complete meaninglessness, which is full of both horror and fascination. He also knows that this situation is not the result of a mechanical necessity but of a destiny which implies freedom and guilt. In being aware of all this, the man of today is near the boundary-situation that Protestantism proclaims.

### V. THE PROTESTANT MESSAGE

Now it can be said what the Protestant message for the man of today must be and what it cannot be.

The Protestant message cannot be a direct proclamation of religious truths as they are given in the Bible and in tradition, for the situation of the modern man of today is precisely one of doubt about all this and about the Protestant church itself. The Christian doctrines, even the most central ones—God and Christ, church and revelation—are radically questioned and offer occasion for a continuous fight among theologians as well as among nontheologians. They cannot in this form be the message of the church to our time. So long as the genuine representatives of the Protestant message do not understand this, their work is entirely hopeless in the widest circles and especially among the proletarian masses. It cannot be required of the man of today that he first accept theological truths, even though they should be God and Christ. Wherever the church in its message makes this a primary demand, it does not take seriously the situation of the man of today and has no effective defense against the challenge of many thoughtful men of our day who reject the message of the church as of no concern for them. The modern man might well say to the church, using her own language: "God does not demand that man, in order to experience the unconditional judgment, the 'No' and the 'Yes' from above himself, shall first accept a religious tenet about God or shall overcome all doubt concerning him." This sort of legalism lays upon man no less heavy a burden than legalism in morals. The one, like the other, is broken through by the radically conceived doctrine of justification. The profoundest aspect of justification, in our situation and for the man of today, is that we can discern God at the very moment when all known assertions about "God" have lost their power.

The message of the Protestant church must take a threefold form. First, it must insist upon the radical experience of the boundary-situation; it must destroy the secret reservations harbored by the modern man which prevent him from accepting resolutely the limits of his human existence. Among these reservations are the residues of the shattered world views, idealistic and materialistic. The recognition of our situation as indicated by the word "ideology" should alone be a sufficient warning against these doubtful securities. We have learned that philosophical systems often represent the working of subconscious powers, psychological or sociological, which drive in a direction quite different from their conscious meaning. This judgment applies also to the unbroken belief in scientific method as the certain way to truth, which is usually not the attitude of the great scientists but of their half-philosophical popularizers. (Science itself is quite conscious of the crisis of its foundations, in mathematics as well as in physics, in biology as well as in psychology.) This judgment applies also to the pedagogical claim to transform society and to shape personalities. It has become abundantly clear that education as a method presupposes a content, a spiritual substance, to which it must introduce people but which it cannot itself create. The judgment applies to the political creeds, whether they glorify a past tradition or a coming utopia, whether they believe in revolution or reaction or progress. The old traditions have disintegrated; the process has been replaced by horrible relapses; and the utopias have created continuous mass disappointments. The judgment applies to the nationalistic ideologies whose demonic implications have become more and more visible, and it applies to the cosmopolitan superstructure which is envisaged either by pacifistic idealism or by imperialistic will to power. It applies to the recent attempts of all forms of therapeutic psychology to form secure personalities by technical methods which, in spite of their profundity and revolutionary power, are unable to give a spiritual center and ultimate meaning to life. It applies to the widespread activistic flight into job, profession, economic competition, humanitarian activity, as means of escaping the threat of the boundary-situation. The judgment applies to the neoreligious movements offering spiritual security, such as the new forms of mysticism and occultism, will-therapy, etc., which, whatever their merits may be, tend to hide the seriousness of the boundary-situation and to create fanaticism and arrogance. And, finally, the Protestant message should unveil the last, most refined, and most intellectual security of the modern man when he aesthetically dramatizes his shattered state; when, Narcissus-like, he contemplates himself in this situation as in a mirror, sometimes tragically; when he, thus, artfully but self-destructively protects himself from the experience of the boundary-situation. Against all this stands the Protestant message; this is its first function.

Second, the Protestant church must pronounce the "Yes" that comes to man in the boundary-situation when he takes it upon himself in its ultimate seriousness. Protestantism must proclaim the judgment that brings assurance by depriving us of all security; the judgment that declares us whole in the disintegration and cleavage of soul and community; the judgment that affirms our having truth in the very absence of truth (even of religious truth); the judgment that reveals the meaning of our life in the situation in which all the meaning of life has disappeared. This is the pith and essence of the Protestant message, and it must be guarded as such; it ought not to be changed into a new doctrine or devotional method or become a scheme that is used in every sermon; it should not be made into a new form of security—a form that would be an especially disastrous one. It must remain the depth and background of all our pronouncements; it must be the quality that gives to the message its truth and power.

Third, Protestantism must witness to the "New Being" through which alone it is able to say its word in power, and it must do this without making this witness again the basis of a wrong security. The New Being, which for Christian faith is manifest in Jesus as the Christ, is effective in the life of the individual personality as well as in the life of the community, and it is not even excluded from nature, as is indicated by the sacraments. To live out of the power of this New Being is the richness of Protestantism which is the correlate to its poverty; for, just because the Protestant principle, the message of the boundary-situation, breaks down all absolute boundaries before the judgment to which everything is subject, Protestantism can be open for everything, religious and secular, past and future, individual and social. All these differences are transcended through the power of the New Being, which works in all of them, breaking through their exclusiveness and separation. Culture is not subjected to religion, nor is religion dissolved in culture. Protestantism neither devaluates nor idealizes culture. It tries to understand its religious substance, its spiritual foundation, its "theonomous" nature. And Protestantism neither idealizes nor devaluates religion. It tries to interpret religion as the direct, intentional expression of the spiritual substance which in the cultural forms is presented indirectly and unintentionally. In this way the Protestant principle denies to the church a holy sphere as its separate possession, and it denies to culture a secular sphere that can escape the judgment of the boundary-situation.

This attitude of Protestantism toward church and culture implies the answer to the questions: Where is Protestantism to be found? Who proclaims the Protestant principle? The answer is: Protestantism lives wherever, in the power of the New Being, the boundary-situation is preached, its "No" and "Yes" are proclaimed. It is there and nowhere else. Protestantism may live in the organized Protestant churches. But it is not bound to them. Perhaps more men of today have experienced the boundary-situation outside than inside the churches. The Protestant principle may be proclaimed by movements that are neither ecclesiastical nor secular but belong to both spheres, by groups and individuals who, with or without Christian and Protestant symbols, express the true human situation in face of the ultimate and unconditional. If they do it better and with more authority than the official churches, then they and not the churches represent Protestantism for the man of today.

# Chapter XIV

## THE FORMATIVE POWER OF
## PROTESTANTISM

### I. THE PROBLEM

FORMATIVE power is the power of creating a form; Protestantism is the attitude of protest against form. How can they be united? Stated in such a degree of abstraction, they are irreconcilable. But actually they have been united, namely, in historical Protestantism, in the development of its churches, in the life of every Protestant. A union of Protestantism and formative power must be *possible,* since it has been and still is *real.* On the other hand, it is not surprising that this unity is full of tensions, restless, and threatened in its existence. These tensions in historical Protestantism will be the subject of this chapter. We raise the question as to how formative power and protest against form can live together in a church, how form and the protest against form can create a new, overarching form.

It is a general axiom concerning all being that the negative can manifest itself only in connection with something positive (as the lie can exist only through the element of truth in it). According to this axiom, we must say that protest cannot exist without a "Gestalt" to which it belongs.[1] The Gestalt embraces itself and the protest against itself; it comprises form and negation of form. There is no "absolute" negation and there is no "absolute" protest—absolute in the literary sense of "absolved from any involvement." Negation, if it lives, is involved in affirmation; and protest, if it lives, is involved in form. This is also true of Protestantism. Its protest is dependent on its Gestalt, its form-negating on its form-creating power, its "No"—however it may prevail—on

1. In the following discussion we shall use the German word *Gestalt* in order to refer to the total structure of a living reality, such as a social group, an individual person, or a biological body. The German word is permissible since "Gestalt psychology" has introduced it into general scientific terminology. We shall use the word "form" whenever we refer to the different organic expressions of the total structure, for instance, the cult of a church or the character traits of a personality.

206

its "Yes." Its "No" would fall into nothingness without the creativity of its "Yes." This union of protest and creation we call "the Gestalt of grace."

The prophetic protest of Protestantism has been proclaimed in recent years by Karl Barth and his friends with such power and out of such depth that the attention not only of world Protestantism but also of large groups outside the churches has been aroused. Perhaps one is justified in saying that the radical character of this protest—the impressive and convincing form in which it was directed against both religion and culture—has saved contemporary Protestantism from sectarian seclusion, on the one hand, and from secularism and insignificance, on the other hand. It is not surprising that the impetus of the protest prevented those who pronounced it from raising the question of the Gestalt out of which the protest came. This is not surprising in view of the fact that protest is not only an essential element of Protestantism at all times but is also very urgently needed in our time. Neither the churches nor society has given heed to it as they should. Theology still has no more important task than to express the Protestant protest radically and penetratingly in its own doctrinal work and in its dealing with every aspect of contemporary life. It must issue the protest unconditionally because of the unconditional character of the divine, and it must express it concretely because of the concrete character of every historical situation. A theology that has not passed through the shattering effect of the "theology of crisis" but has dismissed its prophetic "No" with a polite bow or with an easy criticism of its method and form, cannot be taken very seriously. For a long time to come—and in some way always—the Protestant protest must have priority.

And yet the question of the Protestant Gestalt cannot longer be neglected. The fact that it has been overlooked by the "theology of crisis" has already produced some unfortunate effects. The important liturgical movements in Protestantism have been repelled by the radical character of the critical "No." The same is true of the attempts to unite Christianity with the spirit of the youth movement and with the aims of socialism. After a certain amount of co-operation these new attempts had to separate themselves from the theology of crisis. There can be no doubt, however, that they are badly needed. The decline in liturgical taste (in architecture, poetry, and music) during the nineteenth century made a creative reaction necessary. The help given to it by expression-

istic art and by its ability to rediscover the great cultic art of the past
was invaluable. The same is true of the longing of youth for new
symbols over against the utilitarianism of bourgeois civilization, and it
is true also of the attempts to unite Protestantism and socialism. All this
is needed. But these attempts can preserve their Protestant character
and avoid a hopeless competition with Roman Catholicism only if they
pass through the fire of prophetic criticism. The theology of crisis has
lighted this fire. But it was a merely burning and in no way a warming
and illuminating fire. Consequently, these movements went their own,
often very unprotestant, ways. At the same time the theology of crisis
itself took a dangerous turn. It seems as if Barth and his followers, in a
good orthodox style, are interested only in the form of *doctrine* in Protestantism. Moreover, the way in which they work for the doctrine is not
very much affected by the "No" of the Protestant principle; it has itself
not passed through the fire of its own protest. Indeed, it sometimes appears as if the absolute, religious criticism of the theology of crisis has
strangled the relative, scientific criticism found in liberal theology. This
is a very unfortunate result, certainly not intended by Barth and even
less by great and radical biblical scholars like Bultmann, who unite
higher criticism and Barthian theology. But, though not intended, it has
occurred, especially in the younger generation of theologians, who are
no longer conscious of the heroic struggle of nearly two centuries in
which scientific honesty in historical matters conquered sacred superstitions and ecclesiastical compromises. It is a real danger to the future of
Protestantism that the prophetic spirit of the original theology of crisis
will be abused in favor of the re-establishment of an orthodoxy that feels
safe against the Protestant protest.

These are consequences of the failure of the theology of crisis to
raise the question of the Protestant Gestalt in its relation to the Protestant protest. But the question is unavoidable, and an answer must be
found if there is to be a future for Protestantism. What is the Gestalt,
we ask, out of which the Protestant protest can come without destroying
its own foundation? What are the principles of the formative power of
Protestantism? And how can criticism and creation be united in the different directions of its self-realization? Against a possible misunderstanding, it may be emphasized that we do not agree with a type of liberal Protestantism which identifies Protestantism with the attitude of a

permanent protest in the sense of a negative intellectual criticism. Such an attitude is rejected by the Protestant principle.

## II. THE REALITY OF GRACE

By what authority does Protestantism raise its protest against every sacred and secular reality? There must be such an authority which, of course, cannot be any human authority. But if Protestantism tries to protect the majesty of the unconditional against every attempt of a finite reality to set itself up as unconditioned, it must somehow participate in the unconditional. If Protestant criticism is not the criticism with which one finite being challenges other finite beings but a criticism coming from beyond finitude, Protestantism must participate in the infinite. But participating in the infinite, in the unconditional, in a trans-human authority, means living in the reality of grace or—to use the term already explained—in a "Gestalt of grace," in a sacred structure of reality. No Protestant protest is possible unless it is rooted in a Gestalt in which grace is embodied.

Grace-embodied, reality of grace, Gestalt of grace—all these sound strange and dangerous for Protestants. "Grace" is supposed to be something intangible and unsubstantial, while "embodiment" and "Gestalt" seem to point to something that can be grasped and touched. An embodied grace seems to lose its character as grace and to become a "law" in the sense of Catholic sacramentalism. The struggle of the Reformers against the Roman system of legalized grace seems to have been fought in vain if Protestants start speaking of a sacred structure of reality. Such a view of grace, the Reformers asserted against the pope, deprives the church of its spiritual, invisible character, divides the one unconditional grace into many conditioned "graces," makes the hierarchy the proprietor of the power of grace and therefore the authority to which one must submit for the sake of salvation. A concept like "Gestalt of grace" seems to indicate the end of the Protestant protest and the victory of Rome. The grace of forgiveness, which is a divine judgment over every human achievement and above any perceptible form, seems to be replaced by a conditioned, immanent structure which must be constructed by human activity.

We might in this way express our doubt about Protestantism's possession of a formative power. If the doubt were justified, the concept of a Gestalt of grace would have to be rejected. But does the alternative between Romanism, on the one side, and an unstructured (Gestalt-less) Protestantism, on the other side, really exhaust the possibilities? In contrast to the Reformers, we are no longer involved in a life-and-death struggle with Rome. We are able to decide in terms of principles and not of controversy; and we are not bound in our decision to a classical period of Protestantism. It belongs to the nature of Protestantism that it has no classical period. Every period stands under the Protestant protest, even the age of the Reformation.

There is in the center of Protestant doctrine a point at which it presupposes what we call a "divine structure of reality," namely, faith. The divine judgment, in spite of its transcendence and independence, has meaning and power only if it is appropriated by faith, in the church and in the Christian. Faith is the faith of man. It does not come *from* man, but it is effective *in* man. And in so far as faith is in a community or personality, they are embodiments of grace. Faith is created by the hearing of the "Word." The Word is said from *beyond* us, *to* us. But, if it is received, it is no longer *only* transcendent. It is also immanent, creating a divine structure of reality. Thus it creates faith as the formative power of a personal life and of a community. The Word is said from beyond man, but it is said through men. Men must be able to say it, they must be grasped and transformed by it, and this must have happened ever since the Word became manifest in history. Structures of grace must be permanently actual *in* history—though they do not derive *from* history—if in *any* moment of history the Word is to be pronounced.

A theology that wishes to avoid these implications is confronted with the following alternatives: either faith is itself a creation of grace (of the divine Spirit), or it is a human act of subjection to a report about grace. Either the authority of those who preach the Word is the expression of grace working in their personality, or it is the detached description of something outside the preacher. Either faith means being grasped by the power of the unconditional, or it is objective knowledge with a lower degree of evidence. In the second case it is inexplicable how a personality and community without grace can know and preach grace. In the first case it is understandable that grace is preached and faith is created. We decide for this alternative and say that the presupposition of the formative power of Protestantism is the unity of protest and form in a Gestalt of grace.

It is important to emphasize the reality of grace—in whatever terminology—because Protestant theology (as early as in Melanchthon) showed an inclination to intellectualize religion. This is historically understandable. The radicalism of the Protestant protest against any visible representation of the divine made such an intellectualization almost unavoidable. But it cannot be justified. And the recently influential "theology of the Word" should be careful not to confuse the divine "Word," which has appeared as a personal life and is the Gestalt of grace, with the biblical or ecclesiastical word. For Christian theology Jesus as the Christ is the Word (i.e., the divine self-manifestation); and this involves his being in its totality, to which his deeds and his suffering belong, and not his words alone. "Word of God" in Christian theology, therefore, has an obviously symbolic sense. If we say that his total being and not merely his words (or the words about him) is the Word of God, we are saying that the reality of grace and not the speaking about grace is the source of Christianity. The words of the Bible and of preaching claim to speak not only *about* the reality of grace but as an expression *of* this reality, not detached from their object but grasped by it. The reality of grace is the *prius* of all speaking and hearing about it; being moved by the Spirit is the *prius* of faith, not the reverse. But to be moved by the Spirit or to be grasped by the unconditional means to be drawn into the reality and the life of a Gestalt of grace.

The emphasis on the reality of grace protects theology against orthodox (and rationalistic) intellectualism. But it has, at the same time, the function of protecting Protestantism against a new—or a very old— sacramentalism. In every theology there is the danger that the reality of grace will be interpreted in terms of an "objective" reality, i.e., of a reality that is given like any other object, to be known and used by everybody who wants to know and to use it. But the Gestalt of grace is not a Gestalt beside others. It is the manifestation of what is beyond every Gestalt *through* a Gestalt. Here we see the profoundest difference between the Protestant and the Catholic idea of the reality of grace. In the Catholic view the finite form is transmuted into a divine form; the human in Christ is received in his divine nature (the monophysitic trend in all Catholic Christology); the historical relativity of the church is sanctified by its divine character (the exclusiveness of the Roman church); the material of the sacrament is as such filled with grace (the dogma of transubstantiation). In all this, grace is interpreted as a tangible, special reality—an object like other natural or historical objects—and this in spite of its transcendent, and therefore unconditional, meaning. In contrast to this Catholic understanding of the reality of grace (which attempts to make a Protestant protest against dogma, church, and sacrament impossible), Protestantism asserts that grace appears *through* a living Gestalt which remains in itself what it is. The divine appears *through* the humanity of the Christ, *through* the historical weakness of the church, *through* the finite material of the sacrament. The divine appears through the finite realities as their transcendent meaning. Forms of grace are finite forms, pointing beyond themselves. They are forms that are, so to speak, selected by grace, that it may appear through them; but they are not forms that are transmuted by grace so that they may become identical with it. The Protestant protest prohibits the appearance of grace through finite forms from becoming an identification of grace with finite forms. Such an identification is, according to the Protestant principle, demonic *hybris*. And examples of just such a demonic *hybris* must be seen in the hierarchical possession of the sacramental grace, in the orthodox possession of the infallible Word of God and the "pure doctrine," and in the scientific possession of the "historical Jesus" and his new law.

The Gestalt of grace is not something tangible. You cannot see or touch grace in the personal life or in the life of a community. But perhaps we might say that a Gestalt of grace is a possible object of "imaginative intuition." The transcendent meaning of a finite reality is not an abstract concept but a matter of imaginative perception. The New Testament picture of Jesus as the Christ is open to a nonsensuous intuition. Its character as the central Gestalt of grace can grasp us before any conceptual interpretation. Grace, of course, is not perceptible, but the manifestation of grace through a finite medium can be perceived. A Gestalt of grace is a "transparent" Gestalt. Something shines through it which is more than it. The church is church because it is transparent as a Gestalt of grace. The saint is saint, not because he is "good," but because he is transparent for something that is more than he himself is. Faith alone can perceive the grace in a Gestalt of grace; for faith means being grasped and being transformed by grace.

### III. PROTESTANT SECULARISM

The Protestant church, according to its claim, is a Gestalt of grace. It unites protest and form. This is its idea, but not necessarily its reality. In contrast to Catholicism's claim for itself, the Protestant church must emphasize that it is a historical phenomenon, subjected to sociological and psychological conditions. It is not a "transubstantiated" community, but it may be a "transparent" community, a Gestalt of grace. How is that possible? How can the Protestant church incorporate within itself the protest against itself? How can it be the bearer of grace without identifying itself with grace? The Protestant protest against itself must not remain merely dialectical. It must not become— as the doctrine of justification by grace often has become—a part of its dogmatic possession. Speaking dialectically *against* one's self can be a more refined form of speaking *for* one's self. (Observe the fanatical self-affirmation under the cloak of self-negation in some so-called "dialectical" theologians.) The Protestant protest against itself must become concrete, and it has, in fact, become concrete in its history: it is concrete in the very existence of a secular world. In so far as secularism is an offspring of Protestantism and is related to it in co-operation or enmity, we may call it "Protestant secularism." According to the Protestant principle, it is possible that within the secular world grace is operating not in a tangible but in a transparent form. This possibility implies that grace is not bound to any finite form, not even to a religious form. It is sovereign even with respect to forms that by their very nature are supposed to be bearers of grace, such as the churches. The fathers of Continental religious socialism (for instance, as represented by the Blumhardts) recognized that God may speak for a time more powerfully through a nonreligious, and even anti-Christian, movement, such as the early social democracy, than through the Christian churches. For their period (which is still largely our period) they expressed in this way the Protestant protest against ecclesiastical arrogance. They understood that the church whose nature it is to be a Gestalt of grace may lose its true nature and that a secular group or movement may be called to become a bearer of grace, though latently. From this it follows that Protestantism bears a unique relationship to secularism: Protestantism, by its very nature, demands a secular reality.

It demands a concrete protest against the sacred sphere and against ecclesiastical pride, a protest that is incorporated in secularism. Protestant secularism is a necessary element of Protestant realization. The formative power of Protestantism is always tested by its relation to the secular world. If Protestantism surrenders to secularism, it ceases to be a Gestalt of grace. If it retires from secularism, it ceases to be Protestant, namely, a Gestalt that includes within it the protest against itself.

These considerations lead to the first principle of Protestant form-creation: *In every Protestant form the religious element must be related to, and questioned by, a secular element.* How is this possible? Secular forms are forms in which the finite structure of reality is expressed—poetically, scientifically, ethically, politically—and in which the relation of every finite to the infinite is expressed only indirectly. Secularism is not irreligious or atheistic (atheism is an impossibility and an illusion), but it does not express its latent religion in religious forms. And that is just what Protestantism needs as a corrective against the temptation of every religious sphere and every ecclesiastical system, to identify itself with the unconditional to which it points.

Secular forms are open to a continuous transformation by autonomous creativity. Nothing is less Protestant than the Catholic sanctification of a special philosophy, a special art, a special ethics. This is just the way in which the Roman church tries to prevent secular culture from raising a protest against the ecclesiastical forms. But this is not the Protestant way. Protestantism considers secularism as a continuous, ever changing task for its formative power. There is no fixed, not even a classical, solution. There are preliminary affirmations, constructions, solutions; but nothing is final. The Protestant Gestalt of grace is dynamic and flexible. The "present" decides about the special task. Its problems and tensions, its trends and creations, determine the direction in which the formative power of Protestantism must work. This leads to the second principle of Protestant form-creation: *In every Protestant form the eternal element must be expressed in relation to a "present situation."*

What kind of relation to the "present" is demanded in this principle of contemporaneousness? It cannot, of course, mean bondage to the moment. Not the appearance but the depth of the present is decisive. But the depth, the dynamic structure of a historical situation, cannot be understood by a detached description of as many facts as possible. It must be experienced in life and action. The depth of every present is its power to transform the past into a future. It is, therefore, a matter of venture and decision. This holds true also of Protestant contemporaneousness. It involves daring and risk; it has no safe standards, no spiritual guaranties. It pushes forward, and it may find that it has merely forged ahead into the void and has missed its mark. And yet it cannot do other than venture and risk. Protestantism denies the security of sacramental systems with inviolable forms, sacred laws, eternal structures. It questions every claim of absoluteness; it remains dynamic even if it tries to become conservative. All this, of course, does not mean that Protestantism must surrender its own foundation, the Gestalt of grace, and the Protestant principle protecting it. The formative power of Protestantism is not the power of self-negation— the dissolution of form. Protestant form-creation is not venture in general; it is venture on the basis and within the limits of the reality of grace. It transcends every form which it creates, but it does not transcend the reality of grace which is expressed in these forms. Venture *in abstracto* (apart from the Gestalt of grace) is a jump from one finite possibility to another one. This is relativism; it is not Protestant protest. From this follows a third principle of Protestant form-creation: *In every Protestant form the given reality of grace must be expressed with daring and risk.*

The venture of Protestant form-creation does not result in arbitrariness because it is made in obedience to the Protestant principle, on the one hand, to the demands implied in the reality of the present, on the other hand. Venturing without obedience to reality is wilful. But, without venturing, reality cannot be discovered. The "really real" cannot be reached under logical or methodological guaranties. A daring act is demanded, an act that penetrates to the deepest level of reality, to its transcendent ground. Such an act is what in the religious tradition is called "faith" and what we have called a "belief-ful" or "self-transcending realism." Only such a realism is truly realistic. It refuses to be caught by any preliminary level of being and meaning; it cuts through to the ultimate level. In this way belief-ful realism liberates from cynical realism as well as from utopian realism.

But what is "really real" among all the things and events that offer themselves as reality? That which resists me so that I cannot pretend its not-being. The really real is what limits me. There are two powers in the whole of our experience which do not admit any attempt to remove them, the unconditional and "the other," i.e., the other human being. They are united in their resistance against me, in their manifestation as the really real. The unconditional could be an illusion if it did not appear through the unconditional demand of the other *person* to acknowledge him as a person. And, conversely, "the other," if he did not demand an *unconditional* acknowledgment of his personal dignity, could be used as a tool for my purposes; as a consequence he would lose his power of resistance and his ultimate reality. The unity of the personal and the unconditional, or of the ethical and the religious, is the manifestation of the really real, for it resists absolutely any attempt to be dissolved into subjectivity. From this follows a fourth principle of Protestant form-creation: *In every Protestant form the attitude of a belief-ful realism must be expressed*. Protestant formative power must grasp reality in its unconditional and irresistible seriousness and must not build on a place before or beyond the really real.

### IV. PROTESTANT FORM-CREATION AND RELIGIOUS KNOWLEDGE

Having developed four principles that should determine every Protestant form, we shall now give some examples for a possible application of these principles. Let us turn, first, to the sphere of religious knowledge. The life of a Protestant church includes the seeking for, and expressing of, the truth out of which it lives. It finds this truth as something given, formulated in the tradition but requiring experience, reinterpretation, and new formulation. It knows about the Protestant protest against every tradition, and it knows that this protest is real and concrete in secular knowledge about man, history, and nature. Therefore, it must receive secular knowledge as an element of its own self-interpretation. In some quarters it has been said that secular thought should not be allowed to enter Protestant theology. But philosophy and theology are not a priori in conflict. Whether they are or not depends on the special character of both. In any case, Protestant theology should do frankly what all theology always does, even if it denies passionately any connection with philosophy, it should relate itself to philosophy, and courageously so, though under the criterion of the Protestant principle.

The way in which this can be done we have called "belief-ful realism." Religious knowledge is knowledge of things and events in their religious significance, in their relationship to their transcendent ground. Religious knowledge is the knowledge of the really real. It is not the development of a tradition, it is not the discussion of antiquated problems, it is not the answer to the question of the meaning and truth of ancient concepts. Religious self-interpretation may do all this also. But, first and foremost, it is a turning toward reality, a questioning of reality, a penetrating into existence, a driving to the level where the world points beyond itself to its ground and ultimate meaning. If, out of such a penetration into reality, concepts and words grow which are its genuine expression, they may become keys to an understanding and a new interpretation of the tradition. Protestant theology is not for traditional reasons obliged to speak of the creation of the world and its mythical connotations, but it must analyze the creatureliness of all things and their relation to the creative ground. The religious-mythical term "creation" must be interpreted by the religious-empirical term "creaturely." Nor is it the task of Protestant theology to develop further the traditional problems of Christology and soteriology but rather to describe the New Being, which is manifest in Jesus Christ in relation to nature and history. This "Being" which is *in* history, though not *from* history, is the present problem of the "person and the work of the Christ." It is an actual problem with which reality confronts us at every moment; it is a realistic problem of our present situation. And our answer to it may become a way to understand the realistic meaning of the answers to similar questions given in former periods. Nor is it the task of Protestant theology to defend or deny the Jewish-Christian eschatological imagery. Its task is rather to ask: What is the ultimate meaning in all historical activity? How do we interpret time in the light of the eternal which breaks into it? The "end of time" must be understood as a quality of time, namely, as the quality of historical time which is directed toward the ultimate goal, toward salvation and fulfilment. And it is not the task of Protestant theology to continue discussing the nature and attributes of God, enriching or restricting the traditional statements, but rather it is its task to contemplate the real in such a way that its divine ground becomes transparent in it and through it. The profoundest demand of all is that we learn to speak of God in such a way that he appears not as an object above all other objects, nor as a mere symbol, but as the really real in everything that claims reality. Obviously, that can be done only in the power of a Gestalt of grace, i.e., in faith. We do not know when and where it might be done. We cannot bring it about by willing and acting. It occurs, or it does not occur. But, if it occurs, it is not only revealing for our time but also illuminating for the past, making its concepts and words contemporary, pointing to their depth and reality. *Protestant formative power is at work wherever reality is interpreted with respect to its ground and ultimate meaning.*

### V. PROTESTANT FORM-CREATION AND RELIGIOUS ACTION

Religious action in contrast to ethical action is "cultus" (*colere deum*). It is interdependent with religious thought. The idea of the Gestalt of grace gives new meaning and vitality to the cultus in Protestantism. "Cultus" becomes the term for the perceivable expression of the Gestalt of grace. The Protestant cultus, which traditionally was centered around the preaching of the word, gains a larger field. It liberates itself from the confusion between "the Word of God" and the written or spoken word of Christian preaching. The Word of God is his self-communication which can occur in many forms and is not bound to the human word. It may occur through actions, gestures, forms—of course, not *ex opere operato* (by their mere performance) but, nevertheless, without any accompanying word. Sacraments, visible symbols, bodily, musical, artistic expressions are "Word of God" even if nothing is spoken—that is, for those who accept them spiritually (as the spoken word is Word of God *only* if it is received spiritually).

The Protestant cultus in this wider sense poses a difficult problem for us. The cultus uses special forms in which the Gestalt of grace expresses itself. But, according to the Protestant principle, these forms through their beauty and sacred tradition are temptations to identify grace with some special expressions of grace. Therefore, a corrective is needed which must be derived from the principles of Protestant form-creation. The principles that are especially pertinent here are secular autonomy and the demand of contemporaneousness. The opposition to the cultus on this basis has taken on such dimensions that the majority of people within the Protestant nations have no approach whatsoever to the cultus. This is due not only to the consequences resulting from an exaggerated emphasis on the sermon but also to the feeling that the decisive elements of our present life are not reflected in this cultus. In spite of all the improvement of the liturgical form achieved by the rediscovery of the treasures of the liturgical past, the reform of the cultus has not been able to overcome this feeling. It has brought an aesthetic progress (in contrast to the aesthetic poverty of the later nineteenth century). But it has not created a religious impression strong enough to elicit a new attitude to the Protestant cultus; for being grasped aesthetically is not being grasped by the ultimate.

Religious action—cultus—like religious knowledge, must create its forms out of the experiences of the daily life and the actual situation. The cultus is supposed to give an ultimate meaning to the daily life. It is not so important to produce new liturgies as it is to penetrate into the depths of what happens day by day, in labor and industry, in marriage and friendship, in social relations and recreation, in meditation and tranquillity, in the unconscious and the conscious life. To elevate all this into the light of the eternal is the great task of cultus, and not to reshape a tradition traditionally. It is an infinite task, demanding venturing courage and vision, especially in a period of radical transformations such as ours. In the measure in which Protestantism takes up this task successfully, the liturgical tradition will become contemporaneous and powerful. *Protestant formative power is at work wherever reality is transformed into an active expression of a Gestalt of grace.*

### VI. THE SPIRIT OF PROTESTANTISM AND AUTONOMOUS CULTURE

The formative power of Protestantism expresses itself not only in the religious sphere (in the narrower sense of the word) but also in the totality of the personal, social, and intellectual existence in the whole of a civilization (the Anglo-Saxon term) or culture (the German term). This problem, of course, transcends the limitations of this chapter and is treated, at least partially, in several other chapters of this book. Only a few ideas about Protestantism and culture will be derived here from the principles developed above.

The more that Protestantism is able and willing to accept secular criticism of itself, the more it acquires the right and the power to criticize secularism. The secular world must be permanently subjected to such a criticism because it has the tendency to separate itself from the Gestalt of grace in spite of its essential relation to it. Secularism wants to escape the prophetic judgment and promise, both of which seem to threaten secular autonomy. It is afraid of the will-to-power of organized religion from which it had to liberate itself in a tremendous struggle. The secular world does not want to return into heteronomy and ecclesiastical servitude. Protestantism stands above this alternative. It has no ecclesiastical aspirations but subjects them, wherever they appear, to the same criticism to which it subjects arrogant secularism, scientific, political, or moral. It tries to create a Protestant secularism, a culture related to a Gestalt of grace as its spiritual center.

To the extent to which this attempt is successful, the secular forms in thought and action approach the specially religious ones, without becoming religious themselves. They remain secular, but they show the spiritual influence that permanently emanates from a Gestalt of grace, even if it appears as weak as the Protestant churches often do. Under this "silent" influence of Protestantism on the culture to which it belongs, secular thinking is driven to the question of its own foundation and meaning, i.e., to the question of religious knowledge; and secular action is driven to the question of its ultimate purpose and fulfilment, i.e., to the question of religious action, individual and social. For this "dialectical" relation between the secular world and the Gestalt of grace I like to use the word "theonomy," which indicates that neither ecclesiastical heteronomy nor secular autonomy can have the last word in human culture. The term "theonomy" may be objected to because its use by Catholics has created connotations of a clearly heteronomous character. Therefore, it may be wise to speak, in certain cases, of "Protestant secularism," a term that sharply indicates the ambiguous character of the relation between the Protestant Gestalt of grace and the secular world.

If there is a Protestant secular culture—and it has a very manifest and very powerful reality in most of the Protestant countries—Protestant form-creation is of tremendous significance. It does not determine the secular forms of life, but it creates forms that represent the spiritual meaning of life. Religious thinking and acting represent manifestly what is hidden in secular thinking and acting; they are not something beside the secular or above it or against it or a part of it; they are the representative expression of its ground and aim. Without such an expression, secularism becomes empty and the victim of "demonic" self-destruction. *Protestant formative power is needed in a secular world; and it is at work wherever the autonomous forms become bearers of ultimate meaning.*

The problem of Protestant form-creation confronts us with a far-reaching decision. Either we decide for a mere preaching of the word, unrelated to a Gestalt *of* grace and, therefore, necessarily degenerating into an intellectual report *about* grace and allowing a secular world to remain untouched by it. Or we decide for Protestant form-creation as the expression of a Gestalt of grace in thinking and acting and, therefore, for the possibility of representing the ultimate meaning of the secular world. Both the general situation and the crisis of Protestantism urge upon us the decision for Protestant form-creation. Either the Protestant churches will be reduced to insignificance between Catholicism and secularism, or they will prevail against both of them, in the power of the Protestant principle and of the reality to which it witnesses. Either Protestantism will become a sect, isolated from the main trend of history, or it will become the starting-point of a new embodiment of the spirit of Christianity in which a demonic sacramentalism and an empty secularism are overcome.

# Chapter XV

## THE END OF THE PROTESTANT ERA?

PROTESTANTISM now faces the most difficult struggle of all the occidental religions and denominations in the present world situation. It arose with that era which today is either coming to an end or else undergoing fundamental structural changes. Therefore, the question as to whether Protestantism can face the present situation in a manner enabling it to survive the present historical period is unavoidable. It is true, of course, that all religions are threatened today by secularism and paganism. But this threat, at least as far as pure secularism is concerned, has perhaps reached its culminating point. The insecurity which is increasingly felt by nations and individuals, the expectation of catastrophes in all civilized countries, the vanishing belief in progress—all have aroused a new searching for a transcendent security and perfection. Religion today is stronger than it was before the first World War, at least in the feeling and longing of people. The individualistic atheism of the freethinkers, for instance, has declined in Western countries since the beginning of the present century. The conflict between the natural sciences and religion has been overcome in all important philosophies. But the question as to whether Protestantism in particular has become stronger must be answered in the negative, although sometimes it seems, if one considers the general growth of religious interest and neglects the peculiar situation of Protestantism, that the opposite has been the case.

It is the basic proposition of this chapter that the traditional form of the Protestant attitude cannot outlast the period of mass disintegration and mass collectivism—that the end of "The Protestant era" is a possibility. In order to demonstrate this proposition it must be shown that there is such a tendency toward mass collectivism. In addition, it will be necessary to explain why the Protestant principle is in contradiction to the newly emerging principles of social organization. Finally, it should be asked whether any possibility exists for Protestantism to adapt itself to the new situation without renouncing its essential character.

In speaking of the fact of mass disintegration we refer particularly to the European situation. But, since the cause of this disintegration is the same in the United States and in Europe—namely, the social and intellectual situation of late capitalism—the problem of mass disintegration is relevant in America, too, though more as a threat than as an actually existing reality. By "mass disintegration" is meant the situation in which the group formations which grew up under feudalism and early capitalism break down and give way to amorphous masses, in which the laws of mass psychology operate. In such a situation the individual differentiations and integrations of groups and personalities are supplanted by identical mass attitudes; special traditions are forgotten, old symbols have become powerless; a meaningful personal life, especially among the masses of industrial workers, has become impossible. Disintegration, in the last analysis, leads to meaninglessness in the economic, as well as in the social and intellectual, spheres. The meaninglessness of existence is perhaps the most characteristic phenomenon of the period of late capitalism.

This can be easily explained. Technological innovations and capitalistic economic organization have created those vast masses which inhabit the great cities of all civilized countries. A great number of people do not, as such, constitute a mass. The mass comes into existence at the moment in which all these men are determined by that fate which is practically inescapable for every individual, e.g., within the working and lower middle classes. Since they work in masses in the big factories; since they, as masses, receive the same low wage; since they live as masses in the same type of rundown houses and poor streets; since, as masses, they have the same slight chances of material or intellectual enjoyment, a mass attitude tends more and more to replace more individuated ones, to subject them to the laws of mass feeling and mass emotion, and to lay them open to the appeals of every agitator who is able to use and to abuse the laws of mass psychology. It is characteristic of the behavior of masses that every individual among them acts under the impulsion of those aspects of his personality which he has in common with everybody else, not according to those in which he is an independent, individualized person. Thus the agitators necessarily stimulate those less cultivated and less disciplined elements in every particle of the mass and use them for their own purposes.

All these things are not very dangerous and cannot of themselves constitute the reason for revolutionary changes in the structure of an epoch as long as the industrial society in which these masses exist is in a state of continuous expansion. Indeed, this drive toward expansion gives to all a feeling of the possibility of improvement in their mode of life and even tends to organize the whole of life around the prospect of improvement in social and economic status. But, as soon as the inner contradictions of the whole manifest themselves in the life of the individual and the possibilities of self-advancement begin to disappear, the disintegration of personal life begins. Or, more exactly, the latent and potential disintegration which lies at the roots of modern industrial society becomes a tremendous actuality.

The contradictions inherent in the social order have become real for everyone in the present crisis. These are, fundamentally, (1) the contradiction between the rapidity of technical progress and the dependence of human life on human work, i.e., the fact of structural, inevitable unemployment; (2) the contradiction between productive power and the buying power of the masses, i.e., the fact of the increasing poverty of the masses in contrast to the increase of unproductive capital in the banks, from which is to be derived the necessity of an imperialistic foreign policy and the increasing threat of war; and (3) the contradiction between the assumed liberty of every individual and the complete dependence of the masses on the laws of the market or, in other words, the fact that, after man has overcome the fate which was once implied in the powers of nature, he becomes subjected to the fate implied in economic development. In the late capitalist period the insecurity which is implied by definition in the principle of liberalism becomes a permanent menace to individuals and masses. It threatens more and more every class within society—the lower middle class, the clerks, the farmers, and, finally, even the ruling class. New masses grow out of these groups when their older forms of integration break down; and the individual, having lost his aims, becomes accessible to the influence of any appeal. Permanent unemployment produces a new mass attitude of hopelessness and meaninglessness. The old traditions are destroyed in the mass situation, and new ones cannot be created in this state of perpetual flux. The transcendent meaning of life as it is interpreted in religious ideas and symbols disappears with the secularization of every realm of life; and

THE END OF THE PROTESTANT ERA? 225

the competition of individuals and of groups—the fundamental pattern of modern industrial society—emerges more pronouncedly than ever before between individuals, classes, and nations, driving toward race hatred, revolution, and war. The new generation, growing up under these circumstances, is even more hopeless and directionless than the older generation and longs for change, for revolution and war, as the means of change and as the ultimate and only hope. This picture represents the postwar situation in central Europe. It is, of course, not the description of a reality which exists with equal completeness throughout the Western world, and, if taken in such a way, it would be an exaggeration. Nonetheless, it does describe the central tendency of late capitalist society; and in history the strongest tendency is decisive.

Naturally, in such a situation one question above all others arises in everyone's mind, namely: How is reintegration possible? And the general answer is: by mass organization within a centralized and collective system. There is no other way out. Mass integration in the economic realm means the guaranty of a certain security; in the political realm it means the exclusion of the endless discussion between struggling parties and classes; and in the intellectual realm, it means the production of a common ideology with common symbols and a dogmatic basis for education and intellectual activity. All this presupposes a centralized power and authority, not only with respect to economic and political organization but also with reference to education and religion. The present tendencies in Europe toward an authoritarian, totalitarian state are rooted in this internal necessity of mass reintegration. These never would have succeeded if a very strong feeling for this necessity had not been alive in wide sections of the masses and, above all, in the younger generation. These people do not want to decide things for themselves; they do not want to decide about their political beliefs, about their religion and morals. They are longing for a leader, for symbols, for ideas which would be beyond all criticism. They are longing for the possibility of enthusiasm, sacrifice, and self-subjection to collective ideas and activities. Autonomous thinking and acting is rejected as liberalistic and, consequently, as the cause of meaninglessness and despair in every realm of life. These tendencies are strongest in middle Europe, especially in Germany. But, since they are structural tendencies arising on the basis of the present world situation, they are to be found in every section of the occidental world.

Protestantism stands in complete contradiction to this tendency. This may be observed, first, with reference to the religious basis and then with reference to the intellectual and practical implications of the Protestant attitude. The central principle of Protestantism is the doctrine of justification by grace alone, which means that no individual and no human group can claim a divine dignity for its moral achievements, for its sacramental power, for its sanctity, or for its doctrine. If, consciously or unconsciously, they make such a claim, Protestantism requires that they be challenged by the prophetic protest, which gives God alone absoluteness and sanctity and denies every claim of human pride. This protest against itself on the basis of an experience of God's majesty constitutes the Protestant principle. This principle holds for Lutheranism as well as for Calvinism and even for modern Protestant denominationalism. It is the principle which made the accidental name "Protestant" an essential and symbolic name. It implies that there cannot be a sacred system, ecclesiastical or political; that there cannot be a sacred heirarchy with absolute authority; and that there cannot be a truth in human minds which is divine truth in itself. Consequently, the prophetic spirit must always criticize, attack, and condemn sacred authorities, doctrines, and morals. And every genuine Protestant is called upon to bear personal responsibility for this. Each Protestant, each layman, each minister (the minister in Protestantism is a qualified layman and nothing else), has to decide for himself whether a doctrine is true or not, whether a prophet is a true or a false prophet, whether a power is demonic or divine. Even the Bible cannot liberate him from this responsibility, for the Bible is a subject of interpretation: there is no doctrine, no prophet, no priest, no power, which has not claimed biblical sanction for itself. For the Protestant, individual decision is inescapable.

If we consider the situation of the disintegrated masses, which are quite unable to make such a decision, as well as the situation of the younger generation, which refuses to take upon itself the responsibility for such a decision, we can scarcely see a way for Protestantism to triumph over this difficult world situation. Protestantism itself seems to be participating in the increasing disintegration. As far as liberal Protestantism is concerned, the question arises: How can it furnish a principle of reintegration if its own principles do not themselves transcend the disintegrating secularism? This is true of its thought, in which it depends on the increasingly meaningless intellectual life in general; and it is true of its action, in which it is drawn into the increasingly contradictory social life both within and between national states. Consequently, people who are embarrassed by the meaninglessness of their existence generally prefer the opposing tendencies—fundamentalism, Barthianism, Buchmanism, and many other movements which reject liberalism entirely. These people want to have a principle which transcends their whole disintegrated existence in individual and social life. But the difficulty is that these movements use unintelligible symbols which are powerless for dealing with the present. Barthianism, for example, has shown its power to save the German church from paganization by giving theological aims to a group of struggling ministers, but it has not been able to reintegrate the younger generation or the masses of disintegrated proletarians or even middle-class persons. It is Protestantism merely in the sense of protest and negation. Hence Protestantism still has to discover a possible approach which will enable it to cope with the world situation. The continued existence of Protestantism in the coming era depends on its role in the present and near future.

The consequences of the Protestant principle for intellectual, moral, and social life are obvious. Protestantism is a highly intellectualized religion. The minister's gown of today is the professor's gown of the Middle Ages, symbolizing the fact that the theological faculties as the interpreters of the Bible became the ultimate authority in the Protestant churches. But professors are intellectual authorities—i.e., authorities by virtue of skill in logical and scientific argument. This sort of authority is the exact opposite of the kind that is sought by the disintegrated masses, whose disintegration is to some extent an echo of the endless arguments and counterarguments among their leaders. Bishops, priests, and monarchs have a sacramental authority which cannot be taken away by arguments and which is independent of the intellectual and moral qualities of its carriers. It is a character which can by no means be lost. This sacramental basis is denied by the Protestant protest. The minister is preacher, not priest; and sermons are intended, first of all, to appeal to the intellect. But masses that are disintegrated need symbols that are immediately understandable without the mediation of intellect. They need sacred objectivities beyond the subjective quality of a preacher. The Bible, the dogma, the holy legend, the rites of the holy days as well as of the daily life, the symbolic realities that give meaning to our existence, generally and specially, from birth to death, and the church and its representatives in the past and present were objectivities in this sense. But very few such objectivities remain in the Protestant churches. Instead, under the influence of the Protestant layman, a rationalization of the doctrine—attempts at a reasonable understanding—arose and dissolved the religious mystery more and more. Protestant education in its reasonable and moralistic attitude, although it was capable of educating selected individuals, failed in the education of the masses. More and more individuals became unable to endure the tremendous responsibility of permanently having to decide in intellectual and moral issues. The weight of this responsibility became so heavy that they could not endure it; and mental diseases have become epidemic in the United States as well as in Europe. In this situation, psychoanalysis has seemed more desirable for educated people than religion, especially Protestant religion. In Catholic countries the situation has been different because the confession has been able to overcome many tendencies toward personal disintegration.[1]

Finally, we have to consider the social and political aspects of the Protestant attitude. The most important point is the lack of an independent hierarchy in Protestantism. While the Catholic hierarchy confers a social and political independence upon its church, Protestantism is dependent either on the state or on certain social groups. It is almost impossible for it to be independent of the state because the entire social existence of the church is based on state support. Since the princes became emergency bishops in the Lutheran Reformation, we have had no real bishops in German Protestantism, but only more or less general superintendents, who in some countries have assumed the title of "bishop." In the United States the trustees are the "outstanding members" of the congregation, corresponding to the princes or state secretaries in central Europe. The danger of this situation is the identifi-

---

1. The success of psychoanalysis in Protestant countries has two main reasons: (1) the rigorous moralism which developed in Protestantism after the sacramental grace was taken away and which poisons the personality through repressing vital impulses by moral law and social conventions and (2) the solitude of the deciding individual, who has to bear responsibility and guilt without the help of confession and the related forgiveness which comes from the outside.

cation of the outlook of the church with the interests of a special social group and the practical exclusion of opposition groups from influence on the spirit of the churches. In periods of social disintegration this means the disintegration of the church itself. It can offer but slight resistance against destructive tendencies, and it has very little power to provide an independent principle of reintegration. Furthermore, it could not do so even if it had the power, since Protestantism has no autonomous system of social and political ethics which can serve as a criterion for every social order, as Catholicism has in Thomism.

Hence non-Protestant forces predominate today in the tremendous efforts of mass reintegration which are taking place in the three systems of centralized authority, namely, communism, fascism, and Roman Catholicism. Protestantism is merely on the defensive.

The analysis of the survival possibilities of Protestantism in the present situation may be formulated as follows:

1. Protestantism as a church for the masses can continue to exist only if it succeeds in undergoing a fundamental change. To do this it must obtain a new understanding of symbols and all those things which we have called "sacred objectivities." To continue to live, it must reformulate its appeal so that it will provide a message which a disintegrated world seeking reintegration will accept. It has to remold its forms of life, its constitution, its rites, and its individual and social ethics. But the precondition for any readjustment is that the Protestant leaders become aware of the seriousness of their situation. Protestantism is still in a position where it can appeal to the needs of the present-day world, but perhaps the world will soon cease waiting and will go over to some type of catholicism—more Christian, like Roman Catholicism; or more pagan, like national socialism; or more humanistic, like communism, all of which movements have more power of mass reintegration than Protestantism has.

2. In making readjustments Protestantism can draw on certain resources which are inaccessible to every form of catholicism, i.e., the power of dealing with the secular world in a more differentiated and direct manner than any other religion is able to do. Protestantism denies in principle the cleavage between a sacred and a profane sphere. Since to it God alone is holy in himself and since no church, no doctrine, no saint, no institution, and no rite is holy in itself, every man and every thing and every group is profane in itself and is sacred

only in so far as it becomes a symbol of the divine holiness. This attitude, which contains within itself the danger of becoming exclusively secular, is already understood and realized by the Protestant churches in the United States. The conception of the Kingdom of God as a concern not only for the individual soul but also for social, political, and cultural life is one of those ideas of world Protestantism which have developed primarily in this country. But in Europe, too, Protestantism has certain possibilities which do not exist for Catholicism. Religious socialism was able to emerge in European Protestantism despite the conservative attitude of the churches, while the attempt to arouse such a movement in Catholicism has failed, despite its connection with socialist parties. And we have the same situation in the realms of philosophy, art, psychology, and education. While Catholicism deals with these things from the point of view of having the entire truth and the perfect form of life, Protestantism is always learning, without the claim of being itself the Kingdom of God.

3. The most important contribution of Protestantism to the world in the past, present, and future is the principle of prophetic protest against every power which claims divine character for itself—whether it be church or state, party or leader. Obviously, it is impossible to build a church on the basis of a pure protest, and that attempt has been the mistake of Protestantism in every epoch. But the prophetic protest is necessary for every church and for every secular movement if it is to avoid disintegration. It has to be expressed in every situation as a contradiction to man's permanent attempts to give absolute validity to his own thinking and acting. And this prophetic, Protestant protest is more necessary today than at any time since the period of the Reformation, as the protest against the demonic abuse of those centralized authorities and powers which are developing under the urge of the new collectivism. It is in this Protestant protest that the eternal value of liberalism is rooted. Without this prophetic criticism the new authorities and powers will necessarily lead toward a new and more far-reaching disintegration. This criticism requires witnesses and martyrs. Without these, the prophetic and Protestant protest never has been and never will be actual.

Concerning these three points of view (the Catholic or sacramental element, the profane or contemporaneous element, and the prophetic or critical element) it should be asked whether Protestantism will be able to unite these elements or whether they will be represented by different groups (the first by the Catholic churches, the second by an independent secular world, the third by individuals or groups of a sectarian character). In the latter case Protestantism as embodied in the churches would come to an end. "The end of the Protestant era" would be at hand. Must we then look forward to an occidental world divided into Christian Catholicism, nationalistic paganism, and communistic humanism—i.e., into three systems of authority—as means of mass reintegration? It is not necessary that this be realized in a formal dissolution of the existing Protestant churches. This seems scarcely likely. But the change may go on—and is, indeed, already going on—as a slow, or perhaps not so slow, change of mind in the new generations, a change from an autonomous to a heteronomous attitude, a change toward Catholicism in some and toward national paganism or communistic humanism in the very great majority. To remain a member of a Protestant church does not mean remaining a real Protestant. Those who believe in the divine revelation in a nationalistic leader may be Protestant church members, but they have ceased to be Protestants. Those who believe in the Kingdom of God as something to be realized fully in a coming period of social justice and intellectual truth may never leave the Protestant church, but they are not Protestants in the true meaning of the term. If we apply this criterion we must ask: Where are the Protestants? Where are those for whom the faith of the Reformers is their highest symbol, giving them unity and meaning? There are some with this attitude in all Protestant churches. There are ministers and laymen, professors and students, in all denominations who hold to their Protestantism as the only form in which they can be Christian. But although they themselves are not yet forced into disintegration and meaninglessness, they recognize them as a reality in the masses and as a threat to themselves, and thereby they tend to lose their unbroken Protestant character. Understandably, they try to confirm it through providing a religious reservation beyond the temporal powers of disintegration, decay, and meaninglessness. They cling to the old dogmas or to a belief in a merely transcendent revelation which has no relationship to the temporal or to the salvation of their individual souls. It is a Protestantism of retreat and defense. And though it is often a very strong defense, as the German church struggle shows, it is, nevertheless, a defense and not an attack. Will the survival of Protestantism take the form of a retreat to a reservation, analogous to the way in which the Indians have survived in the United States? Protestantism could survive by this means, but it would cease to have any serious formative influence on the period of transformation which has been going on since the first World War.

Or is there a chance that the Protestant churches as they are will transform themselves into churches which will be able to give a principle of reintegration to the present world? There are many movements in Protestant churches which are attempting to introduce certain elements of Catholicism, such as episcopal authority or a new understanding of sacraments or an enrichment of rites or new forms of meditation and new symbols. But all these measures encounter the obstacle of having no root in the traditional feeling of Protestants; consequently, they very often give the impression of imitations rather than of original creations, and for this reason they lack the power of conviction. Hence to say that Protestantism, if it is to maintain itself, must draw certain lessons from the history of Catholicism does not mean that it should learn in the ordinary way of imitation and repetition. It must seek a new foundation if it is to survive at all in its essential aspects. And this raises the question of a third possible way. If the transformation of the churches as a whole is impossible and if the way of retreat into a reservation would mean the end of Protestantism as a living power in the present, then we must ask: Is there a third way in which Protestantism can continue to exist? If there is such a way it cannot dispense with the imperative of basing itself on the prophetic principle in Protestantism and its capability of dealing directly with the secular world. If it failed to do so, it would not be the Protestantism that we are speaking about. This third way requires that Protestantism appear as the prophetic spirit which lists where it will, without ecclesiastical conditions, organization, and traditions. Thus it will operate through Catholicism as well as through orthodoxy, through fascism as well as through communism; and in all these movements it will take the form of resistance against the distortion of humanity and divinity which necessarily is connected with the rise of the new systems of authority. But this imperative would remain a very idealistic demand if there were no living group which could be bearer of this spirit. Such a group could not be described adequately as a sect. It would approximate more closely an order or fellowship and would constitute an active group, aiming to realize, first, in itself that transformation of Protestantism which cannot be realized either by the present churches or by the movements of retreat and defense. It would therefore be a group in which the Christian message would be understood as the reintegrating principle in the disintegrating world situation of today. This, in its turn, would imply the following conditions for its members: (1) a decision in favor of the Protestant principle in the interpretation of human existence without the necessity of belonging to a Protestant or even a Christian church; (2) a decision in favor of the application of the principle to the present situation as the reintegrating power without the necessity of belonging to a special philosophical or political party; (3) a decision in favor of a general program containing the foundation of the group on the Protestant principle (this would exclude the criticism of this foundation itself); (4), a decision for special programs containing the application of the general program to the needs of the special groups within denominations, churches, nations, parties, races, classes, and continents—programs which are adequate to the task of every one of those special groups but from which are excluded all points contradicting the general program. There is no doubt that there are many objections to be made against the possibility of such a group's appearing. But in their very beginning all movements and their ideas seem very unrealistic with respect to a possible realization. The question is whether their roots lie deeply enough and whether their adequacy to the emerging historical reality is great enough. If there were such a movement, the end of the Protestant era would not yet have arrived.

V. THE PRESENT CRISIS

# Chapter XVI

## STORMS OF OUR TIMES[1]

### I

IT IS my first duty to thank you for the honor of addressing this
important congress, being myself a stranger both to your church,
of which I am not a member, and to your nation, which I have joined
only as a refugee from abroad. However, there is an advantage in my
situation. The boundary between two realms is the most favorable
position for understanding them. Although the power and the unity
of life is stronger in the center, the chance of observing and knowing
it is greater at the periphery. From the boundary line between two
churches, two nations, and two continents I am speaking to you today.

But I stand not only between the spaces but also between the times.
The generation to which I myself, as well as many of you, belong is a
generation between two periods of history. The only thing we can
hope to be is a bridge between the ages. None of our generation is
able to cross that bridge entirely. He who has lived for fourteen years
in the nineteenth century and for twenty-eight years in the unbroken
world of individualism and harmonism before the first World War
is not able to participate wholeheartedly in the period to come. He
can only see it, understand its inescapable approach, and explain its
causes and nature. That is what we can and must do. That is the help
we can give to the younger generation. For this task we have to provide a sufficient amount of scientific objectivity as well as of dynamic
participation in the actual movements of our period. But in spite of
this we shall remain bridges—and only that; and therefore, if the description of the storms of our times is itself somewhat stormy and
revolutionary, it is not my own stormy mood to which this is due but
the revolutionary nature of the process itself.

1. An address delivered at the Fiftieth Church Congress of the Protestant Episcopal
Church, in Indianapolis on May 6, 1942.

These words imply a presupposition, the main presupposition of my address—that the storms of our times are not a bad accident caused by some evil men, without whose interference everything would have remained as before. No evil men can make history unless the soil is prepared on a tremendous scale. Instead of accepting, therefore, the superficial and all too comfortable theory of accident, I shall develop a theory of "structural necessity." Structural necessity is not mechanical necessity; it has neither naturalistic nor deterministic implications. History is dependent on human action and, consequently, on human freedom and decision. But history, on the other hand, is not a series of accidents; it has a special structure in each of its periods, and it has predominant trends and natural tendencies against which individual acts are of no avail. On this character of history all historical understanding and all adequate and meaningful historical action is based. Without such a structural necessity, history could not be interpreted at all, and no prophetic message would ever have been possible.

On the basis of the assumption that present events are results of structural trends in the bourgeois society of the nineteenth and early twentieth centuries, I shall give an analysis of these trends and its implications. I shall drive the analysis to a point where the vision of a possible reconstruction during and after the war may appear. An analysis seems to be a matter of scientific detachment, of disinterested spectatorship. And, of course, without a great amount of objective knowledge and methodical self-restraint no convincing picture of the situation can be given. Fortunately, an immense scientific literature exists, analyzing all the points we have to deal with. Our task is only to elaborate the decisive lines and to combine them in a true and meaningful picture. But in such an analysis, whether it is more special or more general, still another element is contained, an element of personal involvement—in spite of scientific detachment—an element of valuation and decision, or, as it is called today, an "existential" element. Something that concerns our whole existence, our economic and political, cultural and religious existence, cannot be discussed as if we were unconcerned spectators. Therefore, the analytic and the constructive aspects cannot be separated. The analysis is presented for the purpose of a new construction, as the picture of the construction is painted on the background of the analysis.

## II

The main thesis of the following analysis is that the present world war is a part of a world revolution. Although it appears as a war of nations, it is something different, and it can be understood only in terms of the radical transformation of one period of history into another one. The very fact that world wars are possible and that they have become the only possible form of war shows a fundamental change from all former periods of history. Something has come into existence which never had existed before: world as a historical reality! The term "world"—*kosmos*—is derived from the unity and structural harmony of nature. It has been used also in a religious sense, and it has been applied finally to history as well. The concept of "world history" has often been used; but it could be used only as a metaphysical, not as an empirical, term. History as a unity of historical interactions has become possible only through the union of all nations of the earth by technical processes. This has taken place, but it has not been understood yet. The international and national institutions, the general forms of living and thinking all over the world, have not yet reached the insight that there is *world* in the concrete, technical, and historical sense. This is one of the reasons why the rise of the "historical world" first resulted in world wars. The world as a historical reality is being born in the labor pains of two wars. This is an expression of man's tragic situation; but it shows, at the same time, the need of a revolution which would make the institutions of mankind adequate to the new reality. We must become actually what we have become potentially: a "world."

The general character of the revolutionary transformation in the midst of which we are living can be described in the following way: Following the breakdown of the natural or automatic harmony on which the system of life and thought during the eighteenth and nineteenth centuries was based, the attempt is now being made to produce a system of life and thought which is based on an intentional and planned unity. This refers to all realms of human existence.

### A. THE ECONOMIC DEVELOPMENT

The economic sphere is the most important historical factor—not in all times, as some dogmatic Marxists assert—but certainly within bourgeois capitalism. Its development from the nineteenth to the twentieth century can be described in four stages. The first period is that of liberal capitalism in the sense of the classical theory of economic liberalism: many small enterprises appeared on the market in comparatively free competition. The market was surrounded by a large nonindustrial realm, agrarian and colonial, able to buy according to the laws of the market. Under these conditions the harmonistic presupposition that the economic interest of the whole is best guaranteed if everybody follows his individual economic interest agreed with reality to a great extent. The tremendous increase in social wealth and the general standard of living during this period is an experimental test for the relative truth of the theory of automatic harmony in the economic sphere. But the natural development of this period led to a second period (not foreseen in the classical theory) characterized by a monopolistic structure. The small competitors became more and more conquered by the big trusts and were finally annihilated, a process in which the basic element of liberal economy—free competition—was increasingly restricted and confined to a comparatively small group of big competitors. This development entailed some dangerous transformations of the original situation. The large investments made by the monopolistic enterprises could remain profitable only in an expanding economy. In the moment in which the expansion came to an end, either by a decrease in purchasing power or by the industrialization of the agrarian and colonial sectors (as, for instance, during the first World War), the investments could not return sufficient profit, and the crisis—the dark shadow of all economic liberalism—became more and more permanent. The harder competition made obligatory the use of all means of technical progress and produced additional unemployment, thus further reducing the purchasing power of the masses and deepening the crisis.

But more important than the immediate economic consequences of the monopolistic stage of liberal economy are its psychological effects on the masses. These effects have created a revolutionary situation in the whole Western world. There is no more terrible fate than the fate of permanent unemployment. The bombed-out workers of London tell us that the threat of unemployment is worse than the threat of death. Not only is the unemployed, like any other worker in capitalism, a quantity of working power to be bought and sold; he is also a working power which cannot be used. Not the economic misery connected with unemployment but the feeling of absolute meaninglessness is the worst element in it. The faces of the permanently unemployed which I saw in Germany in 1931 and in England in 1936—faces I never shall forget—are witnesses of the destructiveness of unemployment. The fact that this was the actual or threatening fate for millions in all countries of Western civilization is the background of the present revolutionary movements.

The third stage of the economic development—belonging exclusively to the twentieth century—is that of state interference in the system of free enterprise. It became necessary because the state could not permit the destruction of the big monopolies on which the life of the nation was essentially dependent. So the state had to support them in the crisis, in order to avoid a general breakdown and subsequent chaos. The state had to "socialize the losses." After that the interference had to continue in order to prevent the return of the crisis. So a certain amount of state interference became habitual. The classical form of it is the "New Deal." But state interference is only a half-measure and shares the danger of combining the shortcomings of both sides united in it. The interfering state disturbed the dispositions of the free enterprisers; and at the same time the state could not prevent them from counteracting its social purposes with respect to unemployment, wages, the use of natural resources, etc. So state interference could not overcome the dangers of the general situation, and it created a new danger, the political half-Fascist opposition of the monopolistic groups, who felt deprived of their unrestricted economic power by bureaucratic encroachments. In central Europe this has finally resulted in the Fascist organization of economy. It will lead in all countries to a new—the fourth—stage of the economic development.

The character of the fourth stage is the replacement of state interference by state command. It is "commanded economy" or "state capitalism." Whatever this might mean in the practical execution, however many liberal elements can be incorporated, in one point the structure is clear: it will be planned according to the needs of the whole; it will overcome unemployment and the underconsumption of the masses. It will create—whatever the price may be—the freedom from fear and want, from those fears and wants which belong to the later stages of capitalism. The totalitarian countries have made a radical step in this direction. They did it in a distorted and finally self-destructive way. But at least they did it. What are the democracies doing?

A system of harmony—with certain restrictions—did exist not only in the economic realm but also in the sphere of international relations. The political center, identical with the economic center, lay in Europe. There were colonies, dominions, and spheres of influence in the other parts of the world. The United States was completing her continental extension. In Europe, Great Britain—the market-center of Europe—balanced the relations of the Continental powers. In spite of many single disturbances, this system of "balance of power" worked rather well and seemed to confirm the general harmonistic view. At the same time it was an adequate form for the liberal world economy.

But when the imperialistic competition of the great nations led to the first World War, this system of harmony collapsed. During the war Europe lost its controlling position politically as well as economically. The United States and Japan became powers of first rank. Russia was separated from the European concert. The establishment of a French hegemony in Continental Europe proved to be a failure. The establishment of a large number of sovereign national states on the narrow European Continent proved to be disastrous and just the opposite of what the situation demanded. Each of them, maintaining an independent army, diplomacy, and economy, was set against all the others and played a game which brought all of them to the complete loss of independence. The attempt to counteract the evil consequences of this type of sovereignty by the League of Nations failed because the League itself was built on the same principle of national sovereignty. So the second World War showed even more strongly than the first that the harmony of the balance of power has gone and that it must be replaced by a planned unity of nations, in Asia, in America, on the European Continent, and by an all-embracing unity of all nations. To this unity the great Asiatic nations must belong, not as colonies or spheres of European influence but on an equal basis with the Anglo-Saxon and Continental nations. Not only Japan but also China and India are using the present world revolution for the purpose of removing completely the control of the white nations. The Axis powers have seen all this. They have created an enforced unity by conquest and suppression in Europe, and they have driven the white rulers from many Asiatic countries by subjecting them to their own imperialism. They did it, and do it, in a distorted and self-destructive way. But at least they did it! What are our plans?

### C. THE POLITICAL SYSTEM

Democracy is not a political system *in abstracto,* to be imposed at any time in any place. Democracy has definite historical presuppositions without which it cannot work. It presupposes a large amount of natural harmony and conformity. There must be a basic amount of agreement between the parties, in spite of many points of disagreement. "His Majesty's opposition" must be "most loyal." And there must be a great amount of confidence in the representatives on the part of the voters. The delegates must really be *"our* delegates." Both demands presuppose a fundamentally united interest of the whole nation, which is of more importance to everybody than his own special, deviating interests. If this is the case, each citizen can subject himself willingly to the decisions of the majority, accepting them as the "general will" of which his will is a part. Working democracy presupposes a basically common interest among all its members, whether it is a real or an imagined interest.

If the harmonistic foundation of a democratic system disappears, the democracy breaks down. If the minority gets the feeling that its basic interests are permanently disregarded by the majority, the opposition ceases to be loyal. It denies the system as such; a totalitarian party is formed for the sake of a revolutionary overthrow of the existing political system. This was the situation in Europe, especially in central Europe. From two sides the discontent with the democratic way arose—from the side of the ruling classes and from the side of the economically disintegrated masses. The masses were afraid that the democratic method never would be able to liberate them from misery and unemployment, even under a government in which their own delegates participated. They had experienced too many disillusionments. And the ruling classes were afraid that the democratic way would finally create a parliamentary majority representing the disinherited masses and threatening the position of the economically ruling groups. So sections of both groups joined the predemocratic, half-feudal revolt of desperadoes of the lower middle classes—the Fascist or National Socialist religious-political "Order." The democratic system could not stand this attack from three sides. It fell with its harmonistic foundation. The situation in the originally democratic countries is not so grave as it was in central Europe, except for France. The basic conformism in which democracy is rooted is still alive in England, America, and some smaller nations. But even here the danger-point was nearly reached in the great economic crises, and American democracy was saved only because the power of the central bureaucracy was strengthened to such a degree that a complete catastrophe could be prevented. Today the war has produced a bureaucratic centralism in all countries, even in those in which the democratic method is still used. The critical situation for the democratic system will arise after the war, when the reorganization of a world in ruins will create tasks for which the ordinary democratic methods cannot be used at all. The necessity of a central organization of the European economy alone—not to speak of Asia—demands a basic transformation of the political system.

The abominable form of the totalitarian methods in Europe should not close our eyes to the emergency out of which they have arisen: the breakdown of harmonism. And they should not prevent us from recognizing that a return to the former ways of liberal democracy is impossible. The dictators understood this situation. Can we claim the same?

### D. THE CULTURAL MOVEMENT

The cultural life after the period of the Enlightenment was based on the presupposition that the intellectual and moral development of the individual would lead to a cultural "common sense," able to create a harmonious and progressive civilization. The autonomous search for truth by the "parliament of sciences" was supposed to produce a sufficient amount of certain truths to guide the life of society. Education for social adjustment, on the one hand, and a critical spirit, on the other hand, were supposed to produce an even higher moral level and social progress from generation to generation. Freedom for personal experiences unrestricted by tradition and dogma was supposed to create common symbols of an ultimate, uniting, and obligatory character. The law of harmony seemed to overcome the dangers of a radical cultural liberalism.

This assumption was not entirely wrong. It was partly justified as long as a strong cultural heritage existed, and with it a natural conformity. On this basis the freedom of every individual for autonomous thought and criticism did not endanger the social unity. But when, with the increase of the social and political contrasts, the ideological harmony disappeared, unrestricted freedom of criticism became disastrous, and authoritarian trends developed. This was the European cultural situation during the years before Hitler came to power.

The picture of western Europe, from Great Britain to Italy, as I saw it in the years 1936 and 1937, was the picture of a complete cultural disintegration, especially in the younger generation. This disintegration expressed itself in four main ways of feeling among most of the younger and many of the older people.

First of all, a feeling of *fear* or, more exactly, of indefinite anxiety was prevailing. Not only the economic and political, but also the cultural and religious, security seemed to be lost. There was nothing on which one could build; everything was without foundation. A catastrophic breakdown was expected every moment. Consequently, a longing for security was growing in everybody. A freedom that leads to fear and anxiety has lost its value: better authority with security than freedom with fear!

Related to the feeling of insecurity and fear was a general *uncertainty*. About 1930 a book appeared by the French writer Viennot, *Incertitudes allemands* ("German Uncertainties"), in which the German situation before Hitler's rise to power was described. The title also fitted the situation in France, Belgium, and other countries, as history has shown. The younger generation was tired of making decisions about everything, including their own existence. They could not bear any longer the burden of autonomous thinking and acting. They could not stand any more a life in which nothing was certain. Consequently, they were longing for a certainty to be gained at any price, even the price of a complete heteronomy and subjection under a leader. The situation may become more understandable if we compare it with the method of progressive education in this country. This method has two aspects: the education for adjustment, namely, to the

standards and forms of the given society; and within this frame the
education for autonomous thinking and discussion. The latter is not
dangerous as long as the former is stable; for then even the most
critical thought does not transcend the limits of the social conformity
to which the pupils are adjusted. But if the given social and intellectual structure disintegrates and the conformity vanishes, the autonomy
of the pupil acts within an empty space and cannot reach that amount
of certainty without which life is impossible in the long run. This,
exactly, was the European attitude.

The third characteristic of the cultural disintegration was *loneliness*.
In the system of harmony the metaphysical solitude of every individual is strongly emphasized by the doctrine that there are "no doors
and windows" from one "monad" to the other one. Every single unit
is lonely in itself, without any direct communication. The horror of
this idea was overcome by the harmonistic presupposition that in
every monad the whole world is potentially present and that the development of each individual is in a natural harmony with the development of all the others. This is the most profound metaphysical
symbol for the situation in the early periods of bourgeois civilization.
It fitted this situation because there was still a common world, in spite
of the increasing social atomization. But when the remnants of a
common world broke down, the individual was thrown into complete
loneliness and the despair connected with it. So the younger generation in all European countries tried to escape this situation, to overcome the solitude of individualism, and to discover a new community.
The youth movements, since the beginning of the twentieth century,
are the most visible expression of this longing.

The fourth and most basic symptom of the cultural disintegration
is the feeling of *meaninglessness* and the resulting cynicism. Not only
the religious symbols of earlier centuries had lost their power of giving a meaning to life, but also the philosophical and political symbols
which were supposed to replace them. So everything was missing
which could make an absolute claim for surrender and devotion. But
youth wants just such a claim. It wants strong, unquestioned, commanding symbols. It looks for religious symbols—and, if it cannot
find them, for quasi-religious ones. Otherwise, youth—and not only
youth—despairs of any meaning in life. Skepticism and cynicism conquer the spirit and open the hearts for the entrance of "demonic"

symbols. He who provides them can easily become a leader, and cynicism is not far from fanaticism.

This was the chance of the Fascist and National Socialist revolutions. The Fascists and National Socialists realized their chance and used it with all possible means. They promised security and certainty and community and a new meaning of life; and they provided all this, though in a demonic and self-destructive way. They sacrificed freedom for security, autonomy for certainty, individuality for community, and personality for an absolute symbol. They fulfilled the longing of a large part of the younger generation. And what have we to offer them?

### E. THE RELIGIOUS SITUATION

The problem of the meaning of life, expressed in uniting powerful symbols of ultimate concern, leads to the question of the religious situation, for being religious means being ultimately concerned. Religion is not exempted from the general trends of theoretical and practical activity. The religious situation was determined by the idea of automatic harmony as much as was the situation in all other spheres. The historical actualization of the idea of harmony in religion is Protestantism. The Protestant protest against the distorted authority, certainty, collectivism, and symbolism of the Roman Catholic church has brought about that kind of religious freedom, autonomy, individualism, and personalism through which the Protestant churches became parts of the modern world. In Luther as well as in Calvin we find the presupposition that the mere hearing or reading of the biblical message would create a religious common sense and that preaching alone is sufficient for the making and maintenance of the Christian church. Wherever the Word is rightly preached, it must create the community of believers. Even this highly idealistic assumption was true for nearly two centuries. A Christian education of more than a thousand years had fashioned the soul of the European nations in such a way that Protestant autonomy did not imperil their spiritual substance. This substance responded spontaneously to evangelical preaching.

But, since the period of the Enlightenment, this substance has slowly been lost, and subsequently the law of harmony ceased to be valid. It was not a catastrophic change, for the enlightened *bourgeoisie* maintained a rationalized and weakened Christian tradition in order to maintain itself and the social and cultural system in which bourgeois society is rooted. But this "pragmatic" justification of the religious tradition could not prevent its full disintegration and the rise of a complete secularization not only against religion but also of religion itself. In this way the Protestant churches were drawn into the general process of the dissolution of the harmonistic system of the modern world. The question is whether or not this means the end of Protestantism in the sense of the Protestant churches and cultures, as one might conclude from the analysis of the present revolution. There are movements in the Protestant churches toward a better understanding of symbolism, toward ritual reforms, toward the strengthening of the church authorities, toward a new valuation of the sacramental reality, toward a new ecumenical church. Will the Protestant churches be able to undergo such a transformation without losing the Protestant principles on which they are built? What help can the Anglican church—and in a more remote way the Greek Orthodox churches—give in this regard? Is the middle way of the Episcopalian church a new creative way, or is it the way of a compromise, uniting the weaknesses of both sides? These questions are fundamental for the analysis of the "storms of our times" in the religious sphere; and the religious sphere is the most important if we really are living not in a war of national imperialisms but in a war which is the expression of a revolutionary transformation of human existence.

Even in this respect the totalitarian leaders understood the situation; they renewed the old Shintoist emperor-cult, or they created a new pagan creed, or they divided authority and symbols with the Catholic church, or they used the eschatological hope as the dynamic force of the social revolution. They produced quasi-religions; but these quasi-religions became such strong and largely victorious competitors of Christianity and Protestantism that again we must ask: What have we done for the fulfilment of the religious demand in the present world revolution?

The picture of our time is consistent in all realms of life. It does not fit equally all countries and all levels of the population. There are differences in space and time—the most thorough disintegration has taken place in Europe, especially in central Europe; Russia has jumped directly from the feudal form to her type of post-bourgeois structure; America lives still in a happy backwardness; Asia tries to avoid the bourgeois stage as much as possible. But in spite of these differences, the main trend is obvious, and the dynamic forces are visible to everybody.

### III

If the nature of this war is "world revolution," then its aim must be "world reconstruction" in such a way that the causes of this revolution will be overcome. This is true of all the spheres in which the system of harmony has disintegrated, and that means in the totality of our existence. Therefore, two ways of finishing this war must be excluded completely: the return to the situation before the outbreak of the war, the "status quo" solution; and the conditioned acceptance of the plans of the Axis powers, the "compromise" solution.

The status quo solution never is suggested in a pure and unrestricted form. Everybody knows that history never repeats itself, and everybody agrees that some drastic changes must be made, especially in the international realm. But most people believe that amendments of the old structure are sufficient to keep it alive. If this were carried through, the consequences would be the following: in the economic realm, monopoly capitalism would be re-established and the state interferences entirely removed—up to the next crisis. A few dozens of sovereign states would again disrupt the European Continent—up to the next catastrophe. Asia would be brought back under the white rulers—up to a fully developed racial war. Democracy would be superimposed on a heap of ruined, despised, and uprooted groups—up to the appearance of fighting dictator-generals. Freedom would be forced on people who are anxiously longing for security; individualism on people who are desperately in need of community; autonomy on people who need leadership; personalism on masses who are in want of uniting, absolute, and catching symbols. These are the implications of the status quo solution, however cautiously it may be framed. It seems that destiny is wiser than the representatives of this solution. It seems that the radical progress of the revolution itself has made impossible such a world-historical relapse.

It needs no proof that the acceptance of the war aims of the Axis, even in a very restricted form, would mean the destruction of all values and symbols of Christianity and humanism. The compromise solution is no solution but the victory of the other side. But, although there can be no doubt about this, there is a properly justified doubt about the willingness of all groups among the allied nations to resist any compromise with the present leaders of the Axis. This doubt is suggested by the very nature of fascism and national socialism. These movements are carried by people who are the products of the disintegration of all social classes, the workers as well as the ruling classes, the intelligentsia as well as the lower middle classes. Although the lower middle-class group is most important for the fascist ideologies, it is not so important for the dynamism of the movement as has often been assumed. The ideology is taken cynically by a large number of leading National Socialists. But the fact that fascism recruits its supporters from all social levels gives it the possibility of appealing to all of them. How strong this appeal was in many countries is well known; and—in spite of all opposite assurances—it is still strong in many sections of the world and in many individuals all over the world.

There are people in the democratic countries who are inclined to a compromise because they realize that every additional year of warfare removes farther away the chance of a return to the past for the status quo solution. And for them the war is not worth while to be fought and—above all—to be paid for if it really proves to be a revolutionary war. This attitude has received much support because of the entrance of Russia into the war and the fear that she and her ideology may become decisive for the reconstruction of Europe and Asia. There are other people who have realized that the status quo solution has no chance at all. They understand the revolutionary character of this war. But they want to give it a direction which is not greatly different from the Fascist methods and aims. They work for an American or British branch of fascism, without calling it such, without accepting its anti-Christian and antihumanistic propaganda, without revealing their real purposes as frankly as the European dictators do. Anti-Semitic, antialien, anti–New Deal, anti-worker propaganda, increasing in this country, is the expression of the American type of fascism. They do not want Hitler's victory, not at all; but they want their own fascism—if they cannot get the status quo. There are similar trends in Britain, less active today than in America, but by no means nonexistent. For all these people, Hitler and Mussolini are not merely the enemies but, at the same time, in a transformed way, the models. Against both groups—the status quo supporters and the compromisers —the real meaning of this war must be emphasized again and again. Nothing is more perilous for the war effort of the allied nations than the lack of a great and powerful war aim. The general demand for a statement of war aims has brought about the Atlantic Charter, which is more than nothing, but much less than what we need. Its failure to include Asia is sufficient to reduce its value greatly. Many private and official groups are working for a statement about postwar reconstruction. This fact proves the general feeling that the merely negative purpose of winning the war is not sufficient. We won one war and lost the peace disastrously. If those who make the peace, and the public opinion behind them, will not realize the demands following from the causes and nature of this war, then the peace will be lost once more. It is not my task to outline a program of war aims on this occasion as I have done before. The analysis itself has shown the direction in which the postwar reconstruction must be conceived: a planned economy with as much individual spontaneity as possible; a federation of federations of nations without military and economic sovereignty of the member-nations; a centralized state power with democratic correctives; a security which guarantees freedom—freedom from want and fear; an authority which is leadership and not command; a community which overcomes loneliness by a more collectivistic form of life, without sacrificing the meaning and right of the individual; symbols expressing in a convincing and uniting way an ultimate, unconditioned, and demanding concern and giving life meaning for the coming generations. This is the direction in which we have to think and to act; it is the direction in which a program must be sought; but it is not the program itself.

Let me finish with three questions by which our attitude to the meaning of this war can be tested.

When we fight against Japan, do we fight a racial war, a war for the maintenance of European imperialism in Asia, or do we fight for the freedom of Asia also from ourselves?

When we fight on the side of Russia, do we fight on her side because it is useful for us to do so for the time being, but with the intention of excluding her once more from European affairs, or do we acknowledge seriously her right to determine, on an equal basis with the Western nations, the destiny of Europe and Asia?

When we fight in Europe, do we go as punishers, educators, cultural and economic conquerors in order to actualize the "American century," or do we go in order to help Europe to survive and to be re-established in new forms and for a new future?

The answer to these three questions is important not only for those at home who think about the peace but also for the thinking soldiers who fight the war and want to know for what they are fighting. What hope do we have for a constructive answer to these three questions? How much hope does the situation in Great Britain give us, how much that in America? I cannot answer this question. But what I do know is that if the meaning of this war is not understood and accepted, night will fall over us for generations.

# Chapter XVII

## MARXISM AND CHRISTIAN SOCIALISM

MARXISM has never been accepted indiscriminately and without a serious criticism by the religious-socialist movements. A large part of the theoretical foundation of religious socialism was dedicated to a thorough discussion of the doctrines of Marx and the Marxians. The result of these discussions, in most cases, was partly a rejection, partly an acceptance and an essential transformation of the Marxist teachings by leading religious socialists. Has this situation changed? Has the gap between Christianity and Marxism deepened, either because Marxism has lost its significance and its power to interpret the present world, or because Christianity has developed in an entirely divergent direction? There are, indeed, elements in Marxism which have become obsolete, and there are developments in Christianity which tend to disrupt any connection between it and the ideas of Marx and his followers. But this does not mean that all elements in Marxism have lost their significance and that the entire Christian theology has turned against Marxism. On the contrary—it seems to me that important elements of the Marxist method of thinking are merged with theological thought to such a degree that they are not recognized any more as taken over from Marxism. This is especially true of the realistic and pessimistic interpretation of the human situation by neosupernaturalism and dialectical theology. In order to come to a decision about this question we must first remember why and in which respect Marxism was appreciated and criticized by religious socialism.

### I. THE THEOLOGICAL APPRECIATION OF MARXISM

The main reason for the theological appreciation of Marxism is a striking structural analogy between the prophetic and the Marxian interpretation of history. This has often been carried through and needs only to be mentioned. Both prophetism and Marxism are historical interpretations of history, that is, interpretations in which history has a meaning of its own and is not only a continuation of the general natural process or a place of preparation for the supra-natural. History has an aim toward which it is moving and the fulfilment of which is the meaning of every historical event. And since history has an end, it also has a beginning and a center, a point where its meaning becomes visible and in the light of which an interpretation of history becomes possible. Both prophetism and Marxism regard the fight between good and evil forces as the main content of history, describing the evil forces mainly as the forces of injustice and envisaging the ultimate victory of justice. This interpretation creates in both cases an eschatological mood, a tension of expectation, a directedness toward the future which is entirely lacking in all kinds of sacramental and mystical religion. Both prophetism and Marxism attack the existing order of society and personal piety as the expression of a universal evil in a special period. They passionately challenge concrete forms of injustice, threatening those responsible for it, especially the ruling groups, with the judgment of history and imminent destruction as the inescapable consequence of social injustice. Both prophetism and Marxism believe that the transition from the present stage of history into the stage of fulfilment will occur in a catastrophe or in a series of catastrophic events, the end of which will be the establishment of a kingdom of peace and justice and the symptoms of which are already recognizable to the divining or analytic spirit. The feeling that the catastrophic coming of the "new" is "at hand" is strong in both of them. Both prophetism and Marxism believe that certain minority groups within a selected nation or class are the real bearers of the historical destiny, that through their action the meaning of history is carried into reality. The free actions of these groups are considered as the instruments of the historical destiny. Freedom and historical destiny are not contradictory for prophetic and Marxist thinking. Mechanistic necessity, as well as accidental contingency of the process of history, is denied by both. Prophetic, as well as genuine Marxist, dialectics are above the level of this alternative.

The structural analogy between prophetism and Marxism is not confined to their interpretations of history. It also refers to main elements in their doctrines of man. This is true not only of the prophetic but also of the Christian doctrine of man generally. Man is not what he ought to be; his true being and his real existence contradict each other. Man is fallen, if not from an original actual goodness, at least from a stage of undeveloped innocence. He is estranged from himself and his true humanity, he has been dehumanized, he has become an object, a means of profit, a quantity of working power—according to Marx. He is estranged from his divine destiny, he has lost the true dignity of his being, the image of God, he is separated from his fellow-man by pride, cupidity, and the will-to-power—according to Christianity. Christianity and Marxism agree that the nature of man cannot be determined from above history, that man's historical existence is decisive for every doctrine of man. And they agree that the nature of man cannot be determined by the characteristics of the individual man. Man is a social being, and his evil as well as his good is dependent on his social existence. Perdition and salvation are universal and historical. The individual as an individual cannot escape the former and cannot reach the latter. He is a part of a fallen world, whether the fall is expressed in religious or sociological terms; and he can become a part of a new world, whether this new world is conceived of in terms of a supra-historical or an infra-historical transformation. From this it follows that the idea of the truth in both Christianity and Marxism lies beyond the separation of theory and practice. The truth must be "done" in order to be recognized. Without a transformation of reality, no true knowledge of reality is possible. The situation of knowing is decisive for one's ability or inability to know. Only the "spiritual man" can judge everything, according to Paul, and only the man who participates in the struggle of the "elected group" against the class-society is able to understand the true character of being. Expressed in more concrete terms, the church or the fighting proletariat is the place where truth has the greatest chance to be accepted. In all the other spheres the general distortion of our historical existence makes it difficult, if not impossible, to find a true insight into the human situation and through it into being itself. The fate of self-deception or—as Marx called it—of the production of ideologies is inescapable, except in selected groups which are predominantly composed of people in ultimate anxiety, despair, and meaninglessness. On the boundary of all human possibilities the new possibility arises and gains power. If all ideological veils are torn down and self-deception is no longer possible, truth can appear and can be acted upon. And it is revealed only in the measure in which it is acted upon. The protest of the reformers against the "self-made" gods or idols and the protest of Marx against the self-made ideas or ideologies challenge the same spiritual danger of man in his present existence: to make the truth a means of religious pride or political will-to-power. In all these points Christianity and Marxism are united in their opposition to a "Pelagian" or "harmonistic" optimism with respect to the nature of man.

## II. THE THEOLOGICAL CRITICISM OF MARXISM

The basic difference between religious socialism and Marxism is rooted in their different attitudes toward the idea of transcendence. There is a kind of transcendence in Marxism, i.e., the limits of the present possibilities of human nature are transcended by the expectation of a coming stage of justice. A kind of miracle in the transition from the present to the future stage of mankind is presupposed, at least implicitly. And it is obvious that Marxism draws a great deal of its psychological power from this element of transcendence and faith. But this transcendence is not the absolute transcendence of Christianity. It remains in time and space, in history and politics. It is dependent on immanent processes. It transcends the present time, but not time as such. It does not know eternity breaking into time, shaking, turning, and transforming the temporal. Marxism never reaches this transcendence. It is suspicious of it. Religion, because of its supra-temporal nature, is considered to be an ideology, i.e., a system of ideas and symbols which have no basis in reality but which are invented for the sake of making the misery of the disinherited classes more bearable to them and, consequently, for the sake of breaking their revolutionary impulse by a mystical opiate. This is the theory of religion in original, as well as in late, Marxism. Obviously, this theory had to be criticized sharply by religious socialism. Religions of this type are distortions of what religion essentially is. This distortion is always possible and has often become a historical power in the sense in which Marxism describes it. But such a description does not fit prophetic religion and its fight against the demonic powers of history and of the personal life. And even the "sacramental" element in religion is not simply ideology. It is also the basis of the prophetic element because only in the power of the Holy that is present can the Holy that is future be expected and realized. In any case, religious socialism follows the Christian and all great religious messages in affirming the transcendent, invisible, and eternal character of the ultimate fulfilment of history and human life. History is fulfilled above history, not within history.

From this follow some basic differences between religious socialism and Marxism. Although Marx had fought against what he called "utopian socialism," he himself and, even more, his followers did not escape dangerous elements of utopianism themselves. They did not expect, of course, that the class situation could be changed by persuasion of the ruling classes, but they did expect that the economic process, in unity with the revolutionary impulse of the proletarian classes, would create the fulfilment of history—the classless society in which the main evils of the earlier mankind, of its "prehistory" as Marx called it, would be overcome. Religious socialism, on the contrary, has always maintained that the demonic forces of injustice, pride, and will-to-power never will be eradicated from the historical scene, although special manifestations of it, such as capitalism and nationalism, might be conquered. Therefore, religious socialism turned the anti-ideological criticism as much against itself and against all the other socialist and Marxist groups as against the enemies of socialism. The sharpest criticism of the socialist movement comes from religious socialism, while the lack of such a self-criticism, for instance, in the social-democratic parties, contributed much to their catastrophes. For the same reason, religious socialism, contrary to Marxism, upholds the importance of the personal life and its transformation for the revolutionary movement. The personal shortcomings of the leaders of the socialist groups and the lack of a profound education and discipline in the vanguards of the movement are due to the immanentist attitude of Marxism, to its overemphasis on the institutional, and to its lack of understanding of personal factors. For religious socialism the corrupted human situation has deeper roots than mere historical and sociological structures. It is rooted in the depth of the human heart. And in the same way the regeneration of mankind is not possible through institutional and political changes alone, but it also requires changes in the personal attitude of many people toward life. Therefore, for religious socialism the turning-point of history is not the rise of the proletariat but the appearance of a new meaning and power of life in the divine self-manifestation. These differences are of tremendous importance; but they do not prevent the inclusion of basic elements of the Marxist doctrines of history and man by prophetic Christianity.

### III. RELIGIOUS SOCIALISM AND SCIENTIFIC MARXISM

Religious socialists have accepted many of the scientific results of the Marxian analysis of society, especially of economics, because they have found them to be true. And they have maintained and still maintain Marxist theories, as far as they can do so on scientific grounds. They were and are, at the same time, hospitable to any criticism of Marxist ideas as soon as such criticism seems to be demanded by the progress of scientific knowledge. Religious socialism rejects any dogmatism with respect to the Marxist principles. It subjects them to the criteria of every scientific procedure and, beyond this, to the methodical suspicion that they might have become ideologies themselves. But religious socialism rejects dogmatic anti-Marxism as well as dogmatic Marxism and subjects the scientific attack on the Marxian doctrines not only to scientific criteria but also to the suspicion of being an ideological escape. Especially in the present situation, in which Marx is pushed more and more into the background, has the question of ideological anti-Marxism increased in importance.

There are, above all, some philosophical principles in Marxism which can and must be maintained by religious socialism as discoveries of lasting significance, provided that their corrupted forms are recognized as such and rejected. The demand for the unity of theory and practice or, in more recent terms, for "existential thinking" is a lasting insight that Marx has discovered in his fight against theoretical idealism and materialism. But the distortion of this insight into a skeptical relativism, according to which all thinking is only the expression of a special kind of being (psychological or sociological), must be considered not only as a corruption but also as the negation of existential thinking. In the same way it must be acknowledged by religious socialism that Marx is right in emphasizing material reproduction as the foundation of the whole historical process. But the distortion of this insight into a mechanistic economics or into a metaphysical materialism must be rejected. The economic sphere is itself a complex sphere, to which all other spheres essentially contribute, so that they cannot be derived from it, although they can never be separated from it. The dialectical method must be accepted as a method of describing the movements of life and history in their inner tensions, contrasts, and contradictions and in their trend toward more embracing unities. But the distortion of the dialectical method into a universal mechanism of calculable processes has nothing to do with reality and with the original meaning of this method. There are dialectical elements in all life and in every historical totality, namely, elements belonging to a given structure which drive beyond this structure. These structures can be described only in dialectical terms but not at all in terms of mechanical necessity. Existential thinking, historical materialism, and the dialectical method are achievements which should never be lost in religious socialism.

The same is true of several sociological and economic principles of scientific Marxism. Marx's method of analyzing economic phenomena is a sociological method; it takes into consideration, in every moment, the human and social factors and denies the escapist attitude of formal economics which hides the fact that economic action is human action. The recognition of this situation is the second highly important methodological contribution of Marxism. On the basis of this method Marxism has given that analysis of the contradictions of capitalistic society, which, more than anything else, has destroyed the harmonistic beliefs of bourgeois liberalism. Marx himself and most of his followers confined their analysis to the contrast of "capital" and "labor." In the last decades it has become obvious that there are many more contradictory elements in the later stage of capitalism and that the revolutionary vanguard is no longer identical with the proletariat or advanced groups within it. It has become evident that the lower middle classes and bureaucracy in state and business will play a much greater role than Marx anticipated. But all this does not invalidate the main point in his analysis, i.e., the insight into the contradictions in the structure of capitalism. On the contrary, this insight has been deepened and confirmed by the catastrophes of the present world. Any neoliberal attempt to re-establish a harmonistic interpretation of capitalistic society must be rejected by religious socialism. It is an obvious fact that, partly under the influence of Marxism, the economy of free competition has been restricted to a great extent by the increasing power of labor; by frequent and radical interferences of the state in all countries; by the general trend toward state capitalism and the rise of a centralizing bureaucracy. But this transformation, although invalidating some of the anticipations of Marx, is, at the same time, the confirmation of his basic vision. Nobody can understand the character of the present world revolution who has not been prepared for it by the Marxian analysis of bourgeois society, its contradictions and its decisive trends. Every day one may experience the fact that people who are lacking in Marxian education, directly or indirectly, are utterly confused by the rise of communism and fascism and by the present world catastrophe. They simply cannot understand the trends in the former structure of society which, with dialectical (not mechanical) necessity, have brought about the present situation. They explain it as the result of bad accidents created by bad men. Religious socialism, with the tool of the Marxian analysis of society brought up to date, is able to give a meaning to the present world transformation.

### IV. MARXISM AS A LASTING PRINCIPLE AND RELIGIOUS SOCIALISM

It is understandable that ideas can become an element of the general consciousness to such a degree that their original significance is forgotten. Much of what they had to say and which was surprising in the beginning becomes natural. Other parts become antiquated; and so the whole system of ideas seems to belong to the past. A theory of social processes which has partly changed the actual processes may seem to have become wrong just because it was right at the time it appeared. But there are other spiritual creations, the effects of which are not exhausted by their historical successes. They have an infinite, inexhaustible meaning because they represent a lasting type of spiritual possibility. Such types are prophetism, Platonism, and Protestantism. Such types also are religious socialism and Marxism. They return again and again in different shapes, based on their original, classical appearance. Therefore, we must go back to their classical form, and we must reshape them in the light of actual experience. But we cannot dismiss them as merely forms of past history. They would return against our will. We cannot discuss Marxism as a movement of the past as long as we espouse the prophetic spirit as religious socialists. Religious socialism, if it is to keep any meaning and power, must not become another ideological justification of the present democracies, nor must it become a progressive idealism and a system of autonomous harmony. The breakdown of these ideas has created the present situation. Religious socialism, in the spirit of prophetism and with the methods of Marxism, is able to understand and to transcend the world of today.

# Chapter XVIII

## SPIRITUAL PROBLEMS OF POSTWAR RECONSTRUCTION

THE presupposition of every postwar reconstruction is the knowledge of the pre-war disintegration. And the presupposition of every spiritual postwar reconstruction is the knowledge of the spiritual pre-war disintegration. Nobody can doubt that a catastrophe such as the present one never could have happened in an integrated social system; nobody should attribute our period of world wars and world revolutions to the accident of a special national character, for instance, of the Russian or the German or the Japanese character, or to dictatorial leaders, such as Stalin or Hitler, whose rise to power is even more accidental. It should be granted by all those who are able to judge that something was fundamentally wrong in the system of life and thought in the immediate past and that a return to it is neither desirable nor possible. The world war is a part of a world revolution. This statement should be repeated again and again. Many economists and political scientists have shown the causes of the disintegration in their respective realms. Philosophers and historians have given comprehensive pictures of this process; and these analyses have been confirmed by subsequent events. The spiritual disintegration of bourgeois society was foreseen as early as the middle of the nineteenth century by Russian religious thinkers and has been restated by Nicholas Berdyaev and others, supported by ideas of Nietzsche and Spengler. It was the chief topic in the German and French literature of the turn of the century. It has been developed in a combination of Marxist and religious ideas by the movements of religious socialism in Europe and America. And this analysis is not yet finished.

It is obvious that the spirit, that is, the creative, dynamic power of the soul, is not a matter of construction. If spirit is lacking, no construction can possibly produce it. It either is or is not active in individuals or in groups. But if it is active, it creates a body for itself

261

through which it can be manifested and act. Words, forms of life and social institutions, works of culture and religious symbols, are the embodiments of the spirit. And these are subject to conscious cultivation and reconstruction. We refer to them when we speak of "spiritual reconstruction after the war."

Any task of spiritual reconstruction has two sides. Those trends in a spiritual development which can stand criticism from the point of view of the ultimate criteria of thinking and acting must be supported and maintained. Spiritual tendencies should not be accepted simply because they belong to a given historical structure (here positivism is wrong). Neither should general principles be imposed on a spiritual situation which has no organ of receiving them (here idealism is wrong). Much wisdom is needed to avoid these two mistakes, which threaten every reconstruction. The second task, equally important, is the protection of the creative trends of the spirit against distortion and corruption. With respect to the spirit of the Asiatic nations and largely with respect to Russia, this protective task is practically the only one which is demanded of us. The Anglo-Saxon countries cannot be responsible for the spiritual reconstruction of Asia (except perhaps indirectly through the effect of its contact with the West). The protecting side of the work of spiritual reconstruction is equally important in relation to Europe, including the Axis countries. It would be a tremendous mistake if the victorious democracies intended to impose their own forms and standards of spiritual life on the conquered countries in the name of universal principles. Europe, including Germany, will accept what it is ready to accept according to the dynamics of its own spiritual development, but nothing else. The demand just made by a resentful German refugee writer that an army of foreign teachers should be sent to Germany after the war with the purpose of transforming the German spirit is the most certain way of preventing any spiritual reconstruction. Nothing spiritual can be given to the human spirit for which it is not prepared.

## I. THE ANALYSIS

The spiritual disintegration of our day consists in the loss of an ultimate meaning of life by the people of Western civilization. And with the loss of the meaning of life, they have lost personality and community. They have become, whether they know it or not, parts of an objective process which determines their lives in every respect, from their economic situation to their spiritual form. The insecurities and the vicissitudes involved in this process have produced feelings of fear, anxiety, loneliness, abandonment, uncertainty, and emptiness. Their spiritual life oscillates between a cynical and a fanatical surrender to powers the nature of which nobody can fully grasp or control, and the end of which nobody can foresee. In the younger generation of Germany, for instance, cynicism prevailed before national socialism turned it into fanaticism. Today the youngest group in Germany is returning again to cynicism. Because she lost the war, Germany has been an extreme case. But anyone who had contact with the younger generation in western Europe, and even in America, in the years between the two wars must have been impressed and disturbed by their frankly admitted nihilism. This is not surprising. If human beings feel that their destiny is taken out of their hands, that an objective process on which they have no influence throws them on the street today, draws them into a big machine as parts and tools tomorrow, and will drive them into a war of extinction the day after tomorrow, then no other result than utter hopelessness can be expected. The goddesses of the later ancient world—*Tyche* and *Heimarmene,* "chance" and "fate"—have again conquered a civilization and driven millions of people into resigned surrender to forces beyond their imagination. This entails and, at the same time, presupposes the loss of personality as well as of community. The loss of personality was prepared in the naturalistic philosophy of the bourgeois society and found its final expression in the vitalistic and pragmatic dissolution of the self leading to a psychology without psyche and a doctrine of man without a human self. But these theoretical developments—to which strict analogies in literature and art can be found—have become historical forces only because they were the natural expression of the actual depersonalization of man. The technical form of monopolistic production, not only of material but also of spiritual goods, has made the individual, both in his production and in his consumption, a part of an all-embracing machine moved by anonymous forces. While in Europe the mechanization of production was more visible, in America the mechanization of consumption is the most characteristic symptom of this situation. It has created not only standardized machines but also standardized human beings, conditioned by radio, movies, newspapers, and educational adjustment for a subpersonal conformity to this immense process. The ease with which, in the dictatorial countries as well as in America, the whole productive machine, including its human tools, has been brought into a unity for one purpose—the war—shows its completely impersonal and meaningless character.

The loss of personality is interdependent with the loss of community. Only personalities can have community. Depersonalized beings have social interrelations. They are essentially lonely, and therefore they cannot bear to be alone because this would make them conscious of their loneliness and, with it, of the loss of the meaning of life. The striking "lack of privacy" is not an expression of community but of the lack of community. And there is no community because there is nothing to have in common. The monopolistic direction of public communication, of leisure, pleasure, learning, sex relations, sport, etc., does not provide a basis for a real community. Cultural remnants of earlier periods are used to cover up our cultural nakedness. All this is carried through more radically in the totalitarian systems. But the means of carrying it through are better developed in this county. And if these means ever should come into the hands of unchecked dictators—visible or invisible ones—a complete dehumanization would have even more chances in America than in Europe.

The loss of personality and community is the consequence of the loss of an ultimate meaning of life. This has occurred in a development of Western civilization which can be divided into three periods. In the first period, roughly identical with the early and high Middle Ages, the meaning of life was represented by the transcendent symbols and functions of the church, which gave the foundation for personality as well as for community. Personality was established by its direct relation to the ultimate, in guilt and salvation. The eternal meaning of the individual self was guaranteed. The community was established by the participation of every group, according to its special vocation, in the symbols of the universal community. A content for community existed, out of which the spiritual life could draw inexhaustible material for cultural creation. It is important for our task of spiritual reconstruction to keep this period in mind because it has become the standard of criticism and the model of demand for many analysts of the present situation, not only for Catholics. Although personality and community were guaranteed in this period, they were not really developed. The transcendent foundation and its representatives on the top of the hierarchy kept them strictly within the limits of the given system and suppressed as long as possible the autonomous creativity of the individual. When this proved impossible, the second period, roughly identical with the rise and victory of bourgeois society, started. Now reason and its metaphysical and ethical creations replaced or transformed the transcendent foundation of life and its symbols. Spiritual production became personal—in religion through Protestantism, in the arts and sciences through the Renaissance. It still lived from the substance of the past, and, therefore, it still was able to create culture and to maintain community. The so-called "classical" periods of the European nations are based on this union of free creation and God-formed substance. In this their greatness and their short transitory character were rooted. The harmony of individuality and community, which was guaranteed in the first period by the common foundation of both, survived in the second period as natural harmony, guaranteed by the basic conformity of the interests and ideologies of the rising *bourgeoisie*. But there was, so to speak, an undercurrent in the spiritual development of bourgeois society, an element of anti-rational naturalism and pessimism, which came to the surface again and again and which became victorious in the third period. The spiritual heritage was more and more wasted; the autonomous creations became more formalistic, more skeptical, and less universal. The harmony between the individual and the whole broke down. Community was replaced by co-operation for purposes; personality, by a quantity of working power or by technical intelligence and adjustment. In the meantime, the economic and technical process had prepared the monstrous mechanism which has swallowed personality as well as community, and with them a spiritual culture. The third period roughly identical with monopoly capitalism and fascism had come into existence.

These are sketchy indications, much too short for a complete and convincing picture. There is immense material in all realms of life, the use of which would make this picture concrete and irrefutable. This, however, is impossible in the given space. But it would have been utterly unacceptable to speak pleasantly and hopefully about the postwar reconstruction without the weight and seriousness which can be gained only by an analysis of the background of our spiritual disintegration. Perhaps it will be said that the elements pointed to are only elements but not the whole and that an unbalanced stress is laid on them by this analysis. To this the answer is, first, that there are indeed other elements and that without these other elements this article, for instance, would not have been written; second, that the complexity of every historical situation does not obscure the decisiveness of some trends. These dominant trends carry the dynamics of the whole. It is these trends with which we have dealt. Third, it must be said that the analysis of the self-destructive nature of bourgeois society always has been rejected and always has proved to be even truer than the analysts, including the present writer, were able to believe. The fact of the second World War and the self-destruction of the European civilization cannot be refuted.

## II. DEMANDS AND POSSIBILITIES

An abstract statement of the requirements for spiritual reconstruction can be simply derived from the foregoing analysis: the requirement for spiritual reconstruction after the war is the demand for a convincing restatement of the meaning of life, for the discovery of symbols expressing it, and for the re-establishment of personality and community on this new basis. But such a demand includes the demand for an equally radical and inseparable social and political reconstruction. It would, of course, be foolish to assume that demands like these have any possibility of immediate actualization. The world catastrophe cannot be wiped out in a peace conference or in a few years spent in educating some evildoers. Nothing sudden can fulfil the needs resulting from the disintegration of a period of history. The revolutionary transformation, of which this war is a part, is a long process in which not even the forces to be overcome have yet shown their greatest strength. We are still in what we have called the third period. The process of centralized mechanization has not yet reached its final stage. In some countries, as in America, it has just started. We do not know the possibilities of its further progress. There are still large areas in which structures of the two other periods have survived. We do not know how far they will be transformed by the structure of the third period. And even if the dehumanization which has taken place under the reign of monopoly capitalism and fascism had come to an end, this would not mean a quick rehumanization of mankind. Nevertheless, the demands for spiritual reconstruction, as stated above, are not meaningless. It is meaningful even to make as many people as possible realize where they are; what they are missing; what has happened to them; what they have lost; why they are lonely, insecure, anxious, without ultimate purpose, without an ultimate concern, without a real self, and without a real world. Men are still able to feel that they have ceased to be men. And this feeling is the presupposition of all spiritual reconstruction during and after the war, for, in this feeling, humanity makes itself heard in its longing for a meaning of life, for community and personality. It has always belonged and still belongs to the great hopes of mankind that, as new generations grow up, they may be able to receive new creative germs. The new generations themselves do not produce them; spiritual life presupposes maturity, and it spoils the receptive power of the child if it is treated like an adult and is adjusted too early to the given mechanism of social behavior. But, fortunately, no generation of adults has ever succeeded in imposing its pattern of life completely on the following generation. This is one of the greatest hopes for spiritual reconstruction.

The other reason for hope is the fact that the religious and cultural traditions of the earlier periods have survived not only as dead records but also as living realities, moving and forming individuals and groups. Although the churches as large social institutions have adapted themselves to the great historical transformations—sometimes, as in the Middle Ages and the Reformation, even in a leading role they have not completely surrendered to the given social structure. They still resist a complete subjection to the trend toward dehumanization and mechanization. But, more important, they have preserved the message of an ultimate meaning of life which has not yet been exhausted and which, as Christians believe, never can be exhausted. However, this message can become effective for the coming spiritual reconstruction only if it is brought into the center of the present situation as an answer and not as another problem tied up with the general spiritual disintegration. This cannot be done by the churches officially; it is an adventurous task and the duty of a Christian vanguard of a voluntary and half-esoteric -character. The authority of the churches, especially in their ecumenical unity, may be behind those who go this way. But the churches themselves are too much bound by their traditional forms, on the one hand, and by their amalgamation with the present structure of society, on the other hand. The support and protection of a spiritual vanguard will be the main contribution of the churches to the spiritual reconstruction after the war.

But the churches are not the whole of our culture. They are only a small sector within an otherwise secular civilization. Without the participation of the secular spirit in the work of spiritual reconstruction, nothing can be done. It is impossible to return to the hierarchical culture of the first period. The autonomous spirit after having been liberated cannot return into bondage except by a complete re-primitivization or, as it has been called by Spengler, "Fellachization." Therefore, spiritual reconstruction demands a cultural vanguard as much as a religious one. There are personalities in all realms of life who still represent creative culture, who have resisted in themselves the trends of mechanization and dehumanization in the name of human dignity and spiritual values. They have saved their personal selves from the practical naturalism of our existence. But they were not able to change the situation as such. On the contrary, they often have become unconscious servants of the dehumanizing process—the character of which they have not been able to understand. Many noble representatives of the traditions of spiritual culture have served to conceal the barbarism of the social process which made its way without noticing their ideals at all. These people, like many religious people, do not even realize that the second period, which was the period of classical culture, has gone and that no return to it is possible. They do not realize that they have become antiquated in their belief in autonomous culture in our time. They can become bearers of the spiritual reconstruction only if they join the religious vanguards, on the one hand, and the social movements, on the other hand.

Without the collaboration of individuals within the movements for social justice, no spiritual reconstruction can be conceived of. The most penetrating analysis of the dynamics of bourgeois society has originated from their side. They discovered the loss of community very early and saw the necessity of its replacement by social co-operation. They recognized the strict independence of all elements of a social structure, including the spiritual life. They tried to describe a stage in which the freedom and personality of everyone was guaranteed by the integration of the whole. But they were not able to effect the spiritual reconstruction alone. As leaders of mass movements they actually became parts of the whole process against which their protest was directed. They have become, against their will, supporters of the mechanization of life, from which they wanted to protect their followers. This is the dialectic to which large historical movements always are subjected, and it shows once more the irresistible power of the main trends of our period. Nevertheless, the social movements at least expressed their protest, often with revolutionary power and a willingness to accept persecution. In unity with the religious vanguards and the bearers of cultural creativity, they will become a source of spiritual reconstruction.

I have not given a program of spiritual reconstruction. It would have been very unspiritual to try it. I have not dealt with the cultural policy of the peace conference and the armies of occupation. This would have been even less spiritual. I have pointed only to the necessity of protecting spiritual creativity against political encroachments. My idea for the spiritual reconstruction of Europe envisions a large number of anonymous and esoteric groups consisting of religious, humanist, and socialist people who have seen the trends of our period and were able to resist them, who have contended for personality and community (many of them under persecution), and who know about an ultimate meaning of life, even if they are not yet able to express it. The policy of the democracies after the war can only be to protect these groups of spiritual vanguards against political or economic suppression and to use their creativity in the central direction of the world, a direction that will be required for a long time to come. If the victorious governments fail in these matters, the spirit will be forced into the underground, and no spiritual reconstruction will come forth.

TILLICH'S CONCEPT OF THE
PROTESTANT ERA

# TILLICH'S CONCEPT OF THE
# PROTESTANT ERA

JAMES LUTHER ADAMS

"THE Reformation must continue." With these words Friedrich Schleiermacher, over a century ago, raised a protest against the Protestantism and the prevailing mentality of his time and pointed forward to a new Protestant realization. Protestantism and its culture, he believed, were in need of a Protestant reform.

These words of Schleiermacher could well serve as the epigraph of the writings of Paul Tillich. This does not mean that Tillich recommends, any more than Schleiermacher did, a return to the Reformation. Like Schleiermacher, who was also a theologian of culture, schooled in the dialectic of philosophical idealism, Tillich is concerned not only with the religion of the churches but even more with the religious bases and implications of the whole cultural process. In his view, which is based on a realistic philosophy of meaning, religion has to do with man's ultimate concern, his concern with the meaning of life and with all the forces that threaten or support that meaning, in personal and social life, in the arts and sciences, in politics, in industry, education, and the church.[1] It is with respect to the total cultural situation, then, that Tillich would say: "The Reformation must continue"; for we are living at the end of an era.

1. The variety of Tillich's interests is reflected in his prolific literary output, not to speak of his many corresponding practical activities. His larger literary productions published in Germany between 1910 and 1933 include two treatises on the philosopher Schelling and one on eighteenth-century theology; *Masse und Geist* (1922), a work treating modern mass movements and using representative works of art as symbols of changing attitudes; *Das System der Wissenschaften* (1923), a study of the classification, methods, and objects of the sciences; *Religionsphilosophie,* published in Max Dessoir's *Lehrbuch der Philosophie,* Vol. II (1925); *Die religiöse Lage der Gegenwart* (1926), a critical survey of major aspects of contemporary culture; and *Die sozialistische Entscheidung* (1933), a study of philosophical, economic, and political aspects of religious socialism. He has also edited and contributed to two symposia on Protestantism, entitled *Kairos I* (1926) and *Kairos II* (1929), and he has published in German and English over a hundred pamphlets and articles dealing with art, philosophy, theology, economics, sociology, political theory, education, and technology. A volume of collected essays, *Religiöse Verwirklichung* ("Religious Realization"), appeared in 1930. Two volumes of translations of his writings have been published in English, *The Religious Situation* (1932) and *The*

The present era, which, at its beginning in the Reformation and the Renaissance, was ushered in, or so it believed, under the sign of the morning star after a long night of darkness, the age of Enlightenment and of liberalism, which, in the eighteenth and nineteenth centuries of rational and industrial revolution, thought it was nearing its meridian, in the twentieth century has come upon a darkling plain swept with confused alarms of struggle. The contradictions in the mentality and in the social structures of contemporary society (and the world-encompassing destructive tensions resulting therefrom) have impelled large numbers of men to seek new bearings. In fact, our society is already undergoing a revolution that affects all areas of life, a transformation that is most readily evident in the widespread trends toward one or another form of collectivism.

This change constitutes a fate for Protestantism and also for the liberal humanism stemming from the Renaissance and the Enlightenment. These movements have exercised a major influence in the shaping of the modern mentality. Indeed, this influence has been so decisive that Tillich calls the period of the last four centuries the "Protestant" or the "Protestant-humanist" era. But certain aspects of Protestantism and humanism which have played a decisive and positive role in the Protestant era—an era of tremendous accomplishments—have also been a contributory cause of its present contradictions; and they now constitute a formidable obstacle to the overcoming of these contradictions. Indeed, Tillich believes the present situation heralds the end of the Protestant era as we have known it.

If Protestantism is to play a critical and creative role at this juncture, it must break off certain of its attachments to the outlooks and structures of the cultural epoch that is now approaching its possible dissolution; and it must, through a new understanding and application of its principles, assist in the creation of new forms of integration in church and society. In this context the words of Schleiermacher acquire a sig-

*Interpretation of History* (1936), as well as his essay, "The Religious Symbol," translated by the present writer and Dr. Ernst Fraenkel for the *Journal of Liberal Religion,* II (1940), 13–33. In 1933, Dr. Tillich, who had been a leader of the religious-socialist movement in Germany was deprived by the Nazis of his position as professor of philosophy at the University of Frankfort; he then came to the United States, where he has taught in various universities. Since 1934 he has been professor of philosophical theology at Union Theological Seminary, New York City. Many of the themes that have occupied his attention are dealt with briefly in his first chapter, "The World Situation," in the symposium, *The Christian Answer* (1945), edited with an Introduction by H. P. van Dusen.

nificance that he could not have foreseen. They become fighting words again.

The articles included in the present collection have been drawn from Tillich's writings of the last twenty years. Although only a few of the articles deal directly with Protestantism, they are all related to the background and character, or to the problems and the present status, of the religion and the culture in which Protestantism has expressed itself. The problems that are dealt with necessarily extend beyond the confines of organized Protestantism: they have to do with the major social and spiritual issues that confront contemporary society in its present stage of transformation. Tillich's discussion of these problems does not necessarily presuppose on the part of the reader a special interest in Protestantism, or even in religion as ordinarily understood. It does presuppose, however, a feeling for the significance of the moment in which both the "religion" and the "culture" of the past era have reached their limits and in which a fundamental reformation of both is demanded.

In setting forth the principal elements of Tillich's view of the present situation (as it has been presented in his various writings), we shall concern ourselves, first, with his conception of the rise and the decline of the Protestant-humanist era; second, with his philosophy of religion and culture and its implications for the interpretation of the main trends of Protestantism; and, third, with his application of this philosophy to the problems of reconstruction. The first section of this essay will therefore center the attention especially upon what Tillich calls "the bourgeois principle"; the second upon his conception of "the Protestant principle" and upon his philosophical elaboration of this principle in "belief-ful" or "self-transcending realism"; and the third upon what we shall call "the religious-socialist principle."

In confining attention mainly to these aspects of Tillich's thought, we shall forgo any systematic consideration of his Christian theological position. The reason for this omission is twofold. Professor Tillich provides in his own Introduction to the present volume some general characterizations of his theological method and of his fundamental theological presuppositions. Moreover, he is at present engaged in preparing for publication his systematic theology. Hence an extensive and systematic discussion of it may properly be postponed. We turn our attention now to a presentation of his conception of the Protestant-humanist era and of his interpretation of the present religious and cultural situation.

## I

Beginning as a rediscovery of the prophetic message of the majesty of God and emphasizing the doctrines of predestination and of justification through faith, early Protestantism raised a protest against a hierarchical system which had interjected itself between man and God with "a demonic claim to absoluteness." This prophetic message reaffirmed the unconditional character of God. Sin and guilt, the Reformers asserted, cannot be overcome by any mediating human agency. Union with God is received through grace and faith alone. Through this union the sinner paradoxically becomes just before God. Man's love is the consequence and not the condition of this justification through faith. Analogously, the concept of predestination was the doctrinal statement of the experience of regaining the meaning of life without human activity, an experience that is God's work and that has an explanation hidden from man.

In accord with these Protestant affirmations, the absolute doctrinal authority of the church, the constitutional authority of the hierarchy, and the independent power of the sacraments were all renounced as blasphemies, as attempts of man to elevate himself above God and to subject to outer conditions the approach of God to the soul and of the soul to God. In so far as humanism set up human reason as the final arbiter and adopted an anthropocentric orientation, humanism was also renounced on the basis of corresponding objections. The Reformers cut through all these mediations; they also cut through church history and returned to the source of the message of justification, the Bible.

The positive element taking the place of ecclesiastical authority found its initial expression in the claim of freedom of conscience to interpret the Scriptures, a freedom that was expected to issue in a new unity supported by a providentially inspired harmony. This Protestant freedom of conscience was an "ecstatic" rather than a purely autonomous, humanistic freedom; it was interpreted as the "pneumatic," or, as Tillich would call it, the "theonomous," response of the individual member of the church to the message of the Bible. Obedience to the hierarchical priesthood was therefore supplanted by belief in the priesthood of all believers. Clerical domination yielded, in principle, to radical laicism. The Bible, it was assumed, would interpret itself sufficiently for man's salvation. Every individual as a monad in the body of Christ would be able to find truth in the Bible. The saving gospel is there, and the Reformers believed that it would create a unified church wherever it was proclaimed and listened to in faith. Thus, although Protestantism appealed to the individual consciousness and conscience (guided by Scripture and nourished by the religious community), it relied from the beginning upon a hidden automatic harmony. Tillich holds that much of the history of Protestantism and also of modern culture must be understood in terms of this and of corresponding theories of harmony.

Protestantism did not carry through unaided its resistance to the previously accepted authorities; nor was it able alone to establish new integrations in church and society. It eventually made an alliance with the humanism which it had at first opposed as strongly as it had opposed Roman Catholicism. Philosophical and linguistic exegesis was required for the interpreting of the Bible. Protestantism joined humanism to overcome Catholic exegesis. Here it was assumed that autonomous criticism and Protestant criticism would fundamentally agree. This same pattern was adopted also for other areas of common interest. Gradually the "holy" legend of the Catholic church was dissolved by the modern historical consciousness and by humanistic-Protestant historical criticism; humanistic education was combined with biblical education; scholasticism was supplanted by autonomous science, in which theology claimed a leading role (later to be lost); monastic and feudal conceptions of work were replaced by an inner-wordly asceticism and activism (especially on Calvinistic soil). Belief in harmony between divine and natural law gave rise to a new amalgamation of Stoic and biblical ethics. To be sure, there have been and there still are countertendencies within Protestantism. In Europe neofeudal types of authority continued to play a role. Moreover, in many quarters rigid forms of ecclesiastical orthodoxy have ignored the original Protestant protest. As a consequence, they have, in principle, maintained the traditional authoritarian outlook. They have merely substituted for the authority of the Roman Catholic church some new absolute, such as the Bible or the confessions of faith, a Catholicism of the word.

The alliance of Protestantism with humanism gradually developed into an alliance also with a humanist theory of harmony. This development in its outcome must be viewed as simply another dimension of the changes already described; accordingly, it can be best discerned by observing its characteristic negations and affirmations.

The alliance was possible, if not inevitable, because humanism resisted many of the same things that Protestantism resisted. Tillich, employing a conception familiar in modern myth research, characterizes the pre-Protestant, or Catholic, era in terms of its "myths of origin." In general, this sort of myth expresses man's numinous sense of relatedness to the originating or creative powers of nature and history; it provides a feeling of security and support by relating men to sacred powers of origin rooted in the soil, in the blood, in a social group, or in some other support and sanction of a vital and authoritative tradition. For the Middle Ages the superhuman origin of life was found in a primeval revelation, which was preserved as a holy tradition and guarded as a mystery by the priesthood. This holy tradition found objective manifestation in a sacramental system (which included within it the natural powers of origin). Medieval freedoms, securities, and authorities were supported by this comprehensive myth of origin. Innovation could be introduced only in the name of the "origin." All privileges of "domination," including those attached to the feudal ranks, appealed to the same sanction. Since the system was largely controlled by the priesthood, the latter achieved a certain social independence as the bearer of religion and as the consecrating agent for the sacred powers of origin. Against this medieval myth of origin and the corresponding authorities both humanism and Protestantism revolted, humanism in the name of an autonomous humanity and Protestantism in the spirit of ancient prophetism and in the name of the doctrines of justification and predestination.

Protestantism, as we have seen, returned to the Bible, where it found not only its own myth of origin but also a sense of mission, a sanction for pushing forward to a new church and society. This does not mean that the medieval myth of origin was wholly eliminated; rather, it was transformed. Just as in ancient Hebrew religion prophetic and priestly elements were combined, so in Protestantism prophetic elements were grafted onto Catholic sacramental elements. However, in rejecting the claim of the priesthood to be the consecrating agent of the powers of origin, Protestantism initiated a process whereby it would in time weaken its own independence. Partially as a consequence of the principal of radical laicism (implied in the belief in the priesthood of all believers) the modern man has taken a larger share in the shaping of social policy than did his predecessors. Because of these changes, Protestantism has had to depend more and more upon extra-ecclesiastical social forces for support. It entered more and more, especially after the Enlightenment, into alliance with the developing state bureaucracies or with the bourgeois powers and customs.

Humanism also rejected the old myth of origin and introduced a new conception. According to this new conception, man in his possession of universal humanity was believed to be rooted in the divine Logos. In its struggle against authoritarianism, humanism can scarcely be said to have developed a myth of origin, but it did create its own "myth of mission" (a term suggested by Michels and not used by Tillich, though it conveys Tillich's idea); this myth of mission drove humanism forward toward the liberation of man, who as the bearer of reason and truth was to bring in a new rational order of society. This myth came to its full growth when the "enlightened authoritarianism" of the early modern period was replaced by liberal and democratic social myths and forms. This full growth took the form of a theory of natural harmony.

In humanism the Judeo-Christian trust in providence was transformed into a reliance upon a "pre-established harmony" in the cosmos, in the human psyche, and in society. This harmony, it was believed, would progressively engender unity and general well-being if every man had the freedom to follow his own conviction and his own economic interest; in pursuing his own interests, he would be pursuing the interests of the community.

This theory of natural harmony may be understood either from the point of view of the human subject—the mind—or from that of the object——nature and the social, productive forces. With respect to the object, the theory of harmony asserted that, in sense-perception, nature gives herself to man in such a way that a natural knowledge emerges which is adequate for purposes of control; and it asserted that the free sway of all human creative forces—in the cultural area through tolerance, in the economic area through liberal political economy ("laissez-faire"), in the political area through the rule of the majority (democracy)—would lead to the rational shaping of society. In other words, it held that the human being, as soon as he can develop in a manner free from the irrational powers of origin, may through a natural harmony achieve true fulfilment. With respect to the subject, the theory asserted that the categories of the human spirit are the structure-giving elements of nature; hence nature is amenable to rational knowledge and control. Society can be rationally shaped because the human species is undergoing in history an education that will fulfil its rational potentialities. Taken together, then, both the objective and the subjective aspects of the theory of natural harmony presupposed a religious faith in the essential unity and goodness of man and the world and in a spiritual unity between man and nature. It must be noted here that, although certain pessimistic motives of classical Christian thought were ignored, the optimistic world view that was adopted came primarily from Judeo-Christian, rather than from pagan, sources, as did also the activist, world-shaping impulse (which was given marked impetus through Calvinism).

The developments in philosophy during the period of rationalism and enlightenment may be taken as typical of the trends, both practical and theoretical, which gave expression to the theory of natural harmony. From the seventeenth century on, one philosopher after another worked out the implications of the theory of harmony: Spinoza, Descartes, and Leibniz in metaphysics; Shaftesbury and Helvetius in psychology and ethics; Montesquieu, Rousseau, and Adam Smith in political and economic theory; Voltaire and a host of others in the progressivist philosophy of history. Reason, both speculative and technological, both revolutionary and formative, working in the individual and in society, was to usher in the kingdom of universal brotherhood. An original motive power in this drive toward emancipation came, of course, from the recognition of the sacredness of personality, from belief in human rights and human worth. But other ideas also soon appeared, ideas that reflected an increasing tension between the objective and the subjective aspects of the theory.

The enthusiasm for the rational control of nature and society, besides releasing new energies, introduced a new alienation between man and man and between man and nature, an alienation that would in time disrupt the harmony. Employing a characteristically "existentialist" interpretation of the outlook of modern mentality, Tillich asserts that one of the decisive elements of modern thought is the contrast between "subject" and "object," a contrast that tends to stress the "objectivity" or the "subjectivity" of reality. This dichotomy between subject and object superseded the subject-object unity of the high Middle Ages and became the "prime mover" of Western philosophy and also of modern technological, capitalist society. The sense of the immediacy of the origin, of the creative sources of man's life, was gradually lost. Personality and community became merely objective things, thus losing their intrinsic powerfulness and depth. The attitude toward things followed the same course, partially as a consequence of the developing technology; in the human consciousness "things" lost their intrinsic value and depth. Thus personality, community, and things became the instruments of an autonomous secularism; they became merely objects for control and calculation in the service of man's economic purposes. A spirit of "self-sufficient finitude" invaded the common life. Indeed, religion itself lost its sense of the immediacy of the origin and became one sphere among other spheres; even its God became a "thing" among other things, and the language of religion assumed an "objective," literal character that could only elicit skepticism. In philosophy both realism and idealism exhibited the loss of the sense of immediacy, emphasizing in corresponding ways the dichotomy of subject and object. Romanticism attempted to recapture the lost unity between subject and object (and with it the lost splendor of life) by restoring old myths of origin or by developing new ones, but it achieved only the spurious immediacy of irrationalism, either in the archaism of religious revival or in primitivist organicism and vitalism. Romanticism, however, did not much alter the main trend in capitalist society. Positivism became the characteristic philosophy of a technological society, seeking the domination of the object by the subject. In the spirit of this positivism, the dynamic ethos of capitalist society became increasingly determinative for the Protestant-humanist era.

This characteristic dynamic is epitomized in what Tillich calls "the bourgeois principle." Wherever technology and capital have been at work in the modern world, this principle has been operative. Its success is to be observed in its permeation of almost the entire planet, in a world domination which no one can escape. The definition of this principle can be formulated most succinctly in terms of its goal. The goal of the bourgeois principle is the radical dissolution of the bonds of original, organic community life, the dissolution of the powers of origin into elements to be conquered rationally. Science, religion, politics, art, the relations between the classes—all have been drawn into the crucible of the bourgeois principle. It is true that the bourgeois principle has never been—indeed, it never could be—the sole support of capitalist society. The principle was itself primarily utilitarian and critical; it unconsciously presupposed previously existing creative powers and supports. Just as Protestantism retained and transformed Catholic elements, so modern capitalist society has presupposed and has in varying ways retained contact with the powers of origin. It has not carried through the bourgeois principle in complete consistency. This fact becomes evident whenever the middle classes feel themselves threatened; they then appeal to myths of soil and blood, to nationalism, as a protection of middle-class interests. Yet the characteristic positive preoccupation following from the bourgeois principle has been the creation of means of objective control; and this preoccupation has displaced the intuitive grasping of intrinsic values; both things and persons have been enervated by subordinating them to economic purposes. The spirit of bourgeois society is the spirit that, after having dissolved the primary ties of origin, subjects a "thingified" world entirely to its purposes. This process of "thingification" has been carried through by the motive power of the theory of harmony and progress.

The amalgam of Protestant and humanist faiths in a principle of harmony has produced the modern age with its tremendous creativity; it has produced the modern ideas of tolerance and education and democracy; it has provided the energy and goal of the age of "free enterprise." The practical implications of the theory of natural harmony become especially clear if one observes the contrast between the social and metaphysical presuppositions of the Protestant-humanist era and those of the Catholic era. Catholicism has relied upon a hierarchy that is supposedly based on an ontological hierarchy of being. It has attempted to make the hierarchical system exercise control in all spheres of society. Where Catholicism has been dominant, it has elicited sharp resistance from these spheres, as, for example, in Italy and France. The Protestant-humanist era, on the other hand, has depended upon a hidden harmony. Accordingly, Protestantism has exhibited a greater co-operation and harmony with the evolving autonomous cultural spheres than has Catholicism. (As we shall observe later, this fact must be taken into account in any attempt to understand Protestant secularism.) Moreover, a certain harmony has prevailed within Protestantism itself, despite the lack of authoritative courts of appeal. "A decisive harmony," says Tillich, "has again and again come about automatically. And so the division of Protestantism into numerous mutually antagonistic churches, sects, denominations and movements did not involve any dangers so long as the common fundamental attitude was both positively and negatively unshaken."

Humanism's faith in harmony was for a time no less confirmed by history than was Protestantism's corresponding faith. The residues of earlier social coherence, expanding markets, and relatively free competition, these and other similar factors made it appear at first that the "law" of harmony expressed the nature of reality. The rise in the standard of living for many, the great increase in wealth, and the "success" of Western imperialism made tragedy in history seem (at least to the middle-class mentality) a thing of the past.

But the prevailing forms of Protestantism and humanism are now reaching their limits. The cunning of history pursues elusive, labyrinthine ways, and it makes unexpected turns. Capitalism with its religion of harmony has culminated not in harmony but in contradiction and crisis. This turn is no accident.

What earlier seemed to be the natural laws of harmony turned out to be contingent historical circumstances. The theory of the harmony of interests presupposed the eighteenth-century society of small producers and merchants, a society not yet controlled by mammoth corporations. Developments unforeseen by classical liberal economics were to bring about tremendous structural changes—and the breakdown of harmony. Already, within a half-century after the promulgation of the theory of the harmony of interests, the liberal utopia began to assume the physiognomy of Lancashire and Manchester. Subsequently, the theory of harmony has more and more become an ideology protecting the interests of the new ruling groups and sanctioning an increasingly destructive application of the bourgeois principle. Instead of producing harmony, the structural changes have in the twentieth century raised "the storms of our times."

These storms have created a darkness so readily visible that it is now almost a work of supererogation to describe it. Whether we think of the far-flung conflicts between imperialisms and of their exploitations in the domestic spheres or in the colonies, of the growth of monopoly and the concentration of wealth and economic power, of the disparity between increasing powers of production and decreasing purchasing power, of the opposition between the classes, of two world wars within our generation, of the inability of capitalism to use the full resources of the economy except in time of war or of depression and unemployment (the normal sequel to "normalcy"); whether we consider the "thingification" of man through the rationalization of industry and through his being made into a mere quantity of working power subject to the laws (or chances) of the market, or the "thingification" of nature through its being viewed as something only to be conquered and used as only something to be shoveled about; whether we think of the prostitution of education to merely utilitarian ends or of the complacently accepted corruption of politics through special interests; whether we think of the irresponsible and commercial vulgarization of the idea industries (radio, movie, and printing), of the increase of agitation, propaganda, and mass-production methods for the influencing of public opinion (with the consequent weakening of individuality and tolerance and responsible discussion), or of the decline of ethically powerful and uniting symbols in the democracies and in the churches—in each and all these tendencies we discern the causes or the consequences of the disruption of "automatic" harmony. This disruption has created a mass society in which reason has lost its depth and dignity (having created a huge impersonal machine which it does not control); in which societal sadism and insensitivity to suffering and injustice are taken for granted; in which the average individual is lost and lonely; in which the fear of insecurity and lack of spiritual roots produce neurosis and cynicism; in which mental-hygiene hospitals and psychiatric counseling have become major institutions; in which the sense of personal insignificance is compensated by egregious group egotism; in which a flat secularism, the spirit of "self-sufficient finitude," prevails in church and society, exhibiting contemporary man's blunted sense of his relatedness to the creative depths of personality, existence, and meaning; and therefore in which there is a void of meaninglessness, yearning for meaning. This is the world, said Henry Adams in 1892, which is ruled from "a banker's Olympus."

Whether one accepts Henry Adams' dictum in its simplicity or not, one must recognize that Protestantism in its alliance with the evolving middle-class humanism has tended in many respects to become merely the religious aspect of capitalism. Humanist and Protestant harmonism have together moved from their originally creative phase through a technological stage to become a passionately conservative force. Just as Roman Catholicism first helped to shape the culture of the Middle Ages and then became fettered in the "Babylonish captivity" of the waning Middle Ages and of a petrified Counter Reformation, so Protestantism has helped to form the Protestant era and then, in differing ways in its different forms and countries, has to a large extent become bound in a new Babylonish captivity within capitalist culture. It languishes (all too comfortably) in this prison, or, to change the figure from a Reformation to a biblical one, it is largely a prostituted, a "kept" religion. It has lost its relatedness to an ultimate ground and aim, and thus it has lost much of its original prophetic power. Its God has become domesticated; it is a bourgeois god. In its major effect its ethics is largely indistinguishable from the "ethics" of the bourgeois principle.

As a consequence the Protestantism that offers "religious" embellishment for the bourgeois principle merely aggravates the contradictions of capitalist society. Its appeal to individual consciousness and conscience (detached from the socializing influences of a nourishing spiritual tradition) and its belief that the freedom of the individual by virtue of the centripetal power of harmony moves toward a common center and then issues forth in health and healing for the individual and the society have become a means of evading basic social-ethical issues and of merely protecting the governing powers of the status quo. Philanthropy and social reform emanating from the churches usually assists these governing powers by moving strictly within bourgeois presuppositions. Through its emphasis on economic and spiritual "individualism" combined with a class-bound moralism, this Protestantism has also helped to dissolve communal symbols and supports. It has been drawn into the general process of dissolution.

It is true that the dissolution described here has not disintegrated spiritual and ethical values in America to the extent visible during recent decades in Europe. As Tillich puts it, "America lives still in a happy state of backwardness." But many of the conditions and attitudes that led to fascism in Europe exist also in America, and they will constitute an increasing threat as the postwar period proceeds.

The foregoing characterization of the present status of Protestantism is, of course, one-sided and incomplete; indeed, Tillich asserts (as we shall observe presently) that genuinely Protestant motives have persisted in the churches and even in certain aspects of secularism. Yet the tendencies described have been largely responsible for, or have accelerated, the decline of the Protestant-humanist era.

In response to these developments, dynamic movements of revolt have for a century been abandoning the characteristic tenets of bourgeois and Protestant-humanist individualism and automatic harmonism and have been moving in the direction of new (and sometimes of collectivist) forms of faith and society. Some of these movements have opposed the churches and liberalistic humanism as the bulwarks of privilege; other movements have appeared within the churches or in the form of neohumanism. The spectrum of revolt is a wide one. Communism, fascism, and Roman Catholic corporatism assume varying shades of red and black. The Christian socialist movements, neoliberal and neo-orthodox, occupy other positions in the spectrum. In certain areas of the spectrum a desire to "escape from freedom" is evident. The burden upon the individual has become almost too heavy to bear. Consequently, many people relinquish individual religious or political responsibility; they are willing to sacrifice their autonomy in the hope of finding on the path of authority a new meaning in life, new symbols and forms of life. The present attraction of Roman Catholicism and communism must be understood partially in this context. All these movements have been seeking a way out of the Protestant-humanist era.

The whole situation is a paradoxical one for both Protestantism and humanism, the partners of the modern era. In a recent essay Tillich has succinctly described the plight in which Protestantism finds itself. The description applies also to humanism. "That which Protestantism denied at its rise," he says, "is today—*in an altered form*—the demand of the age. That demand is for an authoritative and powerfully symbolic system of mass-redintegration: but it was just that—*in a distorted form*—against which Protestantism protested..... The Protestant era is finished, after nearly all the historical conditions upon which it rested have been taken away from it." Indeed, the very manner of the rise of Protestantism would seem to have determined its present limitations.

It is clear that if Protestantism is to play a prophetic and creative role in the new situation, it must effect a break and transformation as disruptive and as boldly productive as the changes made at the beginning of the Protestant era; and the transformation must in its effect on the social structure move in a direction opposite to that of the earlier break and transformation.

The title of the present collection of articles suggests questions that are importunate for Protestantism and humanism at this epochal moment. It will suffice if we here formulate these questions as they concern Protestantism. Will Protestantism escape its Babylonish captivity and assist reformation again? Will it extricate itself from the disintegration of the mass society of the late capitalist epoch? Or has it cast its lot irrevocably with the transitory and exhausted forces that now serve as its ideological expression and protection? Will it be able to exhibit again the self-surpassing power of the historic Christian dynamic by disassociating itself from these forces and by giving a sense of meaning, a direction, and a quality of greatness to new forms of thought and life? Or will the coming era take shape in opposition to organized Protestantism? Will it be in any significant sense a Protestant era? Or will it eventually be called a post-Protestant era because of the emergence of some new type of Christianity which will help to determine a new spirit and form of society?

Obviously, no one can today give the answers to these questions (or to corresponding questions that might be posed concerning liberalistic humanism). The questions serve the purpose, however, of giving concrete relevance to a consideration of the problems, the perils, and the opportunities that now confront Protestantism. But they cannot be properly dealt with in the manner of the soothsayer. In considering the problems which they raise, Tillich aims, as he says, "to drive the analysis to a point where the vision of a possible reconstruction" of Protestantism and contemporary society may appear. Hence the title of the volume means to suggest not only that the Protestant era is now approaching its limits but also that the end of the Protestant era would not be the end of Protestantism. Indeed, a new realization might be more in accord with the nature of Protestantism.

## II

A main trend, a characteristic dynamic, of the Protestant era has been expressed, as we have seen, in the bourgeois principle supported by the theory of natural harmony. But the harmony has not come. Instead, men have lost their sense of relatedness to the creative springs of life; community has been frustrated, and neurotic insecurity is the "order" of the day. In so far as the Protestant spirit has identified itself with the prevailing ethos, it participates in and aggravates the disintegration of our world. The bourgeois principle is insufficient to create community. The questions arise then: By what principle can the bourgeois society be criticized and transcended? By what principle can Protestantism regain a prophetic and newly creative power?

Tillich holds that, even if the Protestant era is finished, Protestantism knows a principle that is not finished. Like every other finite reality, Protestantism in any particular historical realization must reckon always with the possibility of its exhaustion. But the principle of Protestantism is not finite and exhaustible. As a witness to this principle, Protestantism is not to be identified with any of its historical realizations. It is not bound to the Protestant era. It can drive forward to qualitatively new creation. It can also, in the name of its principle, protest against the Protestant era and against organized Protestantism itself. The latter are relative and conditioned realities. This does not mean that they are lacking in significance. They are to be understood in the light of the Protestant principle.

Protestantism here confronts the perennial problem of the one and the many, what Emerson called *the* problem of philosophy. This problem, he asserted (quoting Plato), is "to find a ground unconditioned and absolute for all that exists conditionally." The Protestant principle aims to express the true relation between the unconditional and the conditioned.[2]

Only by appeal to such a principle can Protestantism transcend its cultural entanglements at any particular time and offer both criticism and creative direction in personal and social life.

This principle is presented in a dual aspect. On the one hand, it is a universally significant principle, pointing to the source and judge of every religious and cultural reality. It points to a moving, restless power, the inner infinity of being, that informs and transforms all conditioned realities and brings new forms to birth. Thus Protestantism can lay no exclusive claim to it. On the other hand, the principle refers to the characteristic possibility, the essential power, of Protestantism as a historical movement. It is the principle by which Protestantism is sup-

2. For a definition of "the unconditional" see pp. 299 ff. below; see also Tillich's definition on p. 32.

ported and judged. When Protestantism is not loyal to this principle or when it does not judge itself according to the principle, it is no longer truly Protestant.

Catholicism, in effect, identifies its own historical realizations of the Catholic era with the ground and judge of all religious and cultural realities. Luther called this self-absolutization the "worship of man-made gods." This worship of man-made gods appears in Protestant as well as in Catholic forms, in the sacramentalism of the word as well as in the sacramentalism of holy institutions and objects. It appears also in the "secular sacramentalism" of capitalism and nationalism. This claim to an absolute authority can conflict with similar claims of other authorities. It can also elicit the resistance of autonomous freedom. At the beginning of the modern era the autonomy that was expressed by humanism and that rebelled against ecclesiastical and political heteronomy, vibrated with a residual religious power. But in both ancient and modern times autonomy has again and again shown itself to be precarious and unstable. It loses its original sense of an unconditional demand for truth and justice; it becomes self-inclosed. As we have observed, this is what has happened in capitalistic society, in which the spirit of self-sufficient finitude now prevails. Increasingly, modern autonomy has degenerated into relativism or into a new heteronomy. Among intellectuals who have been deeply affected by modern historicism, the former tendency is widely evident, but in the culture at large the latter tendency is undoubtedly the stronger. The typical bourgeois man accepts the presuppositions of the capitalist mentality and the societal forms of capitalism with the same rigidity and absoluteness as the fundamentalist exhibits in his religion. But heteronomy and autonomy do not exhaust the possibilities open to man.

The Protestant principle stands in contrast to both these attitudes. The negative implication of the word "Protestant," a word that arose out of an actual historic protest against ecclesiastical authoritarianism, makes it eminently appropriate to serve as the name and the historical manifestation of the prophetic protest against every conditioned thing that makes an unconditional claim for itself. This negative implication of the Protestant principle has from the very beginning of the Protestant movement included also a protest against any autonomy that forgets its unconditional source and judge and that rests in its own conditioned self-assertion.

But the Protestant principle is not only negative and critical; it is also creative. Indeed, the critical presupposes the creative element. This positive element is the formative dynamic that sustains the fundamental attitude of seriousness and responsibility which belongs to all creative endeavor. It points to the ground and source of meaning that is present in a singular way in every relative achievement; but it cannot be exhausted or confined in any realization, not even in a definition. This dialectical principle which combines critical negation and dynamic fulfilment is the basis for what Tillich calls the "Protestant Gestalt of grace." The ultimate orientation involved here Tillich calls "theonomy." Before defining "theonomy," however, we must give further consideration to the Protestant principle.

This principle has been apprehended again and again in the history of religion and culture. In the West its lineage derives ultimately from Old Testament prophetism with its message of judgment and fulfilment. For the Christian the decisive expression of the essential power and meaning of reality is (in Tillich's formulation) the New Being manifest in Jesus as the Christ. Here the essential power and goodness reveals itself as *agape,* "love," an ontological and ethical dynamic that overcomes the frustrations, the fragmentariness, and the perversions of human existence, bringing together that which is separated. *Agape* is the source of justice and law, supporting, criticizing, and transforming them. It is, on the one hand, a command, and, on the other hand, it is the power that breaks through all commands. Thus it relates ethical life to the universal and the unconditional, and yet it adapts itself to every phase of the changing world. The Protestant principle presupposes this original critical and dynamic Christian message and its proclamation of the Kingdom of God near at hand. But there is a peculiarly Protestant statement of the principle.

Tillich finds this characteristically Protestant version of the principle in the Reformation assertion of the unconditional character of God and in the idea that the fulfilment of human existence ultimately depends not upon human devices and mediations (of Catholic, Protestant, or secular type) but rather upon justification through faith. But the doctrine of justification has become well-nigh unintelligible to the modern man and even to the modern scholar. The situation is partly due to the fact that in some instances the doctrine has come to mean a rule of faith imposed as a "law"—just the opposite of what was originally intended. Tillich has therefore attempted to give the doctrine a restatement in modern terms by devising a Protestant interpretation of a conception that has been used in existential theology and philosophy, the concept of "the human boundary-situation." This restatement presents Tillich's peculiarly Protestant interpretation of the character of human freedom and fulfilment.

Human existence is the rise of being to the realm of freedom. Being gets free from bondage to natural necessity. It becomes spirit and acquires the freedom to question itself and its environment, the freedom to raise the question concerning the true and the good and to make decision with regard to them. But man is in a sense unfree in his freedom, for he is compelled to decide. "This inevitability of freedom, of having to make decisions, creates the deep restlessness of our existence; through it our existence is threatened." It is threatened because an unconditional demand confronts man to choose and fulfil the good, a demand that he cannot fulfil. Consequently, man as spirit has a cleavage within him, a cleavage that is manifest also in society. There is no place to which he may flee from the demand. And in confronting the demand he can never provide himself with absolute security.

The point at which every self-provided security is brought under question, the point at which human possibilities reach and know their limits, Tillich calls "the human boundary-situation." "Right" belief and "right" action, church and sacrament and creed, piety and mystical experience, and also secular substitutes for any of these things are recognized as false securities. An ultimate and threatening "No" is pronounced upon them all.

But human freedom and existence find support as well as threat at the boundary-situation. This support comes from beyond or beneath the interplay between person and society. What is involved here is the deepest level of man's existence. Just where dependence upon the finite creations of spirit is relinquished, a new confidence and a creative impulse arise from the infinite and inexhaustible depths.

This experience of the boundary-situation is not something that takes place in a flight away from the concrete and the temporal. The boundary is, so to speak, at the edge of a particular complex of spiritual and cultural realities. The specific consequences of the experience of ultimate threat and support will therefore be different in the time of Luther or Pascal from what they were in the time of Jeremiah. But always the transcendent significance of, and judgment upon, temporal realities are envisaged anew. One gains at the boundary a paradoxical sense of the immediacy of origin and of threat. Beneath the dichotomy between subject and object a new, a third, dimension, the dimension of depth, is discerned. The creative and destructive and recreative powers of being erupt into the consciousness. A new relation to things and men appears. Things are no longer viewed merely as objects for use or as technical means without intrinsic worth. They are seen again in their "powerfulness," which is rooted in the inner infinity of being. In place of "the mutual domination between thing and personality," there appears "a mutual service between personality and things," an *eros*-relation." This *eros*-relation becomes manifest also in a new sense of community and of its depth. In place of the community that breaks the personality and bends it under its yoke, there can now emerge a community of free personalities who know themselves as belonging together through their connection with the ultimate supporting and threatening reality. The personality recognizes something holy and unconditional in the dignity and freedom of other persons; for persons, like things, are seen now to be supported by the inner infinity of being. Here, it would seem, we have Tillich's rendering of Luther's idea of the "love of neighbor"—the consequence of justification.

Man does not, however, by his experience of the boundary gain control of the ultimate threat and support. He can *prepare* for receiving the support by exposing himself consciously and without reservation to the claims of the unconditional. But the awareness of the ultimate meaning and of the possibility of fulfilling that meaning in a particular situation is a matter of "destiny and grace." Neither a church nor any other group can subject the ultimate threat and support to human conditions or techniques. For this reason the radical Protestant attributes only a provisional importance to the church and its forms. Here he stands nearer to the secularism that is skeptical of the conventional securities of piety than to any orthodoxy, whether it be "religious" or secular.

In this connection one of the most striking and original aspects of Tillich's rendering of the doctrine of justification should be noted. Luther applied the doctrine of justification only to the religious-moral life. The sinner, though unjust, is "justified." Tillich applies the doctrine to the religious-intellectual sphere also. No act of will accepting "right" belief can be properly demanded by any authority. Devotion to truth is supreme; it is devotion to God. There is a sacred element in the integrity that leads to doubt even about God and religion. Indeed, since God is truth, he is the basis and not the object of any question about God. Any loyalty to truth is religious loyalty, even if it leads to a recognition of the lack of truth. Paraphrasing Augustine, the serious doubter may say: "I doubt, therefore I am religious." Even in doubt the divine is present. Absolutely serious atheism can be directed toward the unconditional; it can be a form of faith in truth. There appears here the conquest of meaninglessness by the awareness of the paradoxical presence of "meaning in meaninglessness." Thus the doubter is "justified." The only absolutely irreligious attitude, then, is absolute cynicism, absolute lack of seriousness.

Returning, now, to the consideration with which the concept of the boundary-situation was introduced, we may restate the implications of the Protestant principle as they relate to heteronomy and autonomy. Both these types of "religion" are overcome by what Tillich calls "theonomy" (a concept that had been used previously by Troeltsch and others). In the face of the destruction or weakening of freedom which accompanies heteronomy and autonomy, theonomy goes beyond them both, preserving and transforming an element from each. It emphasizes the commanding element in the unconditional demand for the ultimate good, for truth and justice. This ultimate ground of meaning and existence is not (as in heteronomy) identified with any conditioned reality or social form; yet it calls for obedience. Here an element of heteronomy is retained and transformed. But the unconditional is not arbitrary; it never demands the sacrifice of the intellect; it is not alien to man; it fulfils his inmost nature, his freedom. Theonomy takes from autonomy this element of intelligibility and self-determination and transforms it. Recognizing that self-sufficient autonomy, as the self-assertion of a conditioned reality, is not able to create a world from within itself and recognizing that every conception of the ultimate good must reflect the cleavage within man and society, theonomy deepens autonomy to a point where the latter is transcended. Theonomy supports autonomy and at the same time breaks through it without shattering it. Thus theonomy brings both heteronomy and autonomy to the boundary-situation, where in differing ways they confront the ultimate threat and support and are transformed. In short, theonomy is the condition in which spiritual and social forms are imbued with the import of the unconditional as their supporting ground and judge.

The critical and creative principle which expresses the ultimate threat and support is what makes Protestantism Protestant. It is, therefore, called the "Protestant principle." But it is clear that this principle is no sectarian principle. It cuts through all sectarianisms (both religious and secular) to that which shatters and transforms all self-inclosed forms. Its first word, therefore, "must be the word against religion"; and this means its first word is against every movement that idolizes established forms, whether religious or secular, orthodox or liberal, ecclesiastical or nonecclesiastical. All these idolizations are merely forms of "pharisaism." The Protestant may not attribute a classical status even to the Reformation or to any other period (e.g., the period A.D. 30–33) in a normative sense. "It is of the essence of Protestantism," Tillich says, "that there can be no classical period for it." The principle protests also against any idolization of religious language, whether it be old or new, whether it be in the Bible or in the church confessions. Reformation must continue in language as well as in other forms. We must "learn to see with our own eyes and name with our own words that which is not bound to any time or any eye or any word." The Word of God is that reality (a word, a person, a thing, or a situation) in and through which the ultimate divine power breaks into the present.

From this it follows that the Protestant principle has not been and never can be in the secure possession of Protestantism or of any religious movement. It can be apprehended by men who are ostensibly anti-religious or anti-Christian. In fact, some aspects of the principle were more nearly expressed by Marx and Nietzsche in nineteenth-century Germany than by most of the churches. "With Marx," Tillich says, it was "the spirit of ancient Jewish prophetism in both language and content, with Nietzsche the spirit of Luther in both language and content." If this struggle—in the one instance for justice and in the other for the creative life as against bourgeois "Christian" inhumanity and conventionalism—was fought against God and religion, it was against a god and a religion that were bound to the standpoint of bourgeois society. Grave deficiencies are to be discerned in both these men and their disciples, but something like the shattering and newly creative power of genuine prophetism was there.

Protestantism (or any other religion) always needs the correction that comes from the "secular" protest against any tendency within it to identify itself with the unconditional. In this function, as well as in the challenge of its creative achievement, secularism on Protestant soil may be called "Protestant secularism." The very existence of this sort of secularism shows that grace is not bound up with explicit religion, i.e., with those forms whose express purpose it is to serve as a medium of grace. It is "a concealed form of grace," a manifestation of "the latent church." It often serves to remind Protestantism of its own principle and in some cases exhibits a better, even if an unintended, apprehension and application of that principle. Protestantism can appropriate this stimulus only if it stands at the boundary between itself and secularism. When there is a vital relation between church and society, "the church is the perpetual guilty conscience of society and society the perpetual guilty conscience of the church."

These implications of the Protestant principle are given corresponding expression in Tillich's definitions of religion and culture. Religion is "direction toward the unconditional." Culture is direction toward the conditioned forms of meaning and their unity. Despite this contrast, however, genuine religion and vital culture have ultimately the same roots. "Being religious is being unconditionally concerned, whether this concern expresses itself in secular or (in the narrower sense) religious forms." All sharp divisions between the sacred and the secular must be eliminated in recognition of a transcendent critical and formative power which is present in both religion and culture. "Secular culture is essentially as impossible as atheism because both presuppose the unconditional element and both express ultimate concerns." Implied here is a dialectical view of religion and culture. Religion, in order to achieve realization, must assume form and become culture; in doing so it is religious in both substance and intention. But culture, even when it is not religious by intention, is religious in substance, for every cultural act contains an unconditional meaning, it depends upon the ground of meaning. Yet when religion becomes culture, it may lose its depth and its sense of relatedness to the unconditional; it may degenerate into an absolute devotion to conditioned cultural realities. On the other hand, culture, even in the act of opposing "religion," may rediscover the unconditional threat and support, and it may bring forth new religious creation. Accordingly, the major types of explicit religions appear in implicit form in the history of "secular" culture. With Schelling, Tillich would say that the history of culture is in a broad sense the history of religion. The Protestant principle, in pointing to that universally operative reality which judges and supports all meaningful existence, interprets religion as present wherever there is a uniting of negation and affirmation, of threat and support, of judgment and grace, of crisis and form-creation. Perverted religion and perverted culture appear wherever this dialectic is absent.

The demand is always placed before Protestantism, then, to transcend itself at the boundary-situation and to move toward new realization. It must effect this realization directly in relation to secular realities. This means that its prophetic and creative power must become manifest in a concrete historical situation; it means also that it must combine prophetic and rational criticism (as it has done almost from its beginning). The Protestant principle, therefore, relates "the line upward," the reference to the eternal meaning, to "the line forward," the direction toward the temporal realization of the eternal meaning in accord with the demands of a rational understanding of a particular historical situation. In emphasizing "the line forward" as well as "the line upward" and in demanding a dialectical relation between Protestantism and secularism, Tillich turns away from pietistic indifference to "the world" and history and stresses the world-affirming and world-shaping dynamic of Calvinism and modern humanism.

In the light of the Protestant principle there can be no *official* philosophy for Protestantism, and there can be no official program for the application of the principle. Yet, if the principle is to achieve relevance in any particular historical situation, it requires both a philosophical elaboration and a program for action. His own philosophical elaboration of the principle Tillich calls "belief-ful" or "self-transcending realism," for it combines realism and a faith that transcends realism. Beliefful realism "is a turning toward reality, a questioning of reality, a penetrating into existence, a driving to the level where reality points beyond itself to its ground and ultimate meaning." It does not look "above" reality to a transcendentalized spiritual world; it looks down into the depths of reality to its inner infinity.

In his introductory chapter to the present volume Professor Tillich gives a characterization of some of the central concepts of this beliefful realism, such as "the kairos," "the Gestalt of grace," and "the demonic"—concepts that have in a special way become associated with his name and through which his influence is today most readily perceptible. Here we shall, therefore, direct attention mainly to the underlying characteristics and to the historical background and context of Tillich's outlook. In doing so, we shall have to give further consideration to certain of the concepts that have already been referred to in a preliminary way.

"Belief-ful realism" may be characterized as an existential and dialectical philosophy of meaning-fulfilment. The word "meaning" in this context suggests the characteristic concerns of the Neo-Kantians—Dilthey, Rickert, and Troeltsch—who combined philosophy of culture with "historical thinking." The word "fulfilment" implies the dynamic conception of history, stemming from Old Testament prophetism and continuing down through the New Testament and the eschatologies of the left wing of the pre-Reformation and the Reformation. The word "existential" recalls the names of Kierkegaard and Feuerbach and also certain contemporary movements. The word "dialectical" suggests the variegated strand of philosophical and theological tradition that has both Greek and Hebrew sources and that reaches down through Jacob Boehme and the German philosophical idealists to Marx and the present.

The concept of "meaning" has become almost indispensable in discussions of philosophy of culture and philosophy of history during the past three-quarters of a century, especially since Dilthey gave it a central place in his "critique of historical reason." So great a role has the concept played in recent times that Tillich says the problem of the meaning of history has become the problem of the present period in contrast to the previous period's major interest in the control of nature. This shift of interest is a symptom of the crisis in the culture.

The writings of the Neo-Kantians, as well as those of the phenomenologist, Edmund Husserl, no doubt provided an intellectual stimulus for Tillich to develop the concept of "meaning" (though the decisive stimulus for Tillich the existentialist was probably offered by "the storms of our times," in which the meaning of life is radically threatened). He starts with the twofold idealistic presupposition that all the spiritual life of man forms an inner unity and that this spiritual life, both as a whole and in its parts, is to be understood only in its religious roots. But in his "self-transcending realism" he goes beyond epistemological idealism and the critical-dialectical method corresponding to it. He is always conscious of the tension between any synthesis and the unconditional quality pointing beyond it. Moreover, he emphasizes the necessity of taking account of the meaningless and the destructive, as a power negating the synthesis; thus he rejects the idealistic conviction that the antithesis should be thought of only as "sublated" in the achieved synthesis. In this way he replaces the idealistic philosophy of Mind by a realistic philosophy of Meaning.

Tillich's concern with the concept of meaning first came to the fore in connection with his interest in art (an interest he has pursued in a somewhat systematic fashion since the years of his service as a chaplain in the first World War). In great works of art Tillich senses something deeper than form and content. In looking at the Michelangelo murals in the Sistine Chapel in Rome, for example, he was impressed by an intuition of reality that seems to have grasped the artist who created the work and that grasps anyone who looks into its depths. This intuition was expressed with special power in the expressionist art of two decades ago and seems to have given special impetus to Tillich's formulation of belief-ful realism. The thing that gives to art its quality of greatness, he says, is its pulsating witness to something sublime and holy that shimmers through or overflows the form and the content. In such creations, as in painting or music, for example, an ambivalent numinous quality is perceptible; it is as if one were hearing the song that the stars sang on the morning of creation and yet were also looking into the abyss of absolute nothingness. The intuition is not dissimilar to the paradox of the philosophical shock experienced when one faces the question of why there is not nothing. It is the experience of "a meaning-reality, the ultimate, the deepest all-shattering and ever newly creating meaning-reality." Tillich speaks of this essential power and meaning of reality as the import of a work of art in contrast to its form or content. This import is intuited, for example, in a painting in which the artist seems to waver between the portrayal of an object and the expression of a meaning that transcends it. In short, the artist reveals a power and meaning that transcend himself as well as the form and the content of the painting, that transcend both subject and object. The relation between form and import requires a much more thorough (and dialectical) discussion than is here possible. Moreover, Tillich would today probably modify some of the formulations presented in his early writing on art.

Tillich employs the distinction between import (*Gehalt*) and content (*Inhalt*) as the basis of an elaborate philosophy of art and culture and science. Indeed, meaning or import is, in his view, the life-blood of metaphysics. The forms of meaning are filled with a living import. This import, he says, is what the mystics have in mind when they speak of the "ground of the soul," "the unconscious," "the primordial will." It refers to a foundation in being, a suggestion by things of "another thing" that is still no other thing.

This sense of the enhancement of existence and meaning by another power is an "ecstatic" experience. Ecstasy operates in such a way as to break through a given form of individual existence, bringing it into union with the ultimate ground of meaning. It is the experience of being grasped by the essential power and meaning of reality, "the really real," the unconditional—that which is man's ultimate concern so long as he remains within the realm of being and meaning. Applying these ideas to art, Tillich says: "It is possible to see in a still-life by Cézanne, an animal picture by Marc, and a landscape by Schmidt-Rotluff, the direct revelation of an absolute reality in these relative things. The world-import experienced in the artist's religious ecstasy shines through the things; they have become 'holy' objects."

It is this living import that Tillich has in mind when he speaks of religion as direction toward the unconditional. This unconditional element is recognized in and beyond all absolutely serious concerns, in all logical and aesthetic, in all legal and social, action. In all these meaningful activities there appears not only a definite concrete meaning but also a sense of the meaningfulness of the whole, the unity of all possible meanings. But more than a totality of meaning is involved, for a mere totality of meaning could sink into a void of meaninglessness. In the totality of meaning there lives an unconditional meaning which is itself not a meaning but rather the basis of meaning. This is the unconditional element in all being and meaning.

The term "the unconditional" is unsympathetic to the average ear, though it was used almost from the very beginning of philosophical discussion in the West. (We have already cited Plato's use of the concept; as we shall observe later, it is quite different from Tillich's.) The term has played an especially significant role in the writings of philosophical idealists since the time of Kant and Schleiermacher. In Tillich's usage it is a philosophical symbol for the ultimate concern of man. It is the *prius* of everything that has being or meaning. This basis or ground of being is something "secret" into which thinking cannot penetrate, because, as something existing, thought is itself based upon it. Tillich therefore sometimes uses Schelling's term *Das Unvordenkliche* to refer to that which is prior to and inaccessible to thought. The term "the unconditional" carries more powerful connotations in German than in English usage. As Tillich uses it, the German term *Das Unbedingte* connotes the majestic and the awful, the ultimate and the intimate, the sovereign, the commanding, that which cannot be tampered with, that which makes demands that cannot be ignored with impunity.

One misunderstands the term "the unconditional" if one confuses it with the Absolute of German idealism, with the eternal essences of Platonism, with the superessential One of mysticism, with the mathematically calculated laws of nature, with the Supreme Being of rational deduction, or with the "Wholly Other" (as characterized by Rudolph Otto or Karl Barth). It should not even be called the "unconditioned" (as some translators have rendered it). In all these terms that which should be thought of as Being itself tends to be conceived as a particular being about whose "existence" there might be an argument. One cannot properly argue for the "existence" of the unconditional; nor can one consistently argue against its reality. To argue about it is to presuppose it, for the very argument must itself presuppose some unconditional demand and reality. To argue that it is a being is to try to make it one conditioned thing among other conditioned things; it is to deprive it of its unconditional character. The unconditional is not a section of reality; it is not a thing or an "existing" entity; it is not an object among objects, not even the highest "object." (Following the dominant theological tradition, Kant, once and for all, disposed of these transcendental projections and reifications made by supernaturalism and rational metaphysics.) The unconditional transcends the distinction between subject and object. To forget this is to make atheism inevitable. Atheism is thoroughly justified in protesting against the extrapolation of a transcendent world behind the existing world. The unconditional is not *a* being. It is a quality or a qualification of all beings and meanings. It is the power of being in which every being participates. It is inexhaustible in its power; it never fully and finally pours itself into the cosmos of forms; it imbues all forms, but it also bursts through them. Hence, as the depth or the infinity of things, it is both the ground and the abyss of being. It is that quality in being and truth, in goodness and beauty, that elicits man's ultimate concern; thus it is the absolute quality of all being and meaning and value, the power and vitality of the real as it fulfills itself in meaningful creativity. But man has no "control" over it; he cannot manipulate it. If he could control it, it would be something conditional. To attempt to manipulate the unconditional would be like trying deliberately to tell one's self a lie; to attempt to ignore it would be like trying to *be* nothing.

Karl Barth, in one of his critical essays on Tillich (written at the height of the controversy between them), rejects the term "the unconditional" as inappropriate for theological discussion. Indeed, he calls it "a frigid monstrosity." In doing so, he reiterates his rejection of philosophy of religion as such, revealing his idolatrous attachment to the words of Scripture and confession. He also forgets that the term is a negative *philosophical* symbol and is not intended to replace the term "God." God is, in Tillich's view, unconditional. But the unconditional is not God. The word "God" denotes analogies taken from "objective" thinking; it is "filled with the concrete symbols in which mankind has expressed its unconditional concern." But it denotes also the unconditional element beyond these analogies. In other words, the term "God" denotes ontic symbols which refer to the ontological structure of being. In this connection, Tillich observes the precarious character of all religious language. If language is to express vividly our experience of being grasped by something unconditional, it must use symbols drawn from the actual world of the subject-object correlation. Yet the use of the "objective" symbols brings with it the danger of objectifying God. It also gives rise to "the half-blasphemous and mythological concept of 'the existence of God.'" To draw the divine down into the world of objects is to commit idolatry. This idolatry before an objectively "existing" God is the ever present danger of all religion. Every truly religious symbol should carry within it a protest against the thingification of God. With this protest (implicit in the concept of "the unconditional") Barth would certainly agree.

Sometimes Tillich expresses this same idea by speaking of the paradoxical immanence of the transcendent. The intention lying behind this formulation is to exclude any spatialization of the infinite and inexhaustible power in things. Hence, Tillich's conception may not properly be called "supernaturalist" or "neosupernaturalist." It does not imply, as one contemporary critic wrongly asserts, that "the whole meaning and the only meaning of natural existence is found in the unconditional reality of God." Such a conception of meaning contravenes Tillich's intention; it implies spatialization, the very thing that Tillich rejects. The unconditional does not "wholly transcend the world" in any spatial sense; it qualifies it; it is its depth-dimension.

Tillich accepts Rudolph Otto's characterization of the numinous or the holy as a masterly phenomenological description of the vivid awareness of the unconditional. He does not, however, accept Otto's Neo-Kantian epistemology, which makes the holy a separate category alongside the categories of truth, goodness, and beauty. Nor does he, with Kant, interpret it in merely axiological terms. For Tillich, "being is older than purpose." To spatialize it as something that may or may not be related to truth and goodness and beauty is to attempt to condition it.

Nor can the *awareness* of the unconditional be spatialized. The term "awareness" is used because it is a neutral term and may be distinguished from knowledge. The term "knowledge" presupposes the separation of subject and object. Awareness of the unconditional is neither the awareness of an "object" nor a discrete theoretical act. Schleiermacher recognized the inappropriateness of "knowledge" as the basis of religious consciousness, but he spatialized the awareness by assigning it to "feeling." "Neither the Hegelian conception which assigns it to the theoretical sphere, nor the view of Schleiermacher which assigns it to feeling, has been able to maintain itself." The awareness of the unconditional involves the whole being; in this sense the awareness is existential.

This aspect of the concept of the unconditional becomes clearer if one relates it to the concept of faith. Faith is not a special function; it is effective in all functions of the human spirit. Nor is it belief in the truth of uncertain or doubtful objects. It has nothing to do with acceptance or probability. Faith is not a "work" of the mind or of the righteous will. It is a gift of grace; it is the consequence of being grasped by the power of the unconditionally real and creative depth in things. If one asks how the human spirit becomes intellectually aware of this unconditional meaning-reality, Tillich answers that it is through phenomenological intuition, an intuition that can be justified through the ontological argument, though he warns against the frequent perversion of this argument which connects it too narrowly with rational dialectic and which thereby degenerates into "objective" spatialized thinking.[3] Tillich formulates the ontological principle in this way: "Man is immediately aware of something unconditional which is the prius of the separation and interaction of subject and object, theoretically as well as practically."

This "ecstatic" intuition is the operation of love, the uniting of that which is separated. But it brings not only a sense of union or kinship with the ultimate power and meaning of reality; accompanying it there is also a sense of separation. Yet the separation is related to the union. The failure to recognize this fact is the error of dualism and of supernaturalism, an error markedly prominent in Barthianism. In one of his early essays on art Tillich says of this union and separation: "If we imagine the import to be the sun and form to be the orbit of a planet, then for every form of culture there is proximity to and distance from the sun or the import. If on the one hand it is the power of the sun which is revealed in the nearness to the sun, it is on the other hand the peculiar power in the movement of the planets which is expressed in the distance from the sun; and yet, it is the sun itself which supports both nearness and distance." The sense of nearness and distance spoken of here bears affinity to Nicholas of Cusa's "coincidence of opposites." This brings us to a consideration of the dialectical character of Tillich's self-transcending realism."

Tillich's philosophy of tension is reminiscent of Plato's dialectic of participation in and separation from the eternal, though Tillich does not, like Plato, idealistically attribute the separation to something in matter radically resistant to form (this would be to deny the doctrine of creation and to move in the direction of Manichaeanism). For him the alienation is due not only to "objective" thinking but also to man's fateful abuse of freedom. But Plato is rejected not only because of his dualism. Even when he speaks of the presence of the good which appears in things (as well as being concealed by them), his interpretation depends upon a nonhistorical view of reality and history. Tillich's interpretation aims to be "historical," or we might say eschatological; the essential tension is not the Platonic contrast between cyclical time and eternity but rather the dialectic between *kairos* (as the divine breaking into time) and *telos* (as the "end" of the linear movement of time).

3. Tillich has compared his own form of the ontological argument with that of Hocking, Wieman, Lyman, Whitehead, and Hartshorne (see his essay, "The Two Types of Philosophy of Religion," *Union Seminary Quarterly Review*, I, No. 4 [May, 1946], 3–13).

In his conception of the cleavage in human existence he stands near to Jacob Boehme, who viewed existence as participating in the depth of being but who interpreted the cleavage as the consequence of the working of a dark, creative, and destructive power which, like Lucifer, drives toward self-inflation. The principal opposition to the divine unity is not a satanic principle of mere negation; it is rather a demonic power that perverts the creative power into a mixture of form-creating and form-destroying energy in history. A demon is something less than God which pretends to be God. The demonic operates not only in the individual's wilful yielding to the temptation to give rein to the libido of sensuality, of power, and of knowledge. It operates even more powerfully in human institutions. Here Tillich, like Augustine, transforms the primitive Christian conception of the demonic so as to make it applicable to social movements. Thus evil is not primarily mere negation; it is a perverse and powerful affirmation. "The simple lack of form," he says, "the weakness of a social structure is naturally not demonic. Demonry is the reign of a superindividual sacred form which supports life and which at the same time contains the force of destruction in such a way that the destructive power is essentially connected with the creative power." This formulation brings us to a consideration of Tillich's rejection of the idealistic conception of synthesis.

One aspect of the structure of Tillich's conception of dialectic is to be observed in his adaptation of Fichte's conception of spirit. Tillich interprets spiritual or cultural life as the synthesis of thought and being in the cultural creations of human mind (this is the basic principle of his classification of the sciences), but the synthesis remains open and ambiguous. Cultural creation is the work of a creatively rational "individual" spirit, like a planet united with and separated from the sun, the living import. This conception of dialectic may be contrasted with the Hegelian conception. Tillich rejects the Hegelian dialectic (which operates in the unambiguous self-explication of the absolute or unconditioned idea) and proposes a dialectic between transcendent and conditioned meaning; the transcendent is viewed as paradoxically and ambiguously immanent in cultural activity. Thus cultural activity (including church activity) is never to be identified with the essential unity and goodness of being. In other words, the shadow-boxing Hegelian dialectic of the unfolding of the absolute idea into ever richer synthesis is transformed by Tillich into an earnest dialectic of meaning. In place of

Hegel's panlogistic synthesis of the absolute idea, Tillich presents the dialectic of a dynamic form-creating and form-bursting power; and in this way he renounces the Hegelian *hybris,* which presumes to grasp pure being and which in reality identifies essence with existence. He finds in the later philosophy of Schelling an impressive rejection of Hegelian logism, a pushing beyond idealism to a realism in which there appears a sense of guilty separation from the inner infinity of being as well as a kinship with it. Thus human activity, both intellectual and practical, tends to be compounded of the demonic and the divine.

The abstract characterization we have given of Tillich's conception of dialectic (which in other aspects relating to theological method is presented in his introductory chapter for this volume) could create the false impression that his outlook is merely an academic exercise. But Tillich's philosophy is not simply another philosophy of the schools. It is existential in the sense that it has been developed out of a direct confrontation with the historical situation. The term "existential" as applied to Tillich's outlook connects him with certain aspects of a movement that has become increasingly influential during the last hundred years and that has exercised an influence in America, especially since the time of William James.

There are, of course, many varieties of existentialism which have appeared from the time of Schelling, Kierkegaard, Feuerbach, and Marx down through Nietzsche and Dilthey to the time of Bergson, James, Dewey, Heidegger, Jaspers, and Tillich.[4] In general, we may say that Tillich is an existentialist in the sense that he takes his place with all those who appeal "from the conclusions of 'rationalistic,' ('objective') thinking, which equates Reality with the object of thought, with relations or 'essence,' to Reality as men experience it immediately in their actual living." The roots of this existentialist philosophy Tillich finds in the pre-Cartesian tradition of supra-rationalism and *Innerlichkeit* represented by Jacob Boehme. Existentialism represents, therefore, the coming-to-the-fore of a type of thinking which, during the period of Cartesian, Hegelian, and bourgeois rationalism, has been a subdominant tradition in modern European thought. Tillich's attempt to overcome the subject-object dichotomy and his use and interpretation of

4. Professor Tillich has recently given a comprehensive survey of the history of existential philosophy in his article on the subject in the *Journal of the History of Ideas,* V (1944), 44–70.

the boundary-situation are part and parcel of his drive toward immediate experience understood as a confronting of the unconditional, as a standing between the finite and the infinite. Here both the divine and the demonic, support and threat, a sense of kinship and nonkinship with the ultimate, passionate tension and responsible decision, are the characteristic existentialist motifs. The contrast Tillich sees between Protestantism as a historical realization and Protestantism as a witness to a principle is bound up with an immediate experience of the insecurity and questionableness of the one and the faith in something more reliable (the form-bursting and form-creating reality) pointed to by the other. These depths of the actual situation, Tillich believes, cannot be known except through an existential involvement and decision.

Nor is this view itself pure theory for Tillich himself. As illustrations of his practical activity, we recall his struggle against national socialism in Germany, his leadership in the religious-socialist movement in Germany, his work of mediation between philosophers and theologians, his acquiring of a religious and social outlook that ranges him between typically European and typically American positions, his close contact with "secular" leaders in the various areas of the common life (artists, scientists, statesmen, psychiatrists and the like), his prodigious work in various groups concerned with the care and education of refugees, his co-operation with the United States government (broadcasting many radio addresses to wartime Germany) and with groups looking toward the strengthening of democratic forces in Germany.

In this connection Tillich makes a special application of his conception of the boundary-situation and of his dialectical definition of religion and culture. Just as we do not understand, he says, the possibilities and limitations of the human condition until we have confronted the boundary of the human, so also we do not really know any particular historical situation or any particular creative tendency until, through actual experience, we have apprehended its possibilities as well as its limitations. The border line between the various spheres of social life and also between various tendencies and outlooks is, he believes, a most fruitful place for knowledge and the most fruitful place for practical decision. Many readers will recall that in his autobiographical sketch (published in *The Interpretation of History*) he presents his life as having been lived on the boundaries between the social classes, between church and society, between idealism and Marxism, and so on.

Much of Tillich's own participation in the life of our time has been conducted through practical activity on these borders.

What with his view of the interdependence of all cultural forces and his insistence upon the insecure and ambiguous character of existence and meaning, it follows that Tillich accepts neither the economism nor the dialectic of Marxism with its crypto-Hegelian and utopian expectation of final synthesis in history. Yet he sees in Marx's revolt against Hegel not only a justified opposition to a philosophy that only "explains" and does not act (an opposition to an "ideology" protecting an exploiting class and state) but also a powerfully prophetic mood arising out of a deep sense of alienation in human society and aiming to achieve a union between theory and practice. Despite the purely immanental, sociological context of Marx's view of man and history, Tillich discerns in it closer affinities to classical Christian conceptions of sin and eschatology than to religious-liberal conceptions. What with his emphasis on responsible participation in the common concerns of public life, it follows that Tillich cannot accept Kierkegaard's aloofness to concrete concerns of social and cultural life. In his view, Kierkegaard represents a bourgeois retreat into subjectivity; hence Kierkegaard achieves by default what Hegel achieves by conservative idealism, namely, a virtual sanctioning of bourgeois complacency. But Tillich takes a decisively positive attitude toward other aspects of Kierkegaard's thought, toward his powerful dialectic between the finite and the infinite, his insistence upon the profound tension between essence and existence, his revolt against Hegelian "completeness" of system, his emphasis upon the anxiety and despair of merely autonomous freedom, and especially his rejection of the detached "spectator-attitude" of the academic philosopher or scientist. It is in connection with these aspects of existential thinking that he quotes with approval Feuerbach's exhortation: "Do not wish to be a philosopher in contrast to being a man .... do not think as a thinker .... think as a living, real being .... think in Existence." With Kierkegaard, Marx, and Feuerbach he therefore stresses the passionate character of all existential thinking, a kind of thinking which, in Tillich's view, grips the whole man in his conscious and unconscious life, in his involvement and participation in the ongoing concerns of society and history, in his relation to the lower strata of society (the "rejected"), and in the inescapability of decision.

Here we should indicate the similarities and dissimilarities of Tillich's thought to the pragmatist school of thought initiated by William James. Tillich stands near to John Dewey, for example, in certain important respects, especially in so far as Dewey stresses the existential involvement of the subject in knowledge and also in so far as Dewey acknowledges the fragmentary and dynamic character of truth and of human fulfilment. On the other hand, Tillich criticizes pragmatism because it has "surrendered itself as 'instrumentalism' to the objective process of nature and society, producing means for ends which are finite and, consequently, not a matter of infinite, passionate concern." In Tillich's view the existential man stands between the infinite and the finite and can never be understood as merely a part of natural objectivity. Tillich also criticizes pragmatist "ethics." In his view its reliance upon experimental "ethics" simply takes inherited values of a liberal society for granted, and thus it cannot from itself provide ethical standards for judging and directing the flux of "experience."

But perhaps the thinker with whom the most instructive comparison can be made is Karl Barth. Tillich has often been classified with him in entirely too simple a fashion. Barth is usually referred to as a representative of existential and dialectical theology. In his article, "What Is Wrong with the 'Dialectic' Theology?" (not reprinted in the present volume), Tillich asserts that this neo-Reformation theology at its beginning supplied a powerful and radical religious criticism of church and culture; in the face of naziism it saved the German Protestant church. But he denies that Barth's theology is dialectical; it is, he says, merely paradoxical. Moreover, by interpreting the divine as "wholly other" and alien to man, it derogates all human culture. It denies significance even to any human questioning concerning the ultimate.[5] By rejecting humanism and autonomy it has created a new heteronomy. Although it opposed the Nazi "Grand Inquisitor" (to use Dostoevsky's term), it has set up its own Grand Inquisitor "with a strong but tight-fitting armor of Barthian supernaturalism" and scholastic confessionalism. Despite its constant reference to crisis, it has come to view everything as being under judgment—except itself. It has "relapsed into the mere reiteration of tradition." It has forgotten the Protestant protest in the name of which it began and is in danger of

5. *Journal of Religion*, XV (1935), 127–45. No doubt it is partially because of his fundamental disagreements with Barth that Tillich has recently characterized his own view as "neo-dialectical."

becoming a merely weakened form of Catholicism. Moreover, in its criticism of culture it has opposed tyranny only for the sake of the church and not for the sake of human rights. And, as a consequence of its supernaturalism and of its Kantian ethical presuppositions, it has for the most part pronounced only an abstract, formal judgment upon the social order—all things are judged and really nothing is decided. This aloofness to the responsibilities of prophetic religion, an aloofness sanctioned by a supernaturalist pessimism, merely assists (by default) the ruling and dominating powers in society. By this aloofness, Barthianism even helped to destroy the religious-socialist movement in pre-Hitler Germany. And it has not yet been able to explicate a positive conception of fulfilment in history. It turns away from a positive decision with regard to the specific situation "here and now." It escapes backward into an otherwordly traditionalism. Despite its avowed existential attitude, which renounces the spectator attitude, it is unable to find a way forward out of the Protestant era.

## III

Tillich's philosophy is one that looks toward meaning-fulfilment in all areas of life. Although many of his formulations of this philosophy reveal the influence of modern intellectual movements, its deepest roots are to be found in the Judeo-Christian apprehension of human existence and fulfilment. This apprehension, implicit in what we have already presented, may be epitomized in three familiar axioms—an affirmation of the essential, if not actual, unity and goodness of existence (mythologically expressed in the doctrine of the divine creation of the world) is combined with the recognition of an underivable contradiction in human existence (mythologically expressed in the doctrine of the Fall—which may not be accepted as a historical event or as an explanation of the human condition but as a description of the cleavage in the human spirit and in human society) and with a confidence that the cleavage, the broken unity and goodness, can be restored by the inexhaustible creative power (mythologically expressed in the doctrine of redemption). This Judeo-Christian apprehension, when truly understood, implies a philosophy of history.

In conformity with the "historical thinking" of ancient prophetism and of the modern historical consciousness, which is in part derived from it, self-transcending realism affirms that the focal expression of these three elements is to be found in history, though the form-bursting and form-creating power arises from beneath the level of freedom and existence. Self-transcending realism is a historical realism. In and through the historical "here and now," in and through the dynamics and structures of history, we experience in widest and deepest dimensions the realization and the contradiction of meaning. Here we encounter in its critical and creative power the ultimate threat and support of human existence. History in all its spheres is the arena of salvation, the realm in which the demands of the unconditional are confronted. Salvation occurs in time and through community, in the overcoming of the demonic powers that pervert both personal and social life. It appears in those forms and structures that give a local habitation to justice and love and beauty. And it is the work of a gracious, affirming, healing power moving toward the fulfilment of being and meaning.

The depth, the tensions, and the possibilities of existence are not really known until one in faith apprehends them through passionate participation in the struggles of history. In other words, the existential attitude implicit in the demand for participation presupposes that the subject comes to know the human situation only by entering into the process of fulfilment, a process in which thought and being are merged and transmuted in the creative life of spirit. The mark of the fullest intercourse with reality is found, then, in the uniting of contemporaneity with self-transcending relatedness to the unconditional; it is found in a belief-ful, timely awareness and action in terms of the unconditional demands relevant to the present situation. Such an awareness and action, therefore, demands a venturing decision, the taking of a risk.

When men (or churches) do not direct their deepest existential concern to this focus of decision and participation in the "here and now," they miss an unrepeatable opportunity for the expression of meaning in history; in other words, they miss the kairos. But action or participation is not sufficient. If the action is not accompanied by a decision for the unconditional, then either demonic self-inflation or lack of seriousness ensues. On the other hand, if decision is not accompanied by participation, then knowledge will be abstractly formal or "untimely." Only from an awareness of the inextricable bond and tension between the concrete historical situation and the unconditioned depth of being and meaning can men avail themselves of truly critical and formative power.

The unconditionality of prophetic criticism, combined with the timely resoluteness of formative will under grace, can alone bring the fulness or fulfilment of time, the kairos. No aspect or area of life is exempt from the demands of this "timely" criticism and form-creation, i.e., timely in the sense of the kairos. Only through "timely" criticism and action can the significantly new come into being; only in this way can the import and demand of the unconditional impinge upon history. This is the practical implication of the Protestant principle.

In viewing the present social situation at the end of the Protestant era, Tillich sees a negative vindication of the Protestant principle in the consequences of the operation of the bourgeois principle, as well as in the degeneration of self-sufficient autonomy into the current heteronomies of racism, nationalism, and capitalism. These heteronomies have often served to protect the bourgeois principle against radical criticism and thus to negate the Protestant principle. A characteristic consequence of the bourgeois principle (which, it will be recalled, always moves toward the dissolution of the bonds of community life through the rationalization of the powers of origin) is to be seen in the dependence of the working class upon the "free" sale of their physical ability to work, a dependence which, in its turn, relies upon the "laws" (or the chances) of the market. Here the perversion of man's essential nature assumes tremendous social dimensions. Even in normal times the fateful threat of insecurity confronts the entrepreneur as well as the worker. This threat, as it has expressed itself in the twentieth century, has more and more torn away the ideological veil which romantic conservative thought and progressivist liberal economics have thrown over the contradictions of capitalist society.

These contradictions, in their most general economic aspects, are three: first, the contradition between the rapidity of technical advance and the slowness of the development of societal forms that enable adjustment to the technical advance; second, the contradiction between the increasing production power and the decreasing consumption capacity of the masses (bigger and better factories have brought a higher proportion of unemployment); and, third, the contradiction between the assumed liberty of every individual and the actual dependence of the masses on great concentrations of economic power (which determine not only the production and prices of goods but also the manipulation of symbols through the idea industries).

The way out of the present era can be found only if men can be released from the "possession" of the demonic powers that now carry through or protect the bourgeois principle, only if men can be caught up and transformed by newly creative powers emanating from the depths of being and history. Tillich is convinced that men will not even approach this "timely" moment unless they come to a passionate awareness of the deep void of meaninglessness that the bourgeois principle and its supporting heteronomies have created. The prevailing "neutrality" of the churches to these issues is only a form of ideological concealment of the perversions of the common life. It is true that no Protestant church can properly espouse an official social philosophy or program; to do so would be to violate the Protestant principle. Yet if the Protestant principle is apprehended in a vital and relevant way, it should lead to a turning-away from the void of meaninglessness and to new creation. It should lead to the forging of a principle pertinent to the present historical situation, a principle that in the spirit of radical Protestantism can overcome the bourgeois principle.

This principle might be called the "religious-socialist principle." Tillich has written extensively on this theme; apart from certain collections of his essays, his largest book (*Socialist Decision*) deals with this subject. Besides this, he was coeditor of a religious-socialist magazine for the Kairos Circle in pre-Hitler Germany. Here it must suffice if we give merely a few hints concerning the meaning of the central principle.

Tillich rejects the legalistic or programmatic type of religious socialism which considers socialism to be the precise demand of the Gospels; it attempts to make the Gospels a socialist textbook. He rejects the romantic type of religious socialism which claims that socialism is itself religion; it rightly asserts that religion does not confine itself to a special religious sphere yet it stifles the radical criticism inherent in the Protestant principle. He also rejects the practical-political type of religious socialism which simply tries to bring about co-operation between organized socialism and the churches; it tends to emphasize merely practical strategies and fails to scrutinize the basic presuppositions of either socialism or religion in their actual forms, and thus it neglects the need for fundamental transformation of either of them.

In his religious socialism Tillich attempts in a dialectical fashion to dissolve the static opposition of prevailing conceptions of religion and socialism; he aims to understand them in their deepest roots and to transform both of them in the spirit of prophetic religion. Accordingly, he aims to interpret religion and socialism in such a way as to point toward a new concrete Gestalt, capable in the deepest sense of meeting the particular needs of our time. The goal of this religious socialism is the radical application of the Protestant principle to both Protestantism and socialism, to both religion and secularism, in order to free Protestantism from bondage to the religious sphere as a separate sphere and also to make possible a religious understanding of the socialism and the secularism of the Protestant era. This type of religious socialism works primarily on theoretical problems. It is not concerned with the development of blueprints for a socialist system of society; its practical effectiveness, as compared with the theoretical, is intended to be small.

Whether or not organized Protestantism will continue its class-bound subservience to the spirit of capitalism is largely a matter of conjecture. There are evidences of change in European Protestantism in the direction of socialism. In the United States there would seem to be a persisting disposition in Protestant circles to rely upon automatic harmony, that is, upon capitalism. In any event, the coming years will bring to birth new forms of collectivism, forms that will vary in the different countries. Religious socialism aims to accept the responsibility of delineating the principles that will be in conformity with the theological demands of self-transcending realism, with democratic ideals, and with economic necessities.

The widespread opposition between Protestantism and socialism is to be understood as the consequence of perversions within both of them. Protestantism's opposition is due not only to its Babylonish captivity to capitalism and nationalism but also to a widely held supernaturalist conception of the Kingdom of God as purely transcendent; it is due to the complacency of Protestant liberalism and to the "religious" indifference of Protestant fundamentalism and Barthian neo-orthodoxy. All these tendencies reveal in varying ways and degrees the absence of a really disturbed consciousness of the magnitude of the struggle that must be made against the demonries of our time. In face of this situation, religious socialism not only demands that Protestantism should come to a new awareness of the Protestant principle and thus be released from bondage; it also tries to present the special demands of the kairos of our time, the demand for a new order of life imbued with new meaning to take the place of an autonomously emptied and heteronomously controlled society.

The opposition of socialism to religion is as false in principle as is the opposition of Protestantism to socialism. The historical roots of socialism are to be found in the prophetic-Protestant-humanist tradition; in the drive forward to the new in history, represented by revolutionary spiritualist movements of the pre-Reformation period and of the left wing of the Reformation; in the autonomous revolt against the powers of origin claimed by an ecclesiastically controlled culture (a revolt moving in the direction of democracy); in the Calvinist and humanist impulse to give a rational, rather than an arbitrary, shaping to society; in the struggle for *man* implicit in all these motifs, as well as in the world-affirming spirit of the Enlightenment. Perhaps the most powerful prophetic element in socialism is what has been called its "epochal consciousness," its awareness of the decisive character of the dynamic structures of a whole period. (The very concept of "the Protestant era" presupposes this prophetic view that the human situation must be understood in terms of the integrating and the disintegrating structures of a period.) Tillich believes that socialism is today more strongly conscious of the kairos of our period than is any other movement, conscious of an impending epochal fate and opportunity. But it is perverted by the possession of certain untimely elements which are either residues of the era which is now in crisis or new forms of idolatry. Some of these elements were originally creative ideas, and they are now therefore, in their untimely form, all the more dangerous.

Socialism (and especially Marxism) has ignored the transcendent reference of the Protestant principle, and through its false claim to be a science it has degenerated into a new legalism and a new heteronomy. By its merely sociologistic interpretation of the cleavages and corruptions of human existence and by its continued reliance on an unbroken bourgeois principle (with its naïve belief in progress) it has transformed originally prophetic expectations for the future into utopianism. Religious socialism aims to correct the false anthropology of Marxism and to overcome its heteronomous and utopian impulses by the achievement of an autonomy deepened by theonomy and by an insistence upon the remoteness of socialism from the Kingdom of God, however clearly "the decision for socialism during a definite period may be the decision for the kingdom of God."

The religious-socialist principle points the direction out of the Protestant era by combining elements that have been either neglected or perverted by both capitalism and socialism. It seeks a new theonomous society in which the powers of origin supporting organic community may be broken and yet fulfilled under the demands of the unconditional; it seeks more than a new economic system, it seeks a total outlook on existence in which all cultural areas retain their autonomy. It rejects the metaphysical core of bourgeois harmonism and socialist progressivism, and it adopts a prophetic philosophy of history in which anticipation of the new (as well as the breaking-away from the old) is combined with the responsibility of planning for freedom. On the basis of these principles, religious socialism would overcome the fear, the insecurity, the loneliness, the thingification of the masses of men; in such a way it would overcome the contradictions of our disintegrating world. It is clear, then, that if Protestantism or any other group is to meet the demands of our kairos, concern for individual salvation will have to be coupled with a concern for "the ultimate meaning and salvation of groups and institutions." But men cannot merely by decision bring about so great a change as this. A power more than human, a power greater than that of the now ruling principalities and powers, greater than that of the present demonries that have men in their possession, must be released. If Protestantism responds to this kairos, the Protestant era will not be at an end. The Reformation will continue.

From the foregoing presentation it should be evident that Tillich's accomplishments are among the most comprehensive and deep going in contemporary theology. The integrity of his thought is to be discovered in his concern with the philosophy of history, a concern that grows out of his conviction that "the meaning of history" is *the* problem of our period and that a new meaning must be expressed in a new society. Some readers, even though they be sympathetic with his analysis of the present historical situation and its demands, will feel that his conception of the planned society insufficiently recognizes the liberal demand for democratic controls. But disagreement on this point should not distract attention from the principal need emphasized by Tillich—the need for recognizing the spiritual and structural character of the required redintegration of society. Within the context of Tillich's philosophy of history, all the other elements of his thought and influence must be understood.

It is, of course, impossible to predict which of these elements of his thought will exercise the most direct influence. Reinhold Niebuhr has pointed out that Tillich has already exercised a critical and creative influence as mediator between widely disparate European and American theological tendencies, bringing them into fruitful tension with one another as no orthodox or Barthian theologian could do. In addition to this, he has long served as a mediator between theology and philosophy, between the churches and the secular movements, between the social outlook of Protestant, capitalist individualism and that of religious and secular socialism. His newly devised concepts and his reinterpretations of old concepts (for example, the unconditional, kairos, the demonic, theonomy, and the Gestalt of grace) will do much to break up the incrusted formulations of familiar modes of thought and thus to overcome the supernaturalism which is still widely held in religious circles. He has thereby introduced a new theological conception of nature and of its relation to history; he has disclosed a covert religious element in certain types of secularism and also the blasphemous, irreligious elements in certain types of religion; he has attempted to correct the liberal theology that has exhausted itself by identifying religion with moralism; and he has transcended certain outmoded oppositions between liberalism and orthodoxy. In all these ways he challenges prevailing conceptions of the essential nature of Protestantism. These characteristic concerns of Tillich's endeavor can be of marked significance for the development of sacramental, as well as of prophetic, elements in the ecumenical movement of contemporary Christianity.

But the form as well as the content of Tillich's thought will determine his influence, both within and outside the churches. As one of his European orthodox critics has (lamentingly) observed, his writings "delight the reader in a remarkably untheological and secular way." Besides this, the reader will be struck by the architectonic, albeit dynamic, structure of his thought.

Through all these major aspects of his thinking Tillich may help prepare us for the religious and secular reformation which alone can overcome the crisis of the Protestant era and give new, timely access to what the poet, Gerard Manley Hopkins, has called "the dearest freshness deep down things."

INDEX

# INDEX

319